THIRD EDITION—REVISED AND UPDATED

HOW TO CLEAN EVERYTHING

An Encyclopedia
of What to Use
and How to Use It

By ALMA CHESNUT MOORE
ILLUSTRATIONS BY TOM FUNK

SIMON AND SCHUSTER · NEW YORK

PUBLISHED BY SIMON AND SCHUSTER
A DIVISION OF GULF & WESTERN CORPORATION
SIMON & SCHUSTER BUILDING
ROCKEFELLER CENTER
1230 AVENUE OF THE AMERICAS
NEW YORK, NEW YORK 10020
DESIGNED BY EVE METZ
MANUFACTURED IN THE UNITED STATES OF AMERICA

LIBRARY OF CONGRESS CATALOGING IN PUBLICATION DATA

MOORE, ALMA CHESNUT.
　　HOW TO CLEAN EVERYTHING.

　　BIBLIOGRAPHY: P.
　　1. CLEANING. I. TITLE.
TX324.M6　1977　　648'.03　　77-24506

ISBN 0-671-22705-X

FOR MY SONS,
PETER, ANTHONY, AND CHRISTOPHER,
whose active participation in household matters
has resulted in a vast extension of my research

ACKNOWLEDGMENTS

In preparing this completely revised edition of *How to Clean Everything*, I have again leaned heavily on my original sources—the departments of the United States Government whose research touches the area of home-making and the companies and corporations which provide us with the household products, furnishings, and labor-saving equipment we use today.

Bulletins, leaflets, and news releases of the Department of Agriculture provided up-to-date information on the control of insect pests, the removal of stains from textiles, mildew control, the care of basic equipment, laundry techniques and related matters. A publication on cleaning and polishing materials was contributed by the Department of Commerce. Material dealing with nursery matters was provided by the latest edition of *Infant Care*, best seller of the Office of Child Development, U.S. Department of Health, Education and Welfare.

Leaflets and booklets supplied by leading New York firms formed the basis of articles on the care and cleaning of jewelry and silver. Supplementary information was courteously given. For help in the field of fine art I am indebted to the maintenance curator of an internationally famous art museum who prefers to remain anonymous.

During the last decade many new textile fibers, floorings, cleaning preparations, and items of equipment have made their appearance in our stores. For information about them I turned to the best source possible—the men who produce them. Reputable firms take great pride in their products and are anxious to have them understood properly and used effectively. They spend much time and effort making their products attractive, efficient, and safe. Usually they provide careful instructions for their use and these should always be read and followed.

Without exception the companies approached for information cooperated wholeheartedly, supplying detailed care and cleaning instructions and discussing candidly the advantages and disadvantages

7

ACKNOWLEDGMENTS

of their products—what they will stand and what they will not. It is impossible to list here all of the firms that helped.

ALMA CHESNUT MOORE

This book is based upon material provided by outstanding manufacturers of household equipment and furnishings; upon bulletins and leaflets prepared by scientists of the Department of Agriculture and other branches of the Federal Government; and upon information provided by experts in specialized fields. The author has checked and counterchecked for accuracy, safety, and clarity. The results obtained by following the directions given will depend to a great extent upon the reader's judgment and skill.

Trade names are used for the convenience of the reader. Their use does not constitute a guarantee or imply that similar preparations are not equally effective.

A NOTE TO THE READER

A general INTRODUCTION by the author will be found starting on page 9. The book itself is divided into two major sections: SECTION I, HOW TO CLEAN EVERYTHING AND WHAT TO USE, pages 13–217, and SECTION II, STAINS: HOW TO REMOVE THEM FROM TEXTILES, pages 219–239. Each of these is alphabetically arranged for your convenience.

A LIST OF MATERIALS USEFUL IN CLEANING will be found on page 15, and MATERIALS FOR STAIN REMOVAL appears on page 221.

Introduction

This book is for women who dislike housework but like nice homes. Though it obviously will give brides an enviable head start, it was not written especially for them, but for those of us with growing families, who have to make every stroke tell or go under.

Cleaning is just one aspect of the role we play, and we want to finish it fast. We get more of a bang out of playing tutor, umpire, psychologist, interior decorator, gardener, or companion to equally harried husbands.

When reminded that we are living in an era of labor-saving devices and packaged products that have practically eliminated housework, we are likely to snicker derisively. Naturally, things are not the same as they were in Grandma's day. Neither, for that matter, is Grandma. But, with due respect to her, we have more interests, and duties, outside the home and less help in it. We know, too, that each new material and gadget brings its special problem and that we had better know how to treat the new textiles and special cloth finishes, how to handle plastics and coddle the dishwasher, or it will be cash out of a hard-pressed budget. Housekeeping has gone scientific.

In the wake of the confusing array of new materials, we face a flood of super-do cleaners, which are supposed to clean anything, or just a million things, "like magic." They go by trade names and some of them are wonderful, but we don't know what they really are and not always what they do best.

Every woman knows that there is no one cleaner for everything and that what is good for one material may destroy another. And every woman also knows that there is no "magic" in cleaning anything . . . just knowledge of what to use and how to use it.

This knowledge has never been obtainable in a single volume. Furthermore, it is not easy to get. Experts in different fields are often reluctant to part with information which they consider part of their stock in trade, or disparage our ability to follow instructions. They say that we don't know one material from another and that we "wreck the

9

stuff." To these charges I am obliged to answer that they are often right. It is not easy to tell one kind of rayon from another, Orlon from silk, some synthetics from leather. As for not following directions, I must add that the directions often are at fault and that, if we are going to "wreck the stuff" by our ineptitude, we might as well wreck it following directions that are correct.

It is true, as charged by one authority, that we have attempted to boil our own linseed oil, to clean oil paintings with sliced potatoes and cut onions and to give sparkle to platinum by soaking it in Javelle water. This advice, however, came through on a radio program, and how are we to know?

Manufacturers' directions should be read carefully and followed exactly, but often they are buried so deep in laudatory paragraphs that we are hard pressed to find them. Sometimes the print is so small that we skip it rather than hunt a magnifying glass. And what about those wavy directions on the insides of bottle labels? Directions get lost, too, even when we file them carefully.

I doubt if any expert could do better than we, especially if he received as little training. Women contemplating marriage and a family should be primed with elementary courses in plumbing, electrical engineering and household chemistry, among other things, but do we get such training? We sail into the world's most difficult job on a rosy cloud, to the accompaniment of soft music and flowers, absolutely innocent of all the problems soon to face us. How close upon the diamond come diapers and dishes. Just thinking about it all makes older women cry at weddings.

This book, first published in 1952 after 10 years of work, was revised in 1960, 1968, and 1978. It is intended to supply concise information about different articles and materials and their care. It has been checked and counterchecked against multiple sources for accuracy and completeness and, finally, by a qualified chemist.

The alphabetic arrangement is intended to make it easy and quick to use, and largish type was selected so that we won't have to squint at it through our bifocals. In the back a special section, also alphabetic, gives directions for treating one hundred and fifty stains.

How to Clean Everything is not intended to convert casually efficient women into demon housekeepers. Consult it as you would your cookbook, when in doubt or faced with a special problem. Happily, the best cleaning method is usually the easiest and safest. But please do take time to read the directions carefully, and follow them exactly.

ALMA CHESNUT MOORE

Avoid Home Accidents

The very fact that poison control centers have been established in our major cities attests the danger that lurks in the modern home. An ever-increasing array of special cleaners, insecticides, and household remedies accumulates on shelves and in cabinets. They make life easier and most of them are harmless when used properly and stored safely. However, each year they take their toll—mostly of toddlers and small children, who use their sense of taste as a means of learning.

Avoid accidents to yourself and to your children by using commercial products safely and by storing them where inquisitive little hands cannot reach them. The rules which follow were provided by the Greater New York Safety Council.

1. Keep all medicines in a safe place. Be especially careful with candy-type medications, which are a particular hazard.
2. Weed out from your medicine cabinet all unlabeled bottles and discard old prescriptions when the illness is over. (Some chemicals deteriorate with age; some, like iodine, become stronger through evaporation.) Flush the contents of containers down the toilet, then rinse the bottles or crush the boxes and put them in the trash can. Keep poisonous mixtures in a separate place, preferably locked.
3. Detergents, bleaches, drain openers, cleaning fluids, insecticides, and polishes—labels intact—should be kept out of the reach of small children. Do not store them under the sink or on a shelf containing food. If you buy a "giant size" do not, for convenience, put small amounts in old "pop" or milk bottles or other food containers. Small children "read" pictures.
4. Before using any special cleaner, read or reread the directions on the container and follow them exactly. And do not ever make the mistake of thinking that because they do a good job separately a mixture will be even better. Combinations can be lethal. For example, if chlorine bleach is combined with a toilet bowl cleaner,

11

ammonia, lye, rust remover, or oven cleaner, toxic gases are released which can cause severe illness or death. (Many scouring powders now contain chlorine bleach.)

5. Wear rubber gloves when using detergents, strong cleaners, steel wool. Wear canvas gloves when doing rough cleanup work.

6. Paints, solvents, denatured alcohol, pesticides, garden sprays, and weed killers are dangerous to pets as well as people. Some are both flammable and poisonous. Store them safely in a cool place and take time to read or reread the directions before using them.

7. Never keep large amounts of gasoline or kerosene in your home or garage. Keep small amounts only in metal safety containers with tight lids. (Heat expansion can cause a glass container to explode.)

8. Think twice before you make electrical repairs. There are tricks to rewiring a lamp, splicing a cord, or adjusting an outlet. Unless you know what you are doing, get competent help. Correctly handled, electricity is a docile helper. Abused, it can be a malevolent genie.

9. As a precaution against fire, keep your home free of junk. Oily or paint-stained rags are a particular hazard; they can ignite spontaneously. Don't keep them. Don't keep accumulations of old magazines and papers.

10. KEEP MATCHES AND CIGARETTE LIGHTERS AWAY FROM CHILDREN.

HOW TO CLEAN EVERYTHING

AND WHAT TO USE

A List
of Materials
Useful in Cleaning

Absorbent (any of the following: cornstarch, corn meal, French chalk, fuller's earth, talcum powder, magnesium carbonate) — Drugstore or grocery

Alcohol (rubbing) — Drug or paint store

Ammonia — Grocery

Baking soda (sodium bicarbonate) — Grocery

Borax — Grocery

Cleaning fluid — Drugstore

Detergents (built and unbuilt. If you do not know which detergents are built and which are unbuilt, see "Synthetic Detergents.") — Grocery

General insecticide — Grocery, hardware store

Linseed oil (raw, boiled) — Paint store

Neat's-foot oil — Shoe repair shop

Rottenstone or very fine pumice — Paint store

Saddle soap — Shoe repair shop

Soaps (built and unbuilt. If you do not know which soaps are built and which are unbuilt, see "Soap.") — Grocery

Trisodium phosphate or Oakite — Paint store, grocery

Turpentine (poisonous, flammable) — Paint store

Upholstery shampoo (soapless) — Department store

Washing soda (sodium carbonate) — Grocery

Whiting — Paint store

This list of chemicals and other materials is not complete, but represents those most generally useful. Other chemicals mentioned in this book might be needed only once, or not at all, and need not be kept on the cleaning shelf. If you are not familiar with these cleaning aids, look them up before buying them. For information about the different soda compounds see "Soda and Soda Compounds." It is sometimes necessary to have your druggist order unusual chemicals for you.

A check list of stain removers appears at the beginning of Section II of this book, "Stains: How to Remove Them from Textiles."

Abrasive Any material used to rub, or abrade, a spot or material falls into this classification. Examples are whiting, pumice, rottenstone and volcanic ash. Some of these materials are available in different degrees of fineness. All have specific household uses, described under various headings in this book. For more detailed information about each one, see "Whiting," "Pumice," etc. These materials can be bought at paint stores, sometimes at drugstores.

Commercially sold scouring powders for kitchen and bathroom use are abrasives, differing widely in their degree of harshness. Some contain strong alkalies such as washing soda and trisodium phosphate.

Absorbent An absorbent is a material useful in removing light or freshly made stains and grease stains by absorbing them. Examples are cornstarch and corn meal, obtained from the grocer; French chalk, talcum powder, magnesium carbonate and fuller's earth, available from the druggist. Absorbents are harmless to all fibers and are easy to apply. This is how they are used.

Lay the stained fabric flat on a clean cloth or towel. Spread a layer of absorbent on the stain and work it around gently. When the absor-

bent becomes caked or gummy, shake or brush it off, or use a vacuum cleaner on rugs. Repeat this procedure until most of the stain is gone. Apply another layer and let it remain overnight or longer, if necessary. Overnight treatment alone often will remove a light stain.

To speed removal of a greasy stain put a layer of cloth or brown paper over the fabric upon which the absorbent has been spread and apply a warm iron for several minutes.

Absorbents are more effective on some stains when they are mixed to a paste with cleaning fluid. They are not recommended for dark, unwashable materials because it is difficult to remove them completely.

Soft cloths, absorbent cotton, paper napkins, and facial tissues are absorbent materials useful for soaking up quickly liquids spilled on rugs, upholstery, and other heavy fabrics that do not absorb them readily. Unless the fluid is greasy, still more of the stain can be removed by wetting and blotting the material.

Acetate Acetate fibers are produced from cellulose, found in nearly all plants. The main source is wood pulp or cotton linters. Purified cellulose is treated with acetic acid to produce cellulose acetate. The cellulose acetate is dissolved in acetone and forced through a spinneret into a shaft containing warm air, where the acetone evaporates, leaving the yarn. Herein lies the test for identifying acetates. A drop of acetone on a snipping will dissolve an acetate and make blends sticky.

But ordinary dry-cleaning fluids and bleaches do not harm it.

Acetate combines many of rayon's qualities with superior drape and luster. It is water absorbent, nonstatic, and colorfast. It can be dyed in a wide range of colors and woven as satin, taffeta, faille, tricot, sharkskin, surah, and twill. In blends it appears as brocades, chambrays, crepes, cords, gabardines, and flannels. Acetate fabrics are less absorbent than rayon and therefore dry faster. They are heat-sensitive but some can stand higher heat than others. (See "Arnel.") They resist shrinking and swelling, mildew (discolor only), insects, sunlight, radiator heat, bleaches.

Acetate fabrics can be hand washed or dry cleaned, depending upon their construction, finish, and dyes. Some are machine washable. Be guided by the label. If the label says it will wash, use these directions.

Dissolve heavy-duty soap or detergent completely in warm (never hot) water and then place the garment in it. Squeeze the water through the garment gently, avoiding any rough handling. Rinse thoroughly in clear lukewarm water. Do not wring or twist it. Roll it in a turkish towel to absorb excess

water, then hang it to dry. (No clothespins.)

Acetates are best ironed when they are nearly dry. (Like silk they sometimes look spotty if they are sprinkled and ironed.) Dial your iron for rayon and press on the wrong side. (Right side touch-up with a press cloth.) A steam iron is best. It is not necessary to remove all the moisture. Let them finish drying on hangers.

Acetate Plastics See "Cellulosics."

Acetic Acid A colorless liquid, acid and pungent in odor and taste, useful in treating certain stains. In its pure state it is a clear, colorless, strongly acid liquid, which crystallizes in cold temperatures. As a stain remover it is used in a dilution of 10 percent. (White vinegar can be used as a substitute. It is 5 percent acetic acid.)

Acetic acid can be used safely on silk and wool. It also can be used on linen and cotton. Do not use a strong solution of acetic acid on acetate.

On stains for which acetic acid or vinegar is recommended, follow this procedure. Moisten the stain with the acid, keeping it wet until the stain disappears. Rinse or sponge with water. If the dye changes color, try moistening the fabric with ammonia. (See "Ammonia" for directions.) Section II on Stains will tell you when to use acetic acid.

Acetone A clear liquid, with an odor resembling peppermint, which can be purchased at drugstores. Acetone is useful in removing stains caused by paint, varnish, lacquer, and airplane cement (freely spread by youthful modelers). It is harm-

17

less to natural fibers except those treated with resin finishes, and to all synthetics except acetate, Arnel, Dynel, and Verel. Acetone affects some dyes, so test it before using on colored materials.

Caution: Acetone is flammable. It evaporates rapidly and its fumes are toxic. Use it in a well-ventilated place and be careful not to inhale it for any length of time. Store acetone tightly stoppered in a cool place.

Acid A sour substance. In chemistry, acids have these common properties: they taste sour; they will dissolve in water and sometimes will restore colors that have been changed by an alkali (good to try). Acids turn blue litmus paper red.

Mild acids like lemon, vinegar, and acetic acid perform a number of homely housekeeping chores, such as cutting soap film and bleaching stains, which are described in their proper alphabetic places. Other acids are violently poisonous and can cause severe burns, but few of these fall within our category. For treatment of stains caused by acids see "Stains," p. 224.

Acoustic Tile A porous material used for ceilings. If painted, treat it like any other painted surface. See "Walls and Ceilings—Painted." If unpainted, clean it with a brush or use a standard wallpaper cleaner or rubber sponge.

Acrilan Acrilan is the trade name for Chemstrand's versatile acrylic fiber, which is chemically similar to Orlon. To produce it, air and natural gas are combined and polymerized (converted to long-chain giant molecules). A liquid solution is then made and spun into fiber, which is crimped and cut into staple lengths for processing into yarn.

Acrilan is used alone and in blends, in a wide range of colors, for all types of knitted and woven clothing fabrics, for blankets, carpets and rugs, deep-pile fabrics, draperies, and upholstery. Acrilan fabrics are soft and warm to the touch and feel like silk or wool, depending on their type. They are completely washable, dry rapidly, retain pleats, keep their shape during wear, and do not shrink. They resist soil, mildew, insects, and damage from sunlight, and are not harmed by common solvents and a wide range of chemicals. Shrinkage is less than 1 percent in boiling water.

Wash or dry-clean Acrilan clothing according to the label.

Acrylic Plastics One of ten main branches of the plastics family. Acrylics are sold under the trade names "Lucite" and "Plexiglas." Although light in weight and delicate in appearance, they are resistant to sharp blows and temperature changes. Acrylics can be tinted in a full range of transparent, translucent and opaque colors. Their surface texture, too, can be varied. Clear acrylics are so absolutely transparent that they can be used for camera viewing lenses and television-image magnifiers. Acrylics weather well and can be used outdoors indefinitely. Their water resistance is good.

A decorative advantage is the ability of these plastics to pick up light at an edge and transmit it invisibly around curves and bends to the opposite side or until it reaches a groove. Acrylics are odorless, tasteless and nontoxic. Their burning rate is low.

Lucite and Plexiglas are used for hairbrushes, lamps, clock cases, salad bowls, small tables, decorative shelves, trays, partitions, roofing, handbags, eyeglasses, bookends, light fixtures, dresser sets, window glazing, and picture frames. Clean them with warm water and soap or detergent, rinse and wipe dry. If the water is too hot the article may soften. Protect acrylic surfaces from lighted cigarettes and high heat. Ink and many household chemicals will not affect acrylics, but keep cleaning fluids, nail polish and nail polish remover, hair tonics, perfumes, and alcohol away.

Do not use abrasives in cleaning acrylics; they scratch the surface. If accidentally scratched, a little wax will help hide the blemish. Deep scratches can be buffed out. Antistatic polishes are available for acrylics.

Acrylic Textiles The man-made fibers which compose the textile group known as acrylics are made from a versatile chemical compound called acrylonitrile. Sources of this compound are such basic raw materials as air, water, natural gas, coal, petroleum, and limestone. To qualify as an acrylic a fabric must be 85 percent acrylonitrile.

Acrylonitrile is important in the manufacture of synthetic rubber. The commercial processes used to produce it were developed during World War II when our sources of natural rubber were cut off and a substitute was crucially important. After the war, acrylonitrile found many additional uses: one was the creation of textile fibers.

To produce textile fibers, acrylo-

nitrile is dissolved in a solvent. It is then extruded (spun into fiber) and the solvent removed.

Acrylic fibers have outstanding qualities and are highly versatile. They are very strong, yet soft and silky to the touch. They have natural warmth and resilience as well as resistance to sunlight and weathering. Acrylic fabrics drape well, wash easily, dry rapidly, and require little ironing. They are more easily dyed than nylon, more absorbent, and of higher bulk. They can be used alone or in blends.

Acrylics are almost shrinkproof. They are resistant to most chemicals, including bleaches and cleaning fluids, and to damage from insects, sunlight, and atmospheric gases. They are heat-sensitive, becoming sticky at temperatures ranging from $300°$ to $490°$ F.

Acrylics are sold under such trade names as Orlon, Acrilan, Zefran, and Creslan. These vary somewhat and are listed separately. For washing, see these listings. See also label in garment.

Adhesive Tape See "Stains," p. 224.

Aerosol Technically, an aerosol is a suspension of fine solid or liquid particles in air or gas, as smoke, fog, or mist. Commercially, the word is used to describe any pressurized product which is self-propelled through a valve, regardless of particle size, the type of propellant used, and the form in which the product is dispensed. While the term "aerosol" is used for food and nonfood foams as well as airborne and surface-deposited sprays of either liquids or powders, they are in reality pressurized products.

19

Air-Cooled Finish A finish applied to fabrics at the textile mill to keep the spaces between the threads open. Such a finish increases the comfort of summertime fabrics. There are no special washing or ironing instructions for air-cooled fabrics.

Air Deodorants See "Deodorants."

Airplane Cement See "Glue, Mucilage, Adhesives" in "Stains," p. 228.

Alabaster A material similar to marble, which is found in various colors, but is most valued when of purest white. Alabaster is soft and can be carved and ground easily to make lamp bases, statuettes and other decorative articles. The finest stone comes from Florence, Italy.

Cleaning instructions are the same as for marble. See "Marble."

Alcohol Alcohol is a spirit distilled from fermented sugar, molasses, and other materials. A powerful disinfectant, it can be used to sterilize thermometers and other instruments. As a solvent it is excellent for cleaning glass and for removing resinous stains from cloth. Ordinary rubbing alcohol will do for stains on textiles for which alcohol is recommended. Test first to see if dyes are affected. Dilute with two parts of water for use on acetate.

Alcohol is flammable; wood alcohol is poisonous.

Alcohol Stains See "Furniture." See also "Stains," p. 224.

Alkali In chemistry, an alkali is "any one of various classes of sub-

stances having the following properties in common: solubility in water, the power of neutralizing acids and forming salts with them, the property of corroding animal and vegetable substances, the property of altering the tint of many coloring matters." Thus, an alkali used in washing or for spot removal may change the color of dyes in fabrics. It will turn red litmus paper blue.

Alkalies in household use include ammonia, lye, and various soda compounds. They have important functions in the home but are harmful to certain materials, including silk, wool, and aluminum. Their uses and limitations are described in this book under individual classifications as "Lye," "Ammonia," "Soda and Soda Compounds." See also "Stains," p. 224.

Allergenproof Encasings Encasings for mattresses and pillows made of especially prepared coated material should not be soaked, even briefly. Wash them in rich, lukewarm suds made of mild, white soap flakes. Squeeze the suds through the material; do not rub it. Rinse carefully in lukewarm water. Squeeze gently to remove water, then roll in a turkish towel to remove additional moisture. Unroll promptly and dry in the shade. Press with a warm (never hot) iron on the uncoated side. Wash plastic film coverings with warm water and a mild soap or detergent. Rinse and dry away from heat.

Allied Chemical See "Polyester."

Alloy Instead of being a pure metal, an alloy is a combination

20

of two or more metals. About twenty-seven hundred alloys are now listed. Metallurgists cook them up as we do pies. See "Bronze," "Pewter," etc.

Alpaca Cloth made from the wool of the domesticated South American llama. See "Woolens."

Aluminum is derived from the chemical alumina, a kind of earth. One twelfth of the earth's crust is alumina in various compounds, in case you are interested, which makes it seem plentiful, but many intricate processes are involved in extracting it for use.

New aluminum utensils can be kept bright and shining for a long time by using mild soap or a detergent and water alone, if care is taken not to burn food in them. Rinse with scalding water and polish with a soft tea towel.

To remove burned or scorched food from the bottom of an aluminum vessel, fill it with water, allow it to boil, then remove the softened food with a wooden spoon or pot scraper. Finish the job with steel wool. Steel wool pads with soap are the best and least damaging cleaner for aluminum. Although it scratches the surface to some extent, the filaments are so fine that no damage is caused. In using steel wool, rub in one direction only,

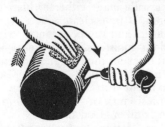

not with a circular motion. Commercial cleaners for aluminum include Alumi-glo, Grid, Mel-Ezy, and Klenz. These work best if the aluminum is washed first in hot water and the cleaner is applied while the metal is hot. Detergents used in electric dishwashers dull the sheen of polished aluminum. Colored aluminum should not go into dishwashers.

Certain alkaline foods, such as spinach and potatoes, tend to darken aluminum; acid foods, like apples and rhubarb, brighten it without injury to the food.

Lime scale, which forms in teakettles in hard-water areas, can be loosened with boiling water and vinegar (half and half). Let it stand in the kettle for several hours, or overnight, then scrape out the deposit with steel wool. If necessary, repeat the process. If the inside of the teakettle is washed frequently, the lime scale will not form.

Caution: Never use aluminum pans for storing foods because chemicals in the foods may cause pitting of the metal. There is no danger of food poisoning involved, but badly pitted, or dented, aluminum is unsanitary and should be discarded. See also "Duralumin," "Coffee Maker."

Amber Amber is the mineralized resin of extinct pine trees, found in beds of lignite (brown coal in which the form of wood can be seen) and in alluvial soil. Pale yellow, but sometimes reddish or brownish in color, it is found mostly along the shores of the Baltic, where it has been tossed up by the sea. Amber is hard, translucent, brittle, and fragrant when

21

heated. Jet, also a fossil substance, is sometimes called "black amber."

If you have beads or a pin of amber, you may, if you look closely, find imprisoned in its translucent depths a tiny insect no longer known on this earth.

A quality of amber is the ease with which it can be charged with negative electricity by a brisk rubbing. This puzzled the ancients, and modern scientists took our word "electricity" from the Greek word for amber. See "Jewelry."

Amethyst See "Quartz"; also "Jewelry."

Ammonia Ammonia is named for Ammon, the ram's-headed sun god of ancient Egypt, since it is supposed to have been prepared originally from camel's dung near the shrine of Jupiter Ammon.

Ammonia is an alkaline gas, dissolved in water. As sold for household use it varies from 5 to 10 percent in strength. For stain removal chemically pure 10 percent ammonia, from a drugstore, is best.

A small amount of household ammonia added to washing or rinse water will help make windows and glassware sparkle and lighten numerous household tasks. This is accomplished through its ability to cut grease. In using, remember that it tends to bleach slightly and to soften paint, so don't use too much.

For stain removal, use ammonia in the following way. On all fabrics except silk or wool and their blends, moisten the stain with ammonia and keep it wet until the stain is gone. Rinse with water. If colors seem changed by the ammonia try moistening the cloth with acetic acid or vinegar. Then rinse with water.

(Dilute the ammonia with an equal amount of water for use on silk or wool and add a small amount of vinegar to the last rinse. If colors are altered follow the directions given above.)

Ammonia is poisonous and should be stored with care, well stoppered and in a cool place. It is caustic to the eyes and skin. If spilled on the skin, flood the area with water, then wash with vinegar or lemon juice.

Warning: If you are using ammonia, do not add another cleaning agent. The combination could be lethal. Ammonia and chlorine bleach, for instance, react to release a deadly gas.

Amyl Acetate This chemical is a compound of acetic and amyl alcohol, useful in removing certain stains, such as fingernail polish and other lacquers. It is safe to use on fabrics damaged by acetone, but if the spilled lacquer contained acetone, damage may already have been done to the fabric. Amyl acetate can be bought at drugstores. For stain removal it should be *chemically pure.* It is flammable and poisonous.

Andirons and Fire Tools These are usually made either of brass or of iron. If iron, clean with a brush or duster and rub occasionally with a cloth moistened with kerosene. This blackens the iron and prevents rusting. If desired, iron fireplace equipment can be finished with heat-resistant, or special andiron, paint, dull or glossy finish.

Brass fittings are cleaned and

cared for like any other articles of this metal. Portions that have become fire-blackened and encrusted with resins from wood will be difficult to restore to their proper luster, but it can be done. Steel wool is most generally recommended but it is difficult to handle and takes hours of scrubbing. Try fine emery cloth, such as metalworkers use, which you can buy in a hardware store. Rub in one direction and polish the brass afterward.

Lacquered brass is merely dusted. If the lacquer starts to crack and peel you may want to remove it and possibly renew the lacquer. Directions for this are given under "Brass."

Fire screens should be kept dusted. If gummy and soiled, clean them with kerosene or wash them with soap or detergent and water, using a brush.

See "Brass" and "Iron."

Angora is a fine yarn or fabric made from the wool of the silky Angora goat. In washing follow the rules for wool. Use lukewarm suds made with an unbuilt synthetic detergent or special wool wash. Rinse carefully; handle lightly. Before shaping it to dry on a turkish towel, shake it out gently to fluff up the yarn.

See "Woolens" and "Sweaters, Wool."

Antiperspirant See "Stains," p. 225.

Antiques The routine care of fine antiques is the same as for other objects of similar material. However, if repairs are required or special cleaning indicated, take a valuable piece to a professional rather than attempt it yourself. Your nearest art museum probably would be glad to advise you.

Antistatic Plastics, and fabrics made of silk, wool, and synthetic fibers especially, tend to accumulate static electricity, particulary in cold, dry weather. The static charge attracts dust to plastic objects and makes garments cling. Special preparations have been developed to reduce static buildup.

To counteract static buildup in washable materials, add a little fabric softener to the wash, rinse, or drying cycle. These can be purchased at most grocery stores. Some are Rain Barrel and First In, added to the wash water; Nu Soft and Final Touch, added to the rinse water; and Cling Free and Petal, added during drying. There are many others, equally good. Liquid antistatic agents can be obtained at notion counters in department stores and in drugstores. In using any of them, follow the directions on the container. Static accumulation varies with the individual. Modify the amount of antistatic to suit your particular charge.

Clothing provided with an antistatic finish at the factory should be washed with soap because detergents remove the finish. Nonwashable clothing can be given an antistatic finish by your dry cleaner.

If static in a carpet worries you, you can apply an antistatic spray made for this job. Use one of the following: Static Proof Pro (Servicemaster Industries, Inc., Downers Grove, Ill. 60515), usually applied by franchised cleaners of the Servicemaster system; Statikil (J. E. Doyle Co., 1220 West Sixth

23

Street, Cleveland, Ohio 44113); Stat-Eze 5 (Fine Organics, Inc., 205 Main Street, Lodi, N.J. 07644); and Carpetstat (Jordan Chemical Co., 1830 Columbia Ave., Folcroft, Pa. 19032).

Ants In battling ants remember that you are dealing with a tough, highly organized insect army, whose infiltration tactics have been perfected since prehistoric ages. A rude classification of the many ant species would be: those that crave sweets and those that like grease.

Winged ants are sometimes mistaken for termites, but it is easy to tell them apart. The ant has a neatly pinched-in waist, whereas the termite has no constriction, and the ant has two pairs of wings of unequal length while the termite has two pairs of almost equal size. Ants crawl over food and carry bits of it to their nests. They do not eat fabrics and leather. Unlike termites, they do not eat wood, though they sometimes establish nests in the decaying woodwork of old homes.

In battling ants, use a liquid household insecticide containing diazinon, lindane, malathion, or propoxur. To treat most places apply it as a surface spray. In the kitchen it may be desirable to use a small paint brush to get the spray exactly where you want it.

Apply the spray generously behind and beneath baseboards, around sinks and window sills, and in cracks and crannies that may serve as runways. Give special treatment to table legs and the bases of cabinets.

If, by watching the invaders, you can locate the nest from which they are launching their raids, that will be just dandy. You can accomplish mass murder.

Ant sprays are effective for all kinds of ants. They seldom have to be applied to the same surface more than once every two or three months. If ants attack from a different sector, spray there.

Ants dislike the odor of kerosene, naphthalene flakes and camphor, but so, probably, do you, especially in the kitchen or pantry. These substances, however, act only as repellents. They do not kill ants.

See "Insecticides" for precautions.

Aramid Aramid ("Nomex," "Kevlar"), developed by du Pont, is an unusually tough textile fiber, resistant to high heat and virtually all chemicals. It is used to make protective clothing for firemen, truck drivers, auto racers, and workers in many industrial fields.

Du Pont claims that an ironing board cover made of Nomex will not char, burn, ignite, or melt if the hottest iron (550° F.) is left face down on it for several months.

Garments made of Nomex can be cleaned by using normal home methods, by dry cleaning, or by commercial laundering. None of these procedures affects its protective features.

Spot clean the garments before washing them, and separate them into two bundles, white and colored. Wash the clothes in hot water with a heavy-duty detergent such as Tide, Cheer, All, or Wisk. Antistatics such as Downy and Cling Free may also be used. Dry clothes at a high temperature and place them on rust-free hangers while they are still hot. Touch up with a hot iron. Starch is not needed or recommended.

Argyrol Stains See "Stains," p. 225.

Arnel Arnel is the trade name for a Celanese triacetate fiber. The fiber-forming substance is cellulose acetate, the same as for acetate, but a different chemical process is used and the resulting fiber has its own individuality.

Arnel has the virtues of an acetate—quick drying, good hand and drape, affinity for dyes, and color-fastness—plus heat resistance and ease of care. Arnel can be heat treated, which makes possible fabrics which do not shrink or stretch out of fit, that resist wrinkles even in humid weather, and hold pleats through repeated washings. The fiber is found in an array of fabrics—flannel, sharkskin, tricot, faille, crepe, taffeta, and challis. Most of these are washable, some by hand, others by machine, depending upon the fiber content and fabric construction. Always check the label.

Arnel tricot, crepe, jersey, faille, and sharkskin can be either hand- or machine-washed in hot water with soap or detergent, and drip dried or tumble dried. They require little or no ironing. Arnel taffeta should be washed by hand and drip dried or tumble dried. These fabrics are ironed when they are dry, with either a steam or dry iron, at the setting for wool. They will stand 450° F. of heat, a temperature that melts nylon and softens most of the synthetic fibers.

Bleaches do not harm Arnel but may affect some colors. Do not use acetone as a spot remover for Arnel.

Artificial Leather See "Leather Goods, Artificial."

Artificial Rubber See "Rubber" (gloves), and "Spandex."

Art Objects Aside from routine dusting, valuable art objects are best handled by experts. Irreparable damage can be done by the wrong cleaning methods. So ask your local art museum where to have them cleaned or repaired. This includes oil paintings, mildewed books, prints and etchings, gilded statuettes, rare laces, etc. Art objects are sometimes ruined by persons who take the precaution of obtaining expert advice but lack the skill to handle the work. So play safe.

Asbestos Asbestos is an indestructible mineral substance, of fibrous construction, as old as the world itself. It is valued in commerce because it cannot be destroyed by fire. Several different minerals are mined as asbestos. As mined—quarried might be a more exact word—asbestos is as heavy as rock. However, it can be separated into delicate, silky fibers, some of which are capable of being woven into cloth.

Asbestos is used as a covering for stove and furnace pipes, as a fireproofing material for buildings, for lamp wicks and gas logs, glass-workers' gloves and firemen's clothing. Theaters are safeguarded against fire by asbestos curtains and even asbestos rugs. The homemaker uses it for mats on the stove, ironing board covers and sometimes, mixed with cotton, in dish towels.

25

Asbestos cloth is a very ancient product. Marco Polo found it in use in China more than seven hundred years ago. This is his description:

"A substance is likewise found of the nature of the salamander for, when woven into cloth and thrown into the fire, it remains incombustible. . . . The fossil substance consists of fibers not unlike those of wool. This, after being exposed to the sun to dry, is pounded in a brass mortar and is then washed until the earthy particles are separated. The fibers thus cleansed and detached from each other, they then spin into thread and weave into cloth. In order to render the texture white, they put it into the fire, and suffer it to remain there for about an hour, when they draw it out uninjured by the flame and become as white as snow. And so again, whenever they become dirty, they are bleached by being put in the fire."

It is not recommended that you throw your asbestos ironing board cover into the fire, however, when it becomes soiled. It contains other fibers. Wash it with soap and water, rinse and replace it on the board to dry. Or wash it on the board with soapsuds and a soft brush. Light scorch stains may be removed by adding household bleach to the wash water. Rinse and let dry.

Asbestos on pipes and gas logs can be brushed with a soft brush or vacuum cleaner attachment.

Ash Trays Wash in soapy water unless made of unglazed pottery. Polish metal ash trays according to the metal of which they are made. For a quick cleanup empty the trays and wipe them with a damp cloth or sponge. Have you a "silent butler" for use during parties? This is a handy gadget. It looks like a little dustpan with a spring-equipped lid.

See "China," "Brass," "Pewter," etc.

Asphalt For stains caused by asphalt or asphalt paint see "Tar" in "Stains," p. 237.

Asphalt Tile A tile made of asphalt, a kind of mineral pitch, used as a flooring especially in basements because it withstands moisture.

Dust asphalt tile with an untreated mop, or with a wet mop wrung out of cool water. Do not use harsh abrasives or strong cleaning powders. Use no oil polishes and no polishing waxes, either liquid or paste. About once a month wash the floor with mild, warm suds, rinse and dry. If desired, coat it with self-polishing wax (a water-wax emulsion), or with a finish recommended by the manufacturer.

Some of the new asphalt tiles, however, may be solvent-resistant, permitting use of a solvent-based wax. To test your floor (or to see if it is really asphalt tile) put a little cleaning fluid or turpentine on an inconspicuous place and study the effect. If the binder in the tile dissolves, causing surface roughness and bleeding of colors, it is asphalt tile and solvent-based polishes should not be used.

Automatic Dryer Clean the exterior of your dryer occasionally by wiping it with a cloth or sponge dipped in warm suds and squeezed out. Rinse with a clean damp cloth or sponge. The use of appliance wax is optional. The ingredients of some waxes are damaging to plastic trim; do not apply wax to plastic parts.

If the basket is spotted after drying starched articles, or stained from tinted items, wipe it with a cloth moistened with a chlorine bleach solution and rinse with a clean damp cloth.

After drying a few loads (some manufacturers say after each load), pull out the lint tray and remove the layers of lint. Occasionally clean out the opening below the lint collector (air intake) with a long-handled brush or with your vacuum cleaner.

Do not store clothing in your dryer.

Warning: Fabrics impregnated with flammable chemicals, such as cleaning cloths and mops saturated with wax, must not be dried in your dryer. Garments which have been cleaned with flammable fluids must be thoroughly cleaned and all traces of flammable fluids removed before being placed in a dryer.

Garments labeled "Dry Away from Heat" must not be put into the dryer. In addition, articles made of foam rubber, such as padded bras, rubber-coated tennis shoes, and galoshes, must not be dried in a dryer.

Automatic dryers are permanently lubricated at the factory and never need oiling.

Automatic Washer See "Washing Machine."

Avicron Avicron is the trade name for a crimped rayon filament yarn produced by American Viscose for carpets and bedspreads. When used in cut-pile construction the yarn takes on a curled surface texture, similar to caracul, upon being wet with water. The crimp cannot be removed with subsequent wetting.

Avlin See "Polyester."

Awnings Duck and canvas awnings cannot be cleaned but stains and mildew can be prevented by drying them properly after a rain. Do not raise them after a storm until they have dried thoroughly. If, however, they were raised during the rain, lower them as soon as you can so that water which has collected in the folds will drain off before stains are formed. Many are treated for mildew resistance.

Awnings should be stored during the winter in a cool, dry place. If your awning man takes them down and stores them for you, have him make any necessary repairs. If they are badly damaged, the frames can be re-covered. A special canvas paint called "Setfast," which has a plastic base, is widely recommended for awnings and outdoor cushions that have become faded. Follow the directions on the can exactly.

Awnings of the newer synthetic textiles do not weather or mildew.

Baby Clothes Use hot water and a mild, low-sudsing detergent or mild laundry soap for cottons. Rinse thoroughly.

Wash woolens, rayons, silks, and synthetics according to directions given under these headings. Woolen clothing and blankets that have been mothproofed should

27

be washed or dry cleaned before they are used again.

See also "Diapers."

Bakelite Trademark for plastics made by the Bakelite Corporation. See "Polyethylene," "Polystyrene," and "Phenolic."

Baking Soda See "Soda and Soda Compounds."

Bamboo Giant grass. See "Furniture—Bamboo."

Basement As a precaution against accidents and fire and for your own satisfaction, your basement should be kept uncluttered, reasonably clean, and orderly. Accumulations of old paper, rags, and shavings are an acute fire hazard. Untidy, badly lighted stairs may cause a broken leg or hip. So, whether yours is a slick modern basement or an old-fashioned, dirt-floor cellar, keep it neat and air it properly.

Air your basement during fair weather when the air outside is cooler than inside. Keep the windows closed during hot humid weather and on rainy days. Avoid storing things on the floor, where it is likely to be damp. Slatted shelves are best for storage because they allow air to circulate on all sides of articles placed on them. Store paints and painting equipment at a safe distance from any source of heat. They are a fire hazard.

Excessive dampness in a basement can be due to several factors. One is condensation of moisture contained in the air on cool surfaces such as walls, floors, and cold-water pipes. Look for leaking pipes and have them fixed. Have the cold-water pipes insulated. And

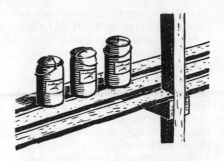

thin, by pruning, heavy base shrubbery that may be impeding the free circulation of air in the basement. The most common cause of excess humidity is laundering. Use of a dehumidifier or an air conditioner can correct this. For a discussion of these, see "Mildew."

Basket A good wetting now and then will prevent basketware from becoming brittle.

Bathtub Clean your bathtub with a damp cloth or sponge dipped in trisodium phosphate (Oakite), Spic and Span, or other chemical cleaner advertised for this purpose. Mild cleaning powders can be used but must be washed away afterwards. Coarse powders scratch the porcelain enamel finish and make the tub more difficult to clean.

Clean the fixtures according to the metal of which they are made. See "Chromium," "Nickel," etc.

Iron rust stains (brown), if light, often can be removed by rubbing them with a cut lemon. For more stubborn stains use a 5 percent solution of oxalic acid (poison) or a 10 percent hydrochloric acid solution (poison). Apply the acid with a bit of cloth or paper toweling, then rinse the tub thoroughly after a few seconds.

Acids, if allowed to stand, damage porcelain enamel. Copper stains (green) sometimes yield to soapsuds containing ammonia. If stubborn, use oxalic acid as described for iron rust stains. (Dripping faucets cause these stains; install new washers.)

To improve the appearance of an extremely stained or discolored tub, use a mixture of cream of tartar and peroxide. Stir in enough peroxide to make a paste and scrub the tub vigorously, using a small, stiff brush. The result will surprise you. Even the dark-brown stains caused by potassium permanganate baths, often prescribed for skin infections, disappear quickly and easily under this treatment.

And now for a few bathroom don'ts. Don't use the bathtub for washing venetian blinds or sharp-edged articles which could scratch it. Don't stand in it or place a stepladder in it to wash walls or a window without first protecting the surface with a rug or nonskid mat. Don't use the bathtub or lavatory as a home photography accessory; photo solutions damage porcelain enamel. Don't let strong solutions of household bleaches, hair bleaches, vinegar, or lemon stand for any length of time in a lavatory. Some of these will etch even acid-resistant enamel. Don't fail to rinse the washbasin thoroughly after cosmetic solutions, hair tints, or medicines have been used in it; they can cause discoloration. And don't leave nonskid mats in the tub to dry; some cause permanent stains.

Bats If bats have shown an interest in sharing your home and are, perhaps, safely ensconced in the attic or in the walls, you will probably save yourself a lot of trouble by calling an exterminator at once.

These flying mammals hunt insects at night and sleep during the day. They do not ordinarily harm people, but they carry rabies and can transmit it to human beings. In addition they are objectionable because of the noise they make and the bad odor they generate. The odor persists long after the roost is broken up and sometimes attracts a new colony unless thorough sanitary measures are taken.

Batproofing a house means making it free of bats and protecting it against their reentry. All openings into the house are covered with sheet metal or quarter-inch mesh. Sometimes the infested area must be fumigated, a job only for a professional exterminator.

Beaunit See "Polyester."

Bedbugs Bedbugs are brown, wingless insects, varying in size from one eighth to one quarter of an inch. They are flat and oval, and emit a disagreeable odor that frequently advertises their presence. Bedbugs hide in the daytime and emerge at night to bite sleeping people.

Bedbugs are spread by the clothing and baggage of travelers and visitors, second-hand beds and bedding, furniture, and laundry.

Brown and black spots on walls and baseboards indicate where these insects hide. In the early stages of an infestation they are found under the tufts and in the seams of mattresses. Later they spread to crevices in bedsteads and, if allowed to multiply, become established behind window and door casings, baseboards, picture moldings, furniture, loose wallpaper, and in cracks in the plaster. An effective spray should be applied in all possible hiding places.

Select a sprayer that can be adjusted to produce either a mist or coarse particles. Both types are required. Lindane, ronnel, malathion, and pyrethrum are effective killers. Use them as a spray rather than as a dust. They can be bought ready-mixed at drugstores, hardware stores, department stores, and large food markets. Prepared mixes often contain other insecticides. Do not use any insecticide on a mattress unless the label declares it safe.

You can, of course, mix your own spray, using one of the emulsifiables with water or kerosene. Labels on the containers will usually give you the proportions and directions for mixing the spray. About 4 ounces is needed for a bed and mattress. Let the bed dry for 1 or 2 hours before making it.

One application of lindane, ronnel, or malathion is usually sufficient because it leaves a coating that acts as a killer for several months. Pyrethrum sprays should contain at least 0.2 percent of pyrethins (measuring units). Most of them also contain the synergist piperonyl butoxide which makes them more effective. They should be applied several times at 1- to 2-week intervals because they do not provide a long-lasting killing surface.

Spray the slats, springs, and frames of beds so that they are thoroughly wet. Spray, but do not soak, mattresses, paying particular attention to seams and tufts.

See also "Insecticides" for precautions.

Bedspreads Machine wash cotton bedspreads and hang them outdoors to dry or put them in a dryer. If you use a clothesline, shake out candlewick and chenille spreads now and then while they are drying to fluff them up. If you double them over the line, with the tufts inside, stray breezes will help fluff the tufts by rubbing them gently together. When dry, brush up the tufts with a clean, dry whisk broom. Do not iron.

If your spread is fringed, you will find it easier to comb out the strands while they are still wet. Crocheted spreads should be stretched gently to their proportions while drying.

Silk and rayon spreads should be dry-cleaned unless the manufacturer's instructions stipulate that they are washable. See "Silk," "Rayon." Launder spreads of synthetic textiles according to fiber. See "Orlon," etc. For cotton spreads with no-iron finishes see "Durable Press."

Bedsprings Box springs are cleaned with a stiff brush, or with the upholstery attachment for the vacuum cleaner. Metal springs should be cleaned with a hand brush, dustcloth, or the round dusting brush of the vacuum cleaner. If necessary, box springs can be scrubbed like upholstered furniture. See "Furniture—Upholstered."

Beetleware Trademark for a urea plastic. See "Melamine and Urea."

Bemberg Trademark for cuprammonium rayon. See "Rayon."

30

Benzene A hydrocarbon obtained commercially from coal tar. It is a clear, colorless fluid with a pleasant odor. Benzene is used as a solvent for gums, resins and fats. Though it is a valuable spot remover, it is highly flammable and should not be stored in large amounts in the home. Keep well stoppered in a cool safe place.

Benzine, Benzol A clear, colorless fluid, commonly called petroleum ether. It is obtained from a distillation of petroleum and contains a mixture of volatile hydrocarbons. It differs essentially from benzene by being such a mixture, benzene being a single hydrocarbon of constant composition. Benzine is used as a solvent for fats, resins and certain alkaloids. It also is highly flammable and should not be used in large amounts in the home or stored there. Friction alone can sometimes generate a spark, which in turn can cause combustion.

Berry For stains caused by berries see "Fruit and Berry," in "Stains," p. 228.

Bicarbonate of Soda See "Soda and Soda Compounds."

Biconstituent A category of man-made textile fibers in which nylon and spandex are blended. The combination of the two fibers makes super-stretch hosiery, sold as Monvelle by the Monsanto Company.

Blanket (Electric) An electric blanket can be washed by hand or in a machine by the soak–wash method. It should never be dry cleaned because solvents used in dry cleaning might damage the insulation on the wires inside. Many laundries specialize in handling such blankets. Ask your laundryman about this service and give him the blanket separately.

If you want to wash the blanket yourself and directions are lacking, the following instruction, based on information from a leading manufacturer, should be safe.

Hand Washing Shake out loose dust gently and soak the blanket for 10–15 minutes in lukewarm suds (100° F.), made with a mild synthetic detergent. Occasionally, press the suds through the fabric. Rinse 3 times in the same way. Squeeze out excess water by hand. Do not wring or twist the blanket.

Tumbler Washer Fill the tub with lukewarm water, add a mild synthetic detergent, and run the machine a minute or two to mix it in. Stop the washer. Immerse the blanket and let it soak, *without tumbling*, for 15–20 minutes. Advance the dial and spin off the wash water. Allow the machine to fill with lukewarm water for a deep rinse. Stop the machine and soak the blanket, *without tumbling*, for 2–3 minutes. Spin off the water and repeat the rinse. Advance the dial to the final spin, and spin for 2–3 minutes.

Top-loading Washer Fill the washer with lukewarm water, add a mild synthetic detergent, and let the machine agitate briefly to mix it in. Use a delicate fabric setting, if available. Stop the washer, immerse the blanket, and let it soak for 15–20 minutes. *Do not agitate.* Advance the dial, spin off the wash

31

water, and allow the machine to fill with lukewarm rinse water. Let the blanket soak for 2–3 minutes. Spin off the rinse water. Repeat the soak rinse. Advance the dial to the final spin. Stop the washer after 2–3 minutes.

Drying Pull and stretch the blanket gently into shape and hang it over two parallel lines to dry—in the shade. Use an automatic dryer only if the directions for your blanket say it is safe. In any case, such a dryer should be used only if it can be operated without heat. The directions are:

Put 3 or 4 bath towels in the dryer and heat at the regular setting for 5 minutes. Turn off the heat. Put the blanket in the dryer and tuck the towels into its folds. Tumble for 10–15 minutes. Remove the blanket (still damp), ease it into shape, and hang it over parallel clotheslines. If clotheslines are not available, spread it over a protected flat surface to complete drying.

Caution: Mothproofing agents should not be used on an electric blanket because of possible damage to the wiring. Wrap your clean blanket in a cloth or in plastic sheeting and store it in the box it came in.

Blanket (Synthetic) If you do not have instructions for washing your *100-percent Orlon acrylic or Dacron polyester blanket,* follow these instructions from the du Pont Company. Plan to do the blankets one at a time. First, shake out the blanket and pretreat spots and soiled bindings with a heavy-duty liquid detergent. Machine wash the blanket for 5 minutes in warm

suds (100° F.) made with a heavy-duty detergent. Stop the machine after 2 or 3 minutes of the final spin-dry cycle. (Use the complete special-fabric cycle if it is available.) Remove the blanket and let it air dry by hanging it evenly on a clean clothesline. Straighten the blanket and smooth the bindings while the blanket is damp.

If desired, a home dryer can be used. Preheat the dryer for about 10 minutes at 180°–190° F. Tumble the blanket for 10 minutes or until it is thoroughly dry.

For hand washing, use lukewarm water (100° F.) and a synthetic detergent. Work the blanket up and down until it is clean. Rinse thoroughly. Squeeze out excess water gently without wringing or twisting. Dry as described for machine washing.

To press bindings, use a steam iron or dry iron at a moderate or synthetic setting, and a press cloth. When dry, the blanket can be brushed with a soft brush to raise the nap.

Union Carbide provides these instructions for *all-Dynel blankets.* Soak them for 10 minutes in warm water (not over 170° F.) with soap or detergent. Agitate them in your washer twice for one and a half minutes (no more). Use a dryer only if the temperature can be kept at "low" and then to "damp dry." If hung when quite damp the wrinkles will fall out. If acetate bindings are pressed, do not let the hot iron touch the nap of the blanket.

Synthetic blankets can also be dry-cleaned.

Blanket (Treated Woolen) Some woolen blankets have been treated with finishes that make them completely machine washable. Because the treatment method varies, the safest advice is to follow the manufacturer's instructions. See "Woolens (Treated)."

Blanket (Untreated Woolen)

Blankets made of wool or wool blends can be washed or dry-cleaned, according to personal preference. If you send them to a laundry be sure you have selected a reliable one and that the blankets arc tagged for special attention.

If you are washing blankets at home, choose a fine warm day with a light breeze blowing. Wash one blanket at a time. First shake it out lightly to remove loose dust, then pay special attention to spots and bindings. Using a soft brush and lukewarm water, work an unbuilt synthetic detergent, such as Woolite, into especially soiled portions.

For washing the blanket, use the same mild detergent and lukewarm water (95°–105° F.). Water that is too hot shrinks wool. Do not use a water softener. They are not needed when synthetic detergents are used. Furthermore, they are alkaline and harmful to wool fibers. Do not use soap: even the gentlest is mildly alkaline.

Too much handling, rubbing, twisting, or agitation in water makes wool mat, pill, and roughen. Recommended today for both hand and machine washing of woolen blankets is the "easy soak" method—better for blankets, easier for you.

Fill your tub or washer with lukewarm water, remembering that wool absorbs a great deal. Dissolve in the water enough synthetic detergent to make a good suds. Place the blanket in the water and let it soak for 15 to 20 minutes. Turn the blanket once or twice by hand, then drain away, or spin off, the water. Refill the tub or machine for the first rinse. This will also be a soak operation. (Do not operate the machine.) Soak the blanket for about five minutes in the lukewarm rinse water, then repeat.

If a light froth of bubbles remains after the second rinse, do not feel that you must rinse a third time. The bubbles are due to the chemical nature of the detergent, which froths even in the hardest water if the merest trace is present. Actually, the detergent rinses out better than soap.

Spin or drain away the last rinse. It is not important to extract a great deal of water from a blanket before hanging it because woolens drip dry quickly. An automatic dryer can be used with caution to hasten the drying. Put 5 or 6 bath towels in the dryer as a buffer load and preheat the dryer for 5 minutes at a high setting. Add the blanket and tuck the towels into the folds. Let the dryer operate on high heat for 10 minutes, then check the blanket. Remove it when it is about three-quarters dry and hang it to complete drying.

Blankets should be hung in the shade on a good tight line, preferably over an old sheet to insure perfect cleanliness. For maximum drying efficiency hang the blankets lengthwise over parallel lines,

placed a foot or two apart. Shake them lightly to fluff the nap. When partially dry, turn them over and shake them out again.

When the blanket is throughly dry, brush up the nap with a clean whisk broom. The warmth of a blanket, as well as its appearance, depends to a great extent upon the amount of nap. Press the bindings gently with a warm iron. If worn, make a note to buy new ones, obtainable at notion counters in department stores.

Blanket Cover If you use blanket covers on your beds, your blankets won't have to be washed very often. A sheet will do if you don't feel like making a special investment.

Bleach (v.) To whiten, either by exposure to the sun or by the use of chemical preparations.

Bleach (n.) Bleaches are chemical agents used to whiten any material, especially white fabrics, and to remove certain stains. They should always be used carefully because, if directions are not followed, they may weaken fabrics and fade colors. Because metals may speed up their action, they should not be used in metal containers.

For home laundry use there are two types of bleach—chlorine and peroxy. Chlorine bleaches are available as liquids, containing sodium hypochlorite, and in granular form, containing organic chlorine compounds. Peroxy bleaches are powders containing sodium perborate or potassium monopersulfate. In using either type, follow the directions on the container. Chlorine bleach (Clorox, Purex, Action, Stardust) is best for untreated cottons, linens, and synthetics;

peroxys (Snowy, Dexol, Clorox 2, Beads O' Bleach) are for fabrics which chlorine bleach damages. Never use chlorine bleaches on silk, spandex, wool, or cottons that have been treated for wrinkle resistance. On fire-retardant fabrics follow the manufacturer's recommendations.

Spreading wet fabrics in the sun is another way to bleach them, but some fibers are weakened by sunlight. If you use this method, expose them briefly and infrequently.

Other bleaches, used in stain removal, are hydrogen peroxide, sodium perborate, and color removers, sold in drugstores. For further information look up the specific bleach you are planning to use: "Chlorine Bleach," "Sodium Perborate," etc.

Blood Stains See "Stains," p. 225.

Bloom A gray discoloration that sometimes appears on highly polished furniture. See "Furniture."

Blueberry See "Fruit and Berry" in "Stains," p. 228.

Bluestone See "Stone Floors."

Bluing Bluing is not essential in the laundry, but many women like the extra whiteness it suggests in clothes and bed linens. If you are using bluing, remember that it is better to use too little than too much. Prepare bluing water according to the directions given by the manufacturer, just before it is to be used. If it stands too long, the clothes may be streaked.

Soluble powder bluing is prepared by dissolving it in a small quantity of water. This liquid is then added a drop at a time to a tub of cool clear water. Block, or ball, bluing is put into a cotton, or flannel, bag and moved through the water until the proper tint is obtained. The tint can be tested on a small garment. All bluings, except bluing soap flakes, are used in the final rinse water. Bluing soap flakes go into the wash water.

Stir bluing water during use and blue a few pieces at a time. The best method is to dip them in and out, one at a time. Never let them soak in the bluing water. Never draw off the bluing water, leaving the clothes in the tub, because this causes streaks.

If cotton clothes are overblued, pour boiling water over them unless finished for wrinkle resistance. Or rinse them in hot water in your washer. See also "Stains," p. 226.

The use of detergents containing fluorescent dyes makes bluing unnecessary.

Bonded Fabrics Bonded fabrics consist of two or more layers of material, at least one of which is a textile. The purpose of bonding is to give fabrics, especially knits, bulk without weight and dimensional stability. Manufacturing processes vary.

At this writing, two methods of bonding are used. The first involves melting one surface of polyurethane (plastic) foam and, while it is molten and sticky, pressing it into a fabric. The second method (flame bonding) uses the same system of melting but an extremely thin layer of foam is applied to the face fabric. Most of this is then burned off and, while the foam that remains is still tacky, a tricot lining material is attached.

Bonded fabrics vary widely in quality, depending on the materials and methods used by the manufacturer. Inferior kinds come apart or shrink excessively when washed or dry cleaned by standard methods. Merely wetting some of them causes them to shrink away and delaminate. At the opposite end of the scale are bonded fabrics that can be dry cleaned or washed successfully by standards applicable to the face fabric. Your only guide is the tag. If the tag says the garment is washable, but specific instructions are not given, wash by hand in cold water with a cold-water detergent and handle gently. A textile manufacturer offers the following advice:

"Unless the garment has a tag giving a money-back or replacement guarantee, give it to a dry cleaner with instructions to use a short cycle of dry cleaning (6 minutes) and air dry. Extensive experimenting has indicated that even the poorest bonded fabrics will not delaminate under these circumstances."

Book Lice Book lice (or psocids) are not harmful or destructive but their presence is annoying. They feed on microscopic molds that grow on furniture, wallpaper, and other household furnishings. Rooms that have been closed or poorly ventilated provide an ideal location for them. They can be controlled by spraying with a 2 percent malathion solution. Little or no discoloration of the sprayed surfaces will result if deodorized kerosene is used as a carrier. See "Insecticides" for precautions.

Books Don't let your books slump on partly filled shelves if you want to preserve their bindings. Use bookends or library brackets. Books should be arranged upright and loosely enough to allow them to be taken out easily without damaging the delicate back bindings. Place them near the edge of the shelf so that air can circulate behind them. Oversized books, such as atlases, art and music books may be stacked flat. A library should be neither too dry nor too damp. Too much dry heat will damage leather-backed books and make the pages and bindings of clothbound books brittle. Dampness will cause mildew and other molds. Bright sunlight will fade the colors of the bindings.

Books can be dusted best with the dusting brush of the vacuum cleaner or with a clean soft paintbrush. Dust outward from the binding. You may flip the pages to get dust out but don't bang books together to remove dust if you want to preserve the bindings.

Leather bookbindings deteriorate from two causes, acidity and lack of oil. Both conditions have been attributed to manufacturing processes but may be due to natural causes—the absorption of acidic gases in polluted air and the gradual destruction of the oil in the leather.

Damage to leather books in good condition can be minimized by replacing the oils lost with use. The treatment should begin when the books are new and be repeated every year or two. Emulsions containing four or five ingredients are sometimes used, but the following simple preparations are all effective: saddle soap, a commercial preparation; neat's-foot oil (for dull leather); petroleum jelly, medicinal grade (white); a mixture of neat's-foot oil and castor oil in equal parts; lanolin oil (4 parts) and neat's-foot oil (6 parts). To prepare this last dressing warm the lanolin oil slowly in a double boiler until it liquefies and then stir in the neat's-foot oil.

These dressings are best applied with the fingers or palm of the hand, or you can use a small swab of felt, cheesecloth, or chamois. Spread the dressing quickly and sparingly over the leather, being careful not to stain the cloth or paper portions of covers. Rub it in gently until it has been absorbed. Wait several hours, then repeat. Oiling leather usually darkens it slightly, and almost inevitably there are areas where the color is of unequal depth.

Leatherbound books that have begun to powder are sometimes improved by lacquering. First smooth the leather very gently, using fine emery cloth or crocus cloth (obtained at hardware stores). Pay especial attention to the places where it is powdery or scuffed. Oil can be applied next, if desired (it cannot be absorbed after lacquering). Light-colored patches can be touched up with an alcoholic solution of a suitable leather dye. Prepared lacquers in aerosol-type sprayers are next applied. Select a thin lacquer recommended for leather (cellulose nitrate, acrylic) and spray a thin even coating on the bindings. When the lacquer has dried, apply a second coating. (Lacquers are flammable; do not work near an open flame.)

Torn pages can be mended with gummed tissue, or with strips cut from rice paper or thin onionskin. Loose pages can be replaced by pasting with a folded strip of paper. After repairs have been made it is a good idea to flank the mended pages with waxed paper before closing the book. This will prevent the pages from sticking together. Press rumpled pages with a warm iron, using a sheet of paper between the page and the iron as a precaution against scorching. Valuable books, in bad repair, should be handled by an expert. Your local library probably can recommend one.

Mildew and other molds are caused by excessive dampness. See "Mildew" for prevention and cure of mildew on books. It is sometimes impossible to remove mildew stains from the pages of books.

Foresight: Think twice before you have a rare book rebound. If it is a first edition, its value will be reduced substantially.

Borax A salt formed by a combination of boracic acid and soda. It is a white crystalline solid, slightly soluble in water. Borax is used in the manufacture of glass and enamel, as a flux for solder, as a cleanser and water softener for laundry, bath and shampoo and as an antiseptic. It cuts grease, loosens dirt and retards the growth of many molds and bacteria which cause putrefaction and unpleasant odors.

Borax formerly was brought to the United States from the East Indies, where it was said to be found on the margins and in the bottoms of certain lakes. Our most important source today is Borax Lake, California.

Caution: Borax is toxic.

Botch Ill-finished or bungled work; what you are likely to make of a cleaning job if you go at it without knowing the proper procedure.

Correcting a botch, if it can be corrected, is likely to entail either a great deal of work or expense. Botches can keep you from saving enough money to get that new end table or spring *chapeau.*

Bottle Use a detergent, or soap, and water and a bottle brush. To remove mineral stains or cloudiness from the bottom of an ornamental bottle, fill it partially with water, add ammonia, and let it stand for several hours or overnight. Then rinse it out.

Nursing Wash bottles, caps, and nipples in clean water and dishwashing soap or detergent. Use a bottle brush. Squeeze water through the nipple holes to be sure they are open. Rinse them well so that all soap or detergent is gone, and let them stand in a rack to dry. Bottles do not need to be boiled, says *Infant Care,* a booklet from the U.S. Department of Health, Education and Welfare, unless the doctor specifically orders it.

Vacuum Clean the inside of a vacuum bottle with hot water and synthetic detergent, or with water and baking soda. Toss in torn bits of paper for mild abrasive action if desirable. Rinse the bottle thoroughly, wipe, and place it upside down to dry. To keep the bottle fresh, leave it uncapped until used again. Never immerse the entire bottle in water, to avoid seepage into the metal barrel. Occasionally, unscrew the metal shoulder of the case and wipe the interior dry to prevent the possible formation of rust.

The inner container of a vacuum bottle usually is made of artificial glass or plastic and should not be subjected to careless handling. Do not use it for carbonated beverages. Fill your bottle to a level just below the stopper.

Stoppers vary. Some snap on, some slide into place when the top is replaced, others twist or screw in. If a cork is used it can be sterilized and sweetened by boiling. If the stopper is a twist-in type, be gentle to avoid breakage. The inner bottle, however, is replaceable.

Brass Brass is an alloy of copper and zinc. Two parts of copper usually are used to one part of zinc. Formerly the copper was combined also with tin and other base metals. "Bronze," from the Italian word bronzo, meaning brass, is used today to identify the ancient alloy of copper and tin.

Tarnished brass is sometimes easier to polish if it is first washed in hot soapsuds. After drying it, remove the tarnish and spots of corrosion by rubbing it thoroughly with a good polish made especially for brass. When it is clean, polish it with a soft flannel cloth or chamois. This will give the brass a bright finish. If a soft finish is desired, substitute for the polish a thin paste made by mixing rotten-stone and linseed oil. Wipe off the excess oil and polish with a clean cloth. Rub antique brass with lemon (mineral) oil and polish it softly.

A piece of lemon dipped in salt, or hot vinegar and salt, will remove corrosion from brass. This is an old-fashioned method but one that can be adapted profitably to small ornaments or miniatures that are difficult to clean. Provided they are not decorated with materials that

hot water will damage, they can be boiled in water containing salt and vinegar. Most of the corrosion will be loosened or removed. You can then finish with brass polish.

Lacquered brass needs only dusting and, occasionally, washing with light mild suds made with lukewarm water. Rinse and dry. If the lacquer becomes damaged it can be removed with acetone or amyl acetate (banana oil). Small articles can be covered with boiling water which soaks off the lacquer. To relacquer, polish it to the desired luster, wipe it with acetone to remove every trace of film, then brush or spray on water-white, transparent metal lacquer. This is not an easy job and unless you are skilled in crafts you had better have your brass redone.

Brass andirons and fire tools that have been long neglected may prove a tough job, owing to burned-in resins from your fire. Fine steel wool (p. 182) may be required for a clean job but will take plenty of time and elbow grease. Easier to handle and very effective is fine emery cloth of the sort used by metalworkers. You can buy it at a hardware store. In using it rub the metal in one direction, not round and round, and when it is clean polish it with brass polish.

After polishing, wash brass thoroughly with soapsuds to remove traces of acid polishes and avoid rapid retarnishing.

Brassière If you are fussy about the fit of your "bra" don't iron it. Replace tired elastic and broken fasteners with "refreshers," available at notion counters. Do not use chlorine bleach on bras with spandex elastic.

Brick Floors, *Glazed* Dust them with a push broom, dry mop, or vacuum cleaner. Wash with a sponge or cloth wrung out of warm soapy water. Rinse and wipe dry. For a very dirty floor use one ounce of sodium hydrosulphite (sold in drugstores as color remover) dissolved in one gallon of warm water. Waxing is optional.

Unglazed Dust with a brush or push broom. Wash with warm water containing one ounce per gallon of a washing powder that contains trisodium phosphate or Oakite. Washing soda also is very effective. Use a sponge or cloth; rinse thoroughly. If especially dirty you can use a stronger solution, but don't forget to rinse the bricks thoroughly with clear water. Floors of unglazed brick are sometimes sealed. In this case, self-polishing waxes may be used to provide a gloss and make them easier to clean.

Brick fireplaces that have faded can be cleaned according to the directions given above. The color can be restored by brushing them over with a cold water paint (consult your paint dealer) of the proper color. In England a material called redding, probably red chalk, is sometimes used with water to restore the color of faded brick fireplaces. "Bath bricks," in various colors, are sold and a little of this is crushed and added to water for use as required.

Tip from Mark Twain: ". . . the bricks were kept clean and red by pouring water on them and scrubbing them with another brick; sometimes they wash them over with a red water-paint they call Spanish-brown." (*The Adventures*

of Huckleberry Finn.) See also "Muriatic Acid" and "Sealers."

Brocade A rich fabric, usually of silk, satin or velvet. It is shot through with gold or silver threads and often ornamented with raised designs of leaves, flowers, etc.

Brocades should be dry-cleaned by an expert. To press, place the material right side down on the ironing board and cover it with a piece of thin white cloth or tissue paper. Do *not* dampen. Press with a warm, never hot, iron.

Bronze Our word "bronze" comes from the Italian *bronzo*, meaning brass. Today's bronze is an alloy of copper and tin, sometimes containing a little zinc and lead. Formerly this alloy was included in the term "brass."

Solid bronze often is given a coating of clear lacquer at the factory to protect the finish. Lacquered bronze needs only dusting and occasional wiping with a damp cloth. Should the lacquer crack or peel, have it redone.

Unlacquered bronze can be washed if required with mild soap or detergent and water. Sometimes hot vinegar or hot buttermilk is used. Rinse and wipe dry with a clean soft cloth. To brighten bronze, rub it with a dry cloth dipped in whiting or rottenstone, or with a polish made for bronze.

Bronze-finished steel often is mistaken for solid bronze. When spots of corrosion appear and a little rubbing reveals a steel base, bronze lacquer or metal paint is called for. Or you might have the article electroplated with a dark copper.

Bronze, an alloy, cannot be applied by electrolysis. However, a new process has been developed recently by means of which molten metals, including alloys, can be sprayed upon metallic surfaces. Large objects can be touched up by this method or done over in a very satisfactory manner. Firms doing such work charge by the hour. Worth looking into, if you have a nice lamp that needs to be refinished.

Broom Why cling to an antique when engineers spend hours designing brooms that have balance and poise? The modern broom is weighted to swing, has a handle this is easy to grip, and a built-in device so you can hang it up.

A broom should never stand on its bristles if you want it to give good service. If yours is not equipped with a ring for hanging, put a screw eye in the end, or bore a hole through the top of the handle and knot a piece of string through it.

Corn brooms should be wet occasionally to keep them from becoming brittle. See also "Electric Broom."

Brushes If you are muddling along with an inadequate supply of good brushes, the time has come to take an inventory of what you have and to investigate the array of new and attractive models that are available.

There is a special brush for every conceivable job and the right one will cut down hours of work. A long-handled bristle brush is dandy for porches and certain types of floors. For a good job on radiators there is nothing better than a brush made especially for the task. A small, soft brush in the laundry is indispensable, once you find how

efficient it is at removing spots on materials, such as wool, which are damaged by rubbing. A nylon bristle brush over the sink is handy for dish washing. Nylon is good, too, for toilet and tub brushes that won't drip. So keep a good supply and take care of them right.

Hair Hairbrushes made of *animal bristles* should be cleaned regularly by washing in warm soapsuds, or suds to which one or two teaspoons of ammonia have been added. Rinse them thoroughly and dry them on a towel placed in the shade, with the bristles down. When they are nearly dry, turn them, bristles up, and place them in the sun. A little alum (about half a teaspoonful) in the final rinsing water will stiffen sluggish hair bristles. Hairbrushes with nylon bristles are washed in lukewarm soapsuds and rinsed with clear water. Brushes with nylon backs and nylon bristles can be sterilized by boiling.

Paint Generally speaking, the material used as a thinner for the paint you are using is the material that will clean the brush after you have finished using it. Different types of commercial paintbrush cleaners are on the market, which also will do a good job if you follow the directions on the container carefully. Some have a starch base and contain soda compounds such as trisodium phosphate. Others contain mixtures of paint solvents to enable them to deal with a variety of paints.

The time to clean a paintbrush is right after you have finished using it. Here are some notes for the different types. Brushes used with shellac should be cleaned with denatured alcohol, then washed with soap and water. Brushes used with water-type paints are cleaned in clear water, or with water and a detergent. Rinse and hang to dry.

Paintbrushes used with lacquer are cleaned with lacquer thinner, or acetone. Wash with a detergent and hang up to dry.

Brushes used for oil paints, varnishes and enamel are cleaned with turpentine, then washed with water and a detergent. Hang them up to dry.

Brushes used for the new rubberized and synthetic resin paints, which are mixed with water instead of oil, can be cleaned with water or water containing a detergent.

Nylon brushes are cleaned in much the same way as other brushes, except that it is a good idea to work out as much of the paint as possible first. Pour a little thinner (the kind used for the paint) onto the brush and work out the paint on a newspaper or board. Then clean the brush in the thinner. If necessary leave it suspended in the thinner overnight, then work it out in the morning, rinse with clean thinner and wash with a detergent. Do not use alcohol to clean nylon brushes, and do not use nylon brushes for shellac or the bristles will be softened.

Important note: Paintbrushes always should be hung up to dry after being washed. They should never be allowed to soak in any solution containing water or the bristles will be loosened. If your paint project (oil paints) is to be continued within a few days, sus-

pend your brush in a jar containing linseed oil and turpentine. This mixture may be half and half, or less than half turpentine. The bristles will remain soft and pliable. When you want to use it again, wipe the bristles off carefully with a clean cloth, then rinse them with turpentine if required.

It is a good idea to wrap your clean brushes in paper or cellophane with the tips exposed, when storing them, as this keeps the bristles nice and straight. Lay them flat, if stored when dry. Or hang them, bristles down, in a rack.

Bulbs See "Electric Bulbs."

Burns on Furniture See "Furniture."

Butter Stains See "Greasy Stains," p. 223.

Butyrate See "Cellulosics."

Calcimine Calcimine is a wash, similar to whitewash. It is sometimes called water paint and is sold under various trade names. Calcimine is not permanent and cannot be washed. However, it is easy to apply and, in rooms not exposed to moisture, may last for several years. If a calcimined wall or ceiling is to be redone, or painted with an oil paint, the old finish should be completely removed. Use a cellulose sponge and a pail of water containing a little washing soda. You may need a scraper. Or ask your paint dealer for advice regarding a newer-type finish that' can go over the calcimine.

Candelabra See "Crystal" and "Lighting Fixtures."

Candles Soiled or finger-marked candles can be cleaned with a soft cloth moistened with denatured alcohol.

Candlesticks Pour warm water into the candleholder to soften and remove old wax. To remove wax from outer surfaces of candlesticks cover your finger with a soft cloth and push the wax off gently with your fingernail.

Wash china candlesticks with warm soapy water, rinse and dry. Wash crystal candlesticks in water containing a synthetic detergent. Rinse and polish with a clean, lint-less cloth.

Metal candlesticks are cleaned according to directions for the metals of which they are made. Candlesticks of weighted or hollow silver should not be immersed in hot water. Lacquered metal candlesticks need only to be wiped with a damp cloth. Hot water and soap will damage the lacquer. "See "China," "Silver," "Brass," etc.

Candle Wax See "Candlesticks," "Furniture," and "Stains," p. 226.

Candlewick See "Bedspreads."

Candy Stains See "Stains," p. 226.

Cane Funiture See "Furniture."

Carafe See "Glass."

Carbon Paper See "Stains," p. 226.

Carbon Tetrachloride Once rated a first-class dry cleaner, because it is nonflammable, carbon tetrachloride today is banned as a killer.

Carborundum A carbon-silicon compound made by electric fusion. Its uses are similar to those of emery. See "Emery."

Carpet Beetle There are three or four species of carpet beetle—a destructive pest—but the common variety is a reddish-brown creature, somewhat fuzzy in appearance and about one quarter of an inch long. Like clothes moths, carpet beetles are harmless in the adult, or winged, form. They flit from flower to flower, imbibing nectar, then in at the open window and the trouble begins.

Carpet beetles deposit their eggs near pleasant sources of food supply for their larvae, such as rugs, hair mattreses and cushions, feather pillows and fur. The eggs hatch and the larvae munch voraciously.

Carpet beetles are hardier than clothes moths and much more active. They may quickly infest an entire house yet many women do not recognize them and blame the damage they do on moths. Certain insecticides will control both moths and carpet beetles. For instructions see "Moths—*Clothes*."

Carpets and Rugs For good appearance and better wear, carpets and rugs should be kept free of the surface dust that dims their colors and of the sharp particles of grit which, unless regularly removed, become embedded and cut their fibers. Areas of heavy traffic and random spills can be cleaned up easily and without pain if you keep a small carpet sweeper handy. Once a week rugs should be vacuum-cleaned thoroughly. Go over each area at least seven times. Spilled foods should be removed

Scrape the lather off with a spatula and wipe away the remaining suds with a clean dry cloth. When the entire rug has been cleaned, sponge it several times with clean water, taking care not to get it too wet. Finally, wipe the rug with a dry cloth in the direction of the nap.

Absorbent powder cleaners also can be used. These include Mainteen, Powder-ene (clay-base cleaners), and Glamorene (wood-flour base). In using, follow the directions on the container.

If the pile of a rug has been crushed by heavy furniture, place a damp cloth over it and apply a hot iron, using no pressure. Brush the spot briskly. Repeat, if necessary. Use this same method on the front and back of corners and edges that curl.

Stain-causing materials, spilled on rugs, should be cleaned up promptly because some stains become permanent if allowed to remain even a few hours. Reweaving the area is then the only solution. When a stain is fresh it can often be removed by just sponging the area with plain lukewarm water.

For spilled foods and stains of unknown origin, follow this procedure. With a dull knife or spatula remove first the solid part of the stain. Next blot up any liquid with a paper towel or with a slightly moistened sponge or cloth. Then sponge the stain with a clean white unstarched cloth, dampened with lukewarm water, working always from the center of the stain toward the edge. Do not scrub roughly; wipe and pat gently to avoid disturbing the pile. If a spot still shows when the area has dried completely, sponge it again with a detergent solution (one teaspoon

promptly and spots and stains should be attended to when they occur to avoid setting.

Periodically, at least once a year, carpets and rugs should be shampooed by a professional or at home with one of the new appliances designed for the task. These can be rented. By finger-tip control they spread a foam of shampoo evenly over the rug. The foam is allowed to dry thoroughly—for several hours or overnight. As it dries it draws the dirt to the surface. When the rug is completely dry you vacuum the soil away. Small rugs can be shampooed by hand with special shampoos. But hand-cleaning a large rug is a backbreaking business and the results are often not satisfactory.

Before attempting to shampoo a rug yourself, clean it with a vacuum cleaner—on both sides if possible. If you use a rug shampoo, read and follow exactly the directions on the container. If using a soap lather, test first in an inconspicuous place to make sure the colors are fast, then, with a soft cloth or brush, using a circular motion, clean a small area at a time.

43

of liquid detergent and one teaspoon of white vinegar in two cups of water). Rinse by sponging with a cloth or sponge squeezed out of clear, lukewarm water. Do not get the rug too wet. Raise the damp part if you can so that air can circulate freely, or dry it with an electric fan or the exhaust from your vacuum cleaner. For greasy stains use a cleaning fluid, sponging from the center of the stain toward the edge.

If the stain requires the use of a special cleaning solution, apply it with a medicine dropper. For difficult or special stains see specific stains in Section II. Follow the directions given, using the methods outlined here.

And now, before moving on to special types of rugs, let's run through some do's and don'ts that apply to them all. **Don't** get rugs too wet during shampooing, and **don't** let furniture stand on a damp rug if you can avoid it. If you can't avoid it, **do** slip folded waxed paper under table and chair legs to prevent stains from casters and glides. **Don't** walk on a dampened rug. If traffic cannot be prevented, make a path by spreading uncolored wrapping paper. **Don't** attempt to pull off sprouting ends of yarn. Snip them off with sharp scissors. **Do** snip off also fiber ends singed by dropped cigarettes—and sponge the place with detergent solution. **Do** lift furniture to move it; **don't** shove it across a rug. **Do** turn your rugs around now and then so that wear will be evenly distributed. **Don't** overlook the value of rubber or plastic glides under casters to keep furniture stationary and to avoid crushing the pile. **Don't** take chances with moths and carpet beetles; protect

wool and wool blends with suitable insecticides. (See "Moths— Clothes.") Cotton rugs and rugs made entirely of synthetic fibers are not attacked unless spotted with food. **Do** air manageable rugs in the sunshine occasionally, if you can. It freshens them and kills insect larvae.

Cotton rugs, scatter size, can be washed in your electric washer or in a tub if the colors are fast. Use plenty of mild suds made with soap and a softener, or detergent, and rinse with large amounts of water. Do not wring or twist them but hang them, dripping, straight on the line in the shade. Shake chenille rugs out lightly now and then and, when dry, shake them vigorously to fluff them up. Oval and round rugs may be laid flat on the grass, or on a paper, to dry without losing their shape. For in-place cleaning of large cotton rugs and carpets, consult your local rug specialist.

Fiber, grass and sisal rugs are vacuum-cleaned or brushed on both sides with a stiff brush and wiped occasionally with a damp cloth. Roll them up frequently to clean the floor underneath, as dirt sifts through them. When very soiled, send them to a rug cleaner. Canvas dye paints and special rug paints can be used to freshen faded rugs of this type. If you undertake this job, be sure to put plenty of newspapers underneath the rug. Use the paint thin and work it into all crevices with a stiff brush.

Fur rugs, when mounted on heavy flannel or wool, can be cleaned with a coarse absorbent, such as corn meal. Spread the corn

44

meal over the rug and then brush it out. Repeat this process, using fresh corn meal each time, until the rug is clean.

Fur rugs otherwise mounted, or unmounted, are cleaned by wiping the fur surface with a cloth wrung out of mild, lukewarm suds, made with a synthetic detergent. Be very careful not to get the pelt wet. Wipe with a cloth wrung out of clear lukewarm water and repeat until all traces of detergent have been removed from the fur. Bluing can be used in the last rinse if the fur is white. Dry flat on the floor. Moths love a fur rug so take due precautions, especially if you are storing it. See "Furs."

Hooked rugs are made by looping wool or cotton strips through a cloth base, such as burlap. They must not be beaten or shaken or these loops will be loosened and the backing broken. Sprouting ends can be clipped off safely if the rug is closely loomed. These rugs, whether made of wool or cotton, are best cleaned by a professional. The rotary scrubbing method usually is recommended.

Ordinary care of hooked rugs is the same as for other rugs.

Matting may be swept with a soft brush or cleaned with a vacuum cleaner. Once a week, after it has been cleaned, it should be rolled up so that the floor underneath can be cleaned thoroughly. This is important because dirt sifts right through the matting. Occasionally wipe the matting with a damp cloth, wrung out of clear water, or water containing one or two teaspoons of ammonia. Don't soak the matting, or you may get a musty smell.

Numdah rugs from India are made of matted goats' hair. They are not woven. Their routine care is the same as for other wool rugs. Do not shake them ever. Have them dry-cleaned; they cannot be washed.

Nylon rugs Nylon carpets and rugs do not require any special treatment. Remove spots and clean them according to the directions given for wool rugs. If spot cleaning disturbs the pile, this can usually be corrected by blotting the area in the direction of the pile lay. If you shampoo the rug, rinse it thoroughly. Vacuum the rug 5 or 6 times if you use an absorbent powder. Residues of either type of cleaner attract soil to any rug. See also "Antistatic."

Resizing If your rug has gone limp, it probably needs resizing. You can resize a small rug yourself, without too much difficulty. Dissolve four ounces of flake glue *completely* in two quarts of *boiling* water. Lay the rug (which has been cleaned thoroughly) face down on the floor and tack it at intervals to hold it straight. Brush the glue solution lightly and sparingly over the back, being careful not to let it soak through the pile. Let the rug dry in this position for at least twenty-four hours before re-laying it.

See also "Rug Cushions" and "Rug Anchor."

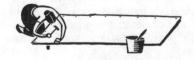

Carpet Sweeper A carpet sweeper should be emptied and cleaned after each use. Snip tangled hair or string with scissors and you can remove it easily from the brush. If badly worn, better get a new brush. Sweeper parts should be oiled about once a month for smooth service.

A carpet sweeper should either be hung up or rested on its side, when stored.

Cashmere Originally the word "cashmere" applied to a rich shawl, made in Kashmir. Later the meaning was extended to the down-soft woolens fashioned from the fine hair which grows at the roots of the hair of Cashmere goats. In modern usage cashmere is applied to a variety of soft woolen materials. Your cashmere sweater probably comes to you through the co-operation of that "hornless, long-necked, elastic-footed animal with the adipose hump (or humps)"—the camel.

Fine woolens deserve the most scrupulous care. In washing cashmeres follow carefully the directions given for woolens, using the finest of detergents made especially for wool. See "Woolens," "Sweaters."

Cast Iron See "Iron."

Castor Oil Castor oil comes from the beans of the castor oil plant. It is not just a medicine with which to intimidate Junior. This oil is an excellent leather conditioner. It is suited especially to types of leather that are to be polished afterward. Clean the leather first; apply a small amount of the oil with a soft cloth pad or with your finger tips; rub it in well and remove the excess oil carefully with a clean soft cloth. See "Leather Goods," also "Books."

Catsup See "Stains," p. 226.

Ceiling See "Walls and Ceilings."

Cellar See "Basement."

Cellophane A plastic made from wood pulp, treated with chemicals.

Cellulose Sponge See "Sponge (Cellulose)."

Cellulose Tape In order to remove traces of cellulose tape from cloth, see "Stains," p. 226.

Cellulosics One of the ten main classes of plastics. Cellulosics are of four types: *acetate*, *butyrate*, *ethyl cellulose*, and *nitrate*. Each type has characteristics that qualify it for specific jobs. All cellulosics are extremely durable even when the sections used are thin. They are light in weight and are available in a full range of bright and pastel colors—opaque, transparent, and translucent.

Cellulosics will take hard use and knocks without breaking and are quite difficult to scratch, but only *butyrate*, which has high water resistance, is designed for outdoor

46

use. The other three types will stand normal moisture. These plastics are not affected by freezing temperatures, but should be kept away from high heat, such as provided by ovens and direct flames. All are tasteless and non-toxic. *Butyrate* alone has a slight odor. *Nitrate* is highly flammable.

Cellulosic plastics are used for toys, partitions, lamp shades, shelf coverings, storage boxes, vacuum parts, ice crushers, juicer bowls, frames for eyeglasses, pipe, and tool handles. Wash them in warm water with mild soap. (They will not stand boiling water.) Do not use abrasives. Protect all types from nail polish, polish remover, and acetone. *Acetate* and *butyrate* are damaged also by alcohols and alkalies. *Butyrate* and *ethyl cellulose* are damaged by cleaning fluids. See also "Plastics."

Cement, *Unpainted* Sweep with a soft broom or vacuum cleaner. Wash with a wet mop or scrub with a brush and rinse. For a thorough cleaning add from two to four tablespoons of washing soda, or trisodium phosphate, to a pail of water and wash with a mop or scrub brush. (A longhandled scrub brush makes the job easier.) Rinse with clear water and allow to dry.

Stubborn grease stains can be sprinkled with washing soda, triso

dium phosphate, or Oakite, moistened with water, and allowed to stand for about an hour. Rinse, and the stain should be gone. If not, repeat the process.

Another method is to sprinkle the stain with an absorbent such as fuller's earth or lime, let it stand for a while, then sweep it up.

Cement patios can be hosed down with water, scrubbed with a stiff broom dipped in thick detergent suds, then rinsed. If grease stains persist, wet the cement and sprinkle dishwasher detergent on them. Let the detergent remain a few minutes, then rinse with a kettle of boiling water.

Painted Sweep with soft broom or vacuum cleaner. Wash with warm soapy water and rinse with a cloth wrung out of clear water. If badly marked, use a mild scouring powder, such as whiting. Rinse with a cloth wrung out of clear water. Dry.

Concrete flooring is being used today for home interiors, with color sometimes added to the cement mixture before it is laid, or the floor is painted with a good deck paint. Self-polishing wax is sometimes used on hard-finished cement and painted cement floors.

To waterproof A coating of sodium or potassium silicate (water glass) will give cement a hard waterproof surface and prevent dust being tracked into other parts of the house. New floors should age 3 to 6 months, however, before it is applied. Use one pint of water glass, available at your hardware store, to four pints of water. Apply to clean dry cement with a brush or a mop and let it dry for twenty-four hours. Rinse with clear water, allow to dry, and recoat. Three or four coatings are desirable for a good hard finish. Special sealers are also made for cement floors. Consult a local specialist or write to your favorite wax company.

Centipede The house centipede is nonpoisonous, seldom bites people, does not damage food or clothing, and destroys other insects, but I have known grown men to quail before it. The thing has altogether too many legs, its antennae are longer than would seem necessary and it goes too fast. To see it scooting along, its legs rippling in fantastic locomotion, gives a fellow creepy sensations along the spine. The same goes for the millipede, a varmint with a trimmer figure but many more legs.

You can destroy both pests by spraying them with a household surface spray containing lindane. Spray openings and cracks around doors, windows, baseboards, and pipes.

See "Insecticides" for precautions.

Ceramics The art of making porcelain and earthenware. The potter's art. See "Pottery," "Porcelain," "China," "Earthenware" and "Tile."

Cesspool See "Septic Tank."

Chalk "A common calcareous, earthy substance of opaque white color," according to Webster's Dictionary. It is a variety of limestone, or calcium carbonate. Whiting is finely powdered chalk that goes into silver polish and other polishes, toothpaste and what have you.

See also "French Chalk."

Chameleon Cloth When you get tired of the colors in this type of printed cloth, you can change them by plunging the garment into a special hot water bath. Because chameleon cloth is made in different ways, the label is your only safe guide for handling it.

Chamois Chamois leather polishers should be washed after use in lukewarm suds made of mild pure soap flakes. Since this leather tears easily when wet, clean it by squeezing the suds through it repeatedly. Do not rub. Rinse in lukewarm water, squeeze out excess water. (Do not wring or twist.) Dry in the shade. Pull it gently this way and that several times while drying to keep the leather soft.

See also "Gloves."

Chandeliers Dust them when you clean the room. Clean them according to the material of which they are made.

See "Brass," "Iron," "Crystal," etc.

Charcoal Charcoal is a form of carbon, a nonmetallic chemical element. It is brother to the diamond and to graphite. You use it, of course, in your outdoor grill, but it has household functions as well. It absorbs odors and a block from your charcoal grill in your

refrigerator will help keep the onions and fish from perfuming the butter. Heating the block in a frying pan will rout the odors it has absorbed. Activated carbon, derived from coconut shell, is many times more efficient than ordinary charcoal for absorbing odors and gases. It is used in some of the air purifiers now on the market.

Checking See "Furniture."

Chenille See "Bedspreads."

Cherry Stains See "Fruit and Berry" in "Stains," p. 228.

Chewing Gum See "Stains," p. 226.

Chiggers See "Mites."

Chimney If a fireplace is used normally, the chimney should be cleaned once a year. If normal use involves burning resinous woods such as pine, more frequent cleaning may be necessary because more soot will be accumulated and the fire hazard will be greater.

A professional chimney cleaner is the best man for this job. He will use a specially designed vacuum cleaner and remove the soot with neatness and dispatch. However, if there is someone rugged about, the following home method can be used:

Fill a burlap sack with straw or excelsior and weight it with a stone or brick. Tie a long rope to it securely. Cover the fireplace opening with a wet cloth to safeguard furnishings. Lower the sack into the chimney and move it up and down the sides to scrape off the soot.

Fire prevention authorities view with doubt other soot-removing procedures such as adding salt to the fire.

As a further precaution, keep your chimney in sound repair. Have it checked for loose bricks, cracks, etc., when it is cleaned.

China (*Chinaware*) Chinaware, as its name suggests, was made originally in the Land of the Lotus, whence it was first exported to Europe in the sixteenth century. It is a usually translucent earthenware and the Chinese made some of their finest from kaolin, a fine porcelain clay named for the hill which supplied it. Some English and French china is made of clay and calcined (powdered by heat) bones. This type is called "bone china." Porcelain is just another name for fine translucent chinaware. The term "china," like the term "porcelain," has been extended to include materials far from the realm of fine craftsmanship. Loosely, earthenware is called "china." And your bathtub is often identified as "porcelain."

The general rule for washing china dishes calls for clean hot water, a mild synthetic detergent, rinsing and drying. Long soaking, hard rubbing and the use of cleaning powders or steel wool damage the glaze and the pattern. Avoid pouring too hot water on cold dishes, or cold water on hot ones, to avoid possible breakage.

China used for egg dishes should be rinsed promptly with cold water, then washed. Hot water will cook the egg to the plate and make it difficult to remove. Tea and coffee stains can be removed by rubbing them with a soft, wet cloth that has been dipped into baking soda

49

or with a commercial porcelain cleaner. However, it is better to avoid the stains in the first place by not letting tea or coffee stand in cups and saucers.

Chinaware and earthenware vary in the treatment they will stand. Ceramic engineers today are producing dinnerware that is not harmed by boiling water or prolonged soaking. Other china, especially very old china, is damaged by such treatment. The instructions which follow are general, safe for all types.

If you have fine china and value it accordingly, you will wash it by hand immediately after use, using a mild detergent if necessary. Salads, salted foods, gravies and similar foods that leave china wet or damp may have an injurious effect if allowed to stand long on china. Soaking china in water may soften ingredients used in its decoration and is especially damaging to gold trim. Rinsing in water that is too hot, or pouring scalding water over china, sometimes meshes the glaze with fine cracks. This is called "crazing."

For hand-washing china, use a plastic dishpan to avoid chipping, or put a mat in the sink. Aluminum pans mark china with fine pencillike lines which are difficult to remove. Electric dishwashers, using harsh detergents, are for everyday china—not delicate, fragile old china and fine dinnerware.

China with raised ornaments may be cleaned with a soft brush.

Prized china should be stacked carefully, as the footing is often unglazed and can scratch the piece on which it is carelessly placed. For storage cover your stacked plates with plastic covers, made for this purpose, or wrap them with a plastic film, such as saran, to protect them from dust. Hang your cups from properly spaced cup hooks. It's a good idea to protect delicate teapot spouts with soft paper if stored on the china shelf. See also "Electric Dishwasher" and "Porcelain Cleaners."

Chintz Chintz is a kind of cloth, usually cotton, printed in colorful flower designs, etc. Glazed chintz has a glossy finish, produced by first treating the material with a sizing, then rolling it between heated cylinders. Wash chintz according to directions given under "Draperies." When the glaze wears off, as it does after a number of launderings, it can be restored professionally. However, you can produce a pretty slick glaze yourself by dipping the chintz into a thin solution of clear starch to which a small amount of wax has been added. Use paraffin or candle wax and stir it thoroughly into the starch solution while it is boiling hot. For a pair of curtains use a piece about the size of a walnut. Iron on the right side. It might be a good idea to test your starch first on a scrap of cloth or a tieback to be sure that it gives the desired effect.

Chloride of Lime Chloride of lime is a combination of chlorine gas and lime. It is valuable as a disinfectant and deodorizer in damp basements and around drains, outdoor toilets and garbage containers.

Chloride of lime and sodium carbonate (washing soda), properly combined with water, make the bleaching solution called "household bleach" or chlorine bleach, which is sold under many trade names.

Chlorine Bleach This is a bleach sold under such trade names as Clorox, Fyne-Tex, Fleecy White, etc. It is easily recognized by its odor. It is useful in the home as a bleach for white cottons, linens and synthetics, as a disinfectant, and as a stain remover. It should not be used on silk, wool, mohair, leather, spandex, or on cotton, linen, or rayons with wash-and-wear finishes created with resins. A yellow stain results and the fabric is weakened. Do not use chlorine bleach on fabrics that are already weak, such as curtains. On colorfast linens and cottons and synthetic materials, it can sometimes be used effectively to remove stains, but the greatest precaution must be observed or the colors will be faded. Always test a sample or inconspicuous place first. Chlorine bleach will weaken even cotton and linen fibers if it is allowed to remain in contact with them too long or if the material is not rinsed thoroughly afterward.

To bleach untreated white cottons, linens or synthetics, use a cupful of bleach in a gallon or more of cold or lukewarm water. After mixing it around, immerse the articles to be bleached. (Do not add bleach to water containing clothing.) Allow the articles to remain in the water until the desired bleaching has been accomplished, but no longer than half an hour or the material will be weakened. Rinse articles thoroughly (three times) with plenty of water.

To remove stains from *washable* materials not damaged by chlorine bleach, use for a *mild* treatment a solution made by dissolving 2 tablespoons of liquid bleach or ¼ cup of granular bleach in 1 quart of cool water. Apply this solution to the stain with a medicine dropper or glass rod, or soak the stained material in it for 5 to 15 minutes. Rinse thoroughly with water and repeat if necessary. For a *strong* treatment, use equal parts of liquid bleach and water. Apply this solution as described above but rinse with water immediately and thoroughly. Repeat if necessary and again rinse thoroughly.

For stains on *nonwashable* materials (*mild* treatment), use a solution made by mixing 1 teaspoon of liquid bleach or 1 tablespoon of granular bleach (Action, Linco) in 1 cup of cool water. Apply it to the stain with a medicine dropper and let it stand for 5 to 15 minutes. Rinse with water and repeat if necessary. Stronger treatment is hazardous, but if you want to try it on a bad stain, follow the instructions given for a strong treatment on washable materials.

Chlorine bleach will remove some stains from bathtubs, sinks, enamelware, tiles, and woodwork. After washing, wipe the stain with a solution containing about 4 tablespoons of bleach to a quart of water. If the stain does not disappear, keep it wet with this solution for 5 minutes. Repeat if necessary. Some manufacturers recommend

51

chlorine bleach as a toilet bowl cleaner and disinfectant. If used for this purpose, no other component should be added. Mixing chlorine bleach with toilet bowl cleaners, ammonia, and other special preparations produces a chemical action which liberates toxic gases. If inhaled, these gases can cause prolonged illness or death.

Chlorine Stains See "Stains," p. 226.

Chlorothene Chlorothene is the trade name of a chlorinated solvent for grease, oil, wax, and allied stains. Chemically it is a special grade of trichloroethane. Having proved its value as a degreasing agent for the metals and machinery of heavy industry, Chlorothene entered the home cleaning field as an almost ideal spot remover. Chlorothene is nonflammable and of low toxicity. See "Cleaning Fluids."

Chocolate See "Combination Stains," p. 223.

Chrome Same as chromium.

Chromium Chromium is a soft, silver-colored, rustproof metal discovered in 1797. It is prepared from its oxide and never found in its metallic state. Chromium takes its name from the lovely colors which its compounds give to minerals into whose composition they enter. In its highest degree of oxidation it forms a chemical salt, ruby red in color. Chromium salts are used in making dyes and paints.

As a metal, chromium is used as a plating on plumbing fixtures, for metal furniture, electric appliances, etc., and is easily recognized by its bluish sheen. It is also used in making stainless steel.

Household chromium usually needs only to be wiped with a soft, damp cloth and polished with a dry one. If very sticky it may be washed with a mild soap or detergent. A little kerosene on a damp cloth, or baking soda on a dry one, is excellent for gummy kitchen lighting fixtures and switch plates.

Harsh metal polishes and cleaning powders should never be used on household chromium. They are totally unnecessary and wear off the plating. Should grease spatters burn on it, rub them off with whiting or baking soda on a damp cloth or use silver polish. Salts also are injurious to chromium and foods containing them should not be allowed to remain on it. Faucets, water pipes, etc., that have become green with corrosion can only be replated or replaced.

Citric Acid This is an acid obtained from many fruit juices, but especially from lemons. It is frequently called "acid of lemons" and is useful as a bleach in treating certain stains. It can be bought at drugstores in dilute or powder form.

Cleaning Fluids Cleaning fluids are effective for stains caused by grease, oil, adhesive tape, and chewing gum. They are available at drugstores and groceries under their chemical names and under a variety of trade names. All should be used with great care.

Nonflammable cleaning fluids Recommended for home use by the Department of Agriculture are perchloroethylene, trichloroethane, and trichloroethylene. They are sold under these names and under various trade names. Trichloroethylene should not be used on Arnel or Kodel.

Warning: Once recommended for its safety features, carbon tetrachloride has now been banned as a grease solvent for household use. Swallowing carbon tetrachloride or inhaling its fumes can be fatal.

Flammable cleaning fluids Petroleum napthas are the most often used of the flammable grease solvents. The names petroleum distillate and petroleum hydrocarbon may be used instead of naptha. Most of the products are sold under trade names. Select a naptha with a high flashpoint; the higher the flashpoint, the less danger that the naptha can be ignited.

Do not use these flammable cleaning fluids near an open flame or where sparks from electric equipment may ignite them. Do not use napthas in a washing machine or put articles that have been cleaned with them into a dryer.

Mixtures Many of the cleaning fluids sold under brand names contain two or more solvents, both flammable and nonflammable. The solvents used may be changed without changing the brand name. Always read the label carefully and follow the manufacturer's instructions.

Clock Clock wheels get tired and

worn out pushing against congealed oil. Have your clock cleaned and oiled, preferably once a year, unless the works are sealed, as in electric clocks.

Cloisonné In this type of enameling each tiny part of the design is first outlined by wire bands. Enamel paste (powdered glass and water) is then filled in and fused under high temperature. Sometimes the whole piece is coated with lacquer. You can wash cloisonné as you would a china dish, with a mild detergent and warm water. Rinse and wipe dry with a soft cloth. Use no abrasives or harsh cleaners.

Clothes Your clothes will look better and last longer if you follow a few simple rules for their care. Hang them up properly. Keep them clean. Mend them promptly.

The time to put your dress or coat on a hanger is when you take it off, not after it has draped a chair for several hours. Button or zip it up so that it won't sag out of shape. Brush woolens carefully after wearing them; it is easier to whisk the dust off then than after it has become embedded in the fabric.

Spots and stains are more easily removed when fresh. If you know what caused the stain and the proper agent for removing it, proceed quickly. Otherwise send the garment to an expert dry cleaner promptly.

In removing clothes, take care not to yank them. Maneuver zippers gently; don't lose your head if you have apparently been locked in or out of your clothes. A little gentle finagling usually will release you from your trap.

53

Sew on that button before you lose it.

Mend that broken seam before it becomes a rip. Your garment will then be ready for the next time, when you are likely to be in a hurry.

Place hats, well brushed, on a hatstand or pack them carefully in a box, using tissue paper to keep them in shape. Mothproof woolens after cleaning, if they are to be stored. Put shoe trees in your shoes.

Good idea: to air garments overnight before putting them into the closet. This enables them to get back into shape and helps remove possible perspiration odors.

See also "Shoes," "Moths" and Section II, "Stains."

Clothes Closet Are you overcome with mortification when a guest opens the wrong door and stumbles into your clothes, or coat, closet? Then it's time to begin all over. Take everything out (a good time to sort and discard doubtful gear) and pray the phone won't ring. If possible, take coats and suits outdoors, brush them carefully and leave them for a good airing. Dust off all boxes, suitcases, hatstands, etc. Clean the walls, shelves, lighting fixtures and hooks. Put nice

fresh paper on the shelves and replace your things neatly, each in its alloted place. Resolve to keep it that way.

If you need a special incentive to undertake this task, the stores are full of nifty space savers and attractive gadgets to dress up a closet and encourage future orderliness.

Clothes Dryer See "Automatic Dryer."

Clothesline If your clothesline is soiled you may ruin the spotless wash you are about to fling to the breeze. Wipe it carefully with a damp cloth before using it. To make a new rope clothesline pleasantly pliable, boil it for several minutes and rinse it in hot water before stringing it up.

Clothes Moths See "Moths."

Clothespins Give wooden clothespins a bath in hot soapsuds if they become grimy. Use mild soap and warm water if you go in for plastic ones. An easy way to wash clothespins is to put them in a nylon mesh bag and place them in your washer.

Coal Oil See "Kerosene."

Coal Range See "Wood and Coal Range."

Cockroaches Here is a bit of information, totally irrelevant to your problem, which may or may not interest you. In scientific circles the cockroach is regarded as a sort of minor miracle, since it has come down to us, practically unchanged by evolution, from the Coal Age, 300 million years ago. Specimens have been found in ancient geological strata that are practically identical to the creature that may be haunting that crevice behind your sink. But, miracle or no, let's get after him. He is a creature of filth and sometimes carries disease. Cockroaches hide during the day and forage at night. They eat food, garbage, starch, glue, fabrics, and paper. Switch on a light suddenly in a dark room and they will reveal their hiding places.

Good housekeeping and the use of a suitable insecticide will usually control cockroaches in homes. In apartment houses, drastic over-all treatment by a professional exterminator is usually necessary. Take the problem to the management.

To destroy cockroaches, apply a household surface spray or dust, after thoroughly cleaning the areas to be treated. If the infestation is severe, spray first and when the spray has dried apply the dust, blowing it with your "gun" into cracks and openings.

Insecticides containing diazinon, malathion, propoxur, or ronnel will control all kinds of cockroach. Insecticides containing lindane will control all kinds except possibly the small German cockroach, ½ inch long, which in many areas has developed resistance to them. If you think you are dealing with the German cockroach, use diazinon, malathion, propoxur, or ronnel.

Household surface sprays in pressurized cans are the easiest to use. Apply enough to moisten the surface thoroughly without running or dripping. Useful as an auxiliary weapon is a space spray (aerosol) containing pyrethrum. It is not recommended as a roach killer but it will penetrate cracks and other hard-to-reach places and drive the insects into the open where surface sprays or dusts can destroy them.

Treat with insecticide all places where roaches may hide: areas under the kitchen sink and drainboard; behind the refrigerator, stove, and washer; cracks around and beneath cabinets, and inside cabinets, especially in the upper corners; around pipes and conduits; behind loose baseboards, moldings, and door and window frames; on the undersides of tables and chairs; and on pantry, closet, and book shelves.

To avoid contamination of food by the insecticide, remove all food, dishes, and utensils from cabinets and pantry shelves before spraying them. Remove and empty the drawers of cabinets. Spray the drawers on the outside. The inside, if thoroughly cleaned, does not need to be treated.

Happy note: There are about 55 varieties of cockroach in the United States, but only 5 are house pests. The others cannot develop indoors, and must either leave or die.

See "Insecticides" for precautions.

Cocktail See "Alcoholic Beverages" under "Stains," p. 224.

Cocoa See "Nongreasy Stains," p. 222.

Cod-Liver Oil See "Stains," p. 227.

Coffee Maker If you are fastidious about your coffee, you will have to be fastidious about your coffee maker. If it is not kept scrupulously clean, traces of oil that remain in it will grow rancid and give the coffee a bitter taste.

If yours is an electric percolator, wash the removable pieces with sudsy water, scald and dry. Wash the inside with warm soapy water after each use. Rinse with clear hot water and dry. Wipe the outside with a cloth wrung out of soapy water, being careful not to wet the heating element unless it is sealed. Wipe with a cloth wrung out of clear water and polish with a clean, soft cloth. Always disconnect your electric percolator immediately after use. The spouts and tubes of percolators require special attention at least once a week. Using a percolator brush, made especially for this job, clean these parts carefully with soap and water. Rinse with hot water.

If your coffee has been off-taste due to oil deposits on the metal, give the coffee maker a special treatment. The following directions are from Westinghouse Electric:

Coffee makers other than aluminum: Dissolve 2 teaspoons of a non-sudsing type of dishwasher detergent (Cascade, Finish) in 1 cup of hot water. Put the solution in the bowl of the coffee maker and add enough hot water to fill the bowl to top cup level. Let the coffee maker go through a complete brewing cycle. With the solution still in the bowl, scrub the spout with a bottle brush. (It may be necessary to repeat this operation if the method has not been used before.)

Next, fill the bowl with water, mix in a tablespoon of baking soda, and again let the coffee maker go through the complete brewing cycle. Wash and rinse. Prevent future accumulation of oil by washing your coffee maker thoroughly after each use, paying particular attention to the spout and tube.

Aluminum coffee maker. Dissolve 2 teaspoons of a cleaner such as Dip-It or Stain-Aid in 1 cup of hot water and put the solution in the bowl of your coffee maker. Fill the bowl to the top-cup marking with boiling water. Let the solution stand for 20 minutes. Do *not* perk. With the solution still in the bowl, thoroughly scrub the stem of the pump and basket assembly with a percolator brush. (If this method has not been used before, it may be necessary to repeat this entire cleaning operation.)

Next, fill the bowl with plain water and add ¼ cup of vinegar. Let it remain for 30 minutes with the basket submerged. Wash and rinse. Prevent a future build-up of oil by washing your coffee maker thoroughly after each use and, when rinsing, running your percolator brush down the stem to remove any deposit. A soaped steel-wool pad can be used to brighten the exterior of aluminum coffee makers and the stem and basket assembly. Do not use it on the interior. A plastic basket can be sweetened by rubbing it with baking soda.

Leave your coffee maker unassembled after cleaning, to air.

Note: Coffee grounds are *not* good for the kitchen drain. They will clog it up right and proper if they get mixed with grease.

Color Removers These are hydrosulfite chemicals, safe for all fibers, which are sold under trade names such as Rit and Tintex. Their primary use is to remove color from cloth that is to be dyed. They should not be mixed in metal containers and they should always be tested on a sample or hidden portion of cloth before being used.

This is how color removers are used to remove stains for which they are recommended in Section II. For a *mild* treatment dissolve ¼ teaspoon in half a cup of cool water. Put a few drops on the stain and cover it with a pad of cotton dampened with the same solution. Let it remain from 1 to 15 minutes. Rinse thoroughly with water and repeat if necessary. For a *strong* treatment on fabrics that will stand it, use the same solution, but boiling hot water instead of cool water. Apply the solution with a medicine dropper and rinse immediately. Repeat if necessary. For large stains on white or colorfast materials follow the directions on the package.

If use of color remover alters dyes, it is sometimes possible to restore the color by prompt rinsing and drying in the open air. Colors that are faded cannot be restored.

Section II on "Stains" will tell you when to use this bleach.

Combs Clean combs made of hard rubber or bone by letting them stand for ten minutes in a basin of warm water containing a couple of tablespoons of household ammonia. Scrub with a small brush. Rinse and dry. Alcohol and Lysol solutions also are good cleaners and disinfectants for hard rubber or bone combs. Nylon combs can be sterilized by boiling.

Wash other plastics in warm (never hot) water, using a mild soap. No ammonia or other chemical which might soften or discolor the plastic.

See "Nylon Plastic."

Comforters Even a well-stitched comforter tends to bunch and mat if it is washed. However, it is sometimes possible to wash successfully a small crib comforter if it is well made with a washable cover and stuffed with a good grade of wool. Test a corner first, though, and don't attempt the job unless you are fairly skillful. Plenty of good, stiff, lukewarm suds made with an ante synthetic detergent are needed. Squeeze the suds gently through it, fold over and roll up loosely to extract the suds. Rinse in clear, lukewarm water several times. Roll gently again to squeeze out the water. Shake very lightly to fluff up the stuffing and hang straight on the line in the shade. A baby's comforter will seem fresher and sweeter if it can be washed in this way. It will not need ironing.

Large comforters stuffed with wool and eiderdown puffs should be dry cleaned. Washable comforters containing Dacron fiberfill can be machine washed in lukewarm suds made with a synthetic detergent or soap and a softener. Set the machine for a 3- to 5-minute wash; use a special fabric cycle if available. Remove after the spin-dry cycle and tumble dry at a low temperature setting for 15 or 20 minutes. Remove from the dryer promptly.

Eiderdowns that float off during the night can be anchored by a special device available at first-class stores. Worth looking into, I

should say, if you have been vic-
timized by a floating fluff.

Concrete See "Cement."

Copper Copper is a red metal,
found in a pure state and in many
ores. It gets its name from the
island of Cyprus and was first
called cyprium metal, or cyprium.

Copper cooking utensils must be
kept scrupulously clean to avoid the
formation of "green rust," a copper
carbonate compound produced by
the action of vegetable juices on
the metal. "Green rust," like all
copper compounds, is toxic. It is
for this reason that most copper
utensils today are lined with
chromium or tin. This lining must
be replaced as soon as it becomes
worn. The reason for going to all
this trouble, and using copper for
cooking, is that it is so excellent
a conductor of heat.

Newly purchased copper vessels
are likely to be covered with a
protective film of lacquer. This
must be removed before they are
used. Cover the utensil with boiling water and let it stand until
the water has cooled and the lacquer will peel off.

Wash copper utensils and ornamental pieces (if not lacquered)
with soap and water, rinse and dry.
Spots caused by corrosion can be
removed if rubbed with (1) hot
vinegar and salt, (2) lemon juice
and salt, (3) copper cleaner, and
(4) buttermilk. Rinse immediately
and dry. Burned-in grease can be

removed with mild scouring powder. For "green rust" use a paste
made by mixing a cleansing powder with a little oxalic acid solution. Sometimes soapsuds and ammonia will turn the trick.

Polishes made especially for copper are to be found in stores. A
good homemade polish consists of
a paste made by mixing equal parts
of salt, vinegar and flour. Rub the
copper with this mixture until it
is perfectly clean, then wash in
hot suds, rinse and polish. Or you
can use whiting or rottenstone
mixed to a paste with olive oil.
Always wash copper thoroughly
with soapsuds after using acids or
commercial polishes or they will
retarnish rapidly.

Wash lacquered ornamental copper in warm, soapy water, if required. Rinse with warm water
and wipe dry. Do not polish. Do
not use hot water or allow it to
soak, as this might crack the lacquer.

Copper Stains See "Bathtub."

Coral Coral is the general term for
the hard calcareous skeleton se-
creted by marine polyps for their
homes. See "Jewelry."

Corduroy This word comes, apparently, from the French phrase,
corde du roi (king's cord), suggest-
ing regal prerogatives. Today's corduroy, tough and durable, is the
mainstay of Junior's wardrobe.

Most cotton corduroys are fast-
dyed and completely washable.
Clean bad spots with a soft brush
before washing. Extract the suds,
then rinse several times in lukewarm water. Tumble dry garment
or dry on hangers after a brief spin.
Clothing to be air-dried should be

quite wet when hung out. When completely dry, brush it in a one-way direction with a soft brush. Corduroy looks better if it is not ironed. Some have a durable-press finish.

Cork Cork stoppers can be sterilized by boiling. Cork used as, for instance, the grip on your glass coffee maker can be rubbed clean with an emery board or emery cloth.

Cork Tile Pleasantly springy, cork tiles are made from shavings of the cork oak tree, ground and pressed together under heat in molds. Naturally porous, they are sealed at the factory by steel disc polishing or with special coatings. Quality tiles, correctly laid, are maintained by frequent waxing with a good polishing wax. Resealing should not be required for years.

The care of waxed wooden floors and cork tile floors is identical. For cleaning, waxing, and removing spots from cork floors, see "Wooden Floors, Woodwork."

Corundum Corundum is a native crystalline alumina. Pulverized, it is used for grinding and polishing gems, etc. Emery is impure corundum.

Cosmetics See "Stains," p. 227.

Cotton (Untreated) Cotton has been used as a textile fiber for so long and in such widely separated parts of the world that no one can be sure where the plant originated or who used it first.

Beautiful cotton prints were produced in India long before Alexander's conquests, and in the Americas the weaving of cotton was an an-

cient art in Mexico and Peru before the white men came. Ready-made for spinning, cotton is produced today in every country where it will grow and is far and away the world's leading textile fiber. It lends itself to innumerable weaves, from sheer lawn and organdy to velvet, corduroy, and carpeting. It can be dyed and printed easily in endless variety. Cotton clothing is absorbent and therefore comfortable and cool to wear. It can be laundered in very hot water—even boiled.

Cotton can be mercerized to make it lustrous, soil repellent, and easier to iron. It can be woven in a special way to make it wind- and water-resistant. It can be finished with synthetic resins that convert it to wash and wear, and by silicone compounds that adapt it to rainwear without sealing the open spaces that permit a fabric to "breathe." Grease- and oil-resistant cottons are available too. The treatments seem almost endless. Some of the finishes disappear with laundering; others are more or less permanent. Most of them do not require any special treatment.

White and colored cottons should always be washed separately. For run of the mill clothing and household "linens," use hot water and heavy-duty laundry soap (with a softener if the water is hard) or a detergent. Hot water gets them cleaner and most dyes will stand it. However, if you have any doubt,

squeeze a sample or inconspicuous corner of the material in a bowl of lukewarm water for a few minutes. If the water colors, the dye is not fast. Wash the article separately, by hand, using a mild soap or detergent and lukewarm-to-cool water. Rinse it in clear cool water and roll it immediately in a turkish towel to remove as much water as possible. Unroll immediately and place it in the shade. Iron it while it is still damp, with a warm iron. (Some cotton dyes are meant to "bleed.")

Stains on cotton materials should be treated before they are washed because many are set by hot water and detergents. Sponge greasy stains with cleaning fluid and treat others according to directions given for them in the section on Stains. Pretreat also especially soiled areas such as neckbands and cuffs by working into them with a soft brush or sponge a thick suds of the detergent you plan to use in washing them. Oversoiled garments—work shirts, play clothes, slip covers, curtains—are more easily and completely cleaned if they are allowed to soak for 10 or 20 minutes in water containing a detergent or a nonprecipitating water softener. If the clothes are greasy, add half a cup of ammonia to the soak water. (The soak may be an agitated prewash in your machine, with lukewarm water and about half as much detergent as you would use in washing them.)

Untreated white cottons without resin finishes can be bleached if desired with either a chlorine or peroxy bleach. Follow the directions on the container. (Bluing and optical whiteners are optional.) Starching gives cottons a neat appearance and helps retard soil. Follow the directions given for the type you select.

For wash-and-wear cottons, see "Durable Press."

Crayon Marks See "Walls and Ceilings (Stains on wallpaper)." See also "Stains," p. 228.

Crazing See "China."

Cream See "Stains," p. 228.

Cream Sauce See "Stains," p. 228.

Cream Soup See "Stains," p. 228.

Creslan Creslan is an acrylic fiber produced by American Cyanamid.

Creslan textiles are 15 percent lighter than wool and 30 percent lighter than cotton. They provide warmth without weight, plus wrinkle resistance, resilience, and dimensional stability. A very special quality is that Creslan, unlike many synthetics, has a unique affinity for a wide variety of dyestuffs and, with this, superior fastness. Creslan also has a distinctive hand. It can be soft, bulky, or crisp—from soft jersey, crisp suiting, downy blankets, and furry rugs, to sturdy carpeting and upholstery. The fiber is moth- and mildewproof, and durable.

Washable Creslan fabrics require no special treatment. Many of them can be handled by automatic washing and drying machines. They require little or no ironing (use synthetic setting). But look for the directions given on the label.

Crickets A cricket on the hearth may be poetic, but crickets in droves are a menace. They eat holes in fabrics and are not particular about the kind. Field crickets enter the house when the weather becomes cool and seek cozy corners near fireplaces, radiators, in kitchens, and warm basements. House crickets breed in dumps and swarm to nearby houses from July to September.

To prevent crickets from entering the house, close all openings and tighten windows, doors and screens. To destroy an infestation, use a household surface spray containing lindane or malathion. Apply it around baseboards, in closets, and in cracks where insects might hide. Dusts containing these insecticides can be used on the bare concrete floors of basements. See "Insecticides" for precautions.

Crochet Crocheted articles can be dry-cleaned or laundered like knitted clothing. See "Sweaters," "Bedspreads."

Crocus Powder A polishing powder obtained by subjecting sulfate, or oxide, of iron to high heat in a crucible. Crocus powder is purple and comes from the bottom of the crucible. The upper portion is scarlet and is known as jeweler's rouge. Crocus is harder than rouge and is used for ordinary polishing. Rouge is used to polish gold, silver, glass, and jewels. Crocus cloth, prepared like emery cloth, can be bought at hardware stores.

Cruet If your vinegar cruet looks cloudy and a mineral deposit has accumulated in the bottom of it, fill it with water, add a little ammonia and let it stand for several hours, or overnight. Rinse with clear hot water.

Crystal This word comes from a Greek word meaning both "ice," or "clear ice," and "rock crystal," since the ancients believed that rock crystal was a modified and permanent form of ice. Rock crystal or, specifically, quartz is used in jewelry today but the word "crystal" is applied commonly to an especially fine type of clear, colorless glass.

Crystal glass contains a great deal of oxide of lead and thus is heavier than ordinary glass. It is used for fine tableware and for ornamental pieces, including cut glass. Crystal is cleaned like any fine glassware.

Crystal candelabra and chandeliers, beautiful accessories in eighteenth-century rooms, require especially delicate handling. Be in the mood for the task and be sure you have plenty of time. Take them apart, being extremely careful not to bend or break the delicate hooks by which they are hung. Wash the crystals carefully in warm water, using a synthetic detergent. Rinse in clear water of the same temperature and dry with a soft lintless cloth, or let them dry on a paper towel. Replace the prisms as before.

Cuprammonium Rayon See "Rayon."

Curtains Sunlight and weather weaken delicate cotton curtains but synthetics (polyester, glass, nylon, etc.) are impervious to such hazards. But handle them gently

to avoid snags and don't let them get really dirty.

Soak untreated white cotton curtains (organdy, dimity, net, etc.) for ten or fifteen minutes in cool or lukewarm water before washing to loosen accumulated dust. Lift them gently, drain off the dirty water, then wash them in thick lukewarm suds. If the curtains are still soiled, make fresh suds and repeat. Handle the curtains gently at all times. Squeeze the suds through them. Do not rub, wring or twist the fabric if you are washing them by hand. Let the water drain off. Rinse three times in lukewarm water, adding bluing, if desired, to the last rinse. Starch lightly all cottons, except organdy with a permanent finish. Many women prefer to hand-launder curtains. However, if you use a washing machine (not for glass fibers), run it from three to five minutes for the first wash and no more than two for the second and let the rinse water drain off or absorb it in a turkish towel.

Colored cotton curtains should be washed separately and should not be soaked unless colorfast. If not colorfast follow the instructions given under "Cotton." Dry in the shade or indoors. Hang

white cotton curtains lengthwise on a tight line, with the hems even to make ironing easier. When nearly dry iron with a warm iron on the reverse side, following the lengthwise threads.

Rayon requires special care because the fibers are sometimes weak when wet. Do not soak rayon curtains; wash them twice instead. Use lukewarm suds and squeeze the water through the material, keeping it under water at all times. Do not rub or twist. Repeat in second suds. Rinse several times in lukewarm water. Fold lengthwise, then across, for the last rinse, dipping the curtain up and down in the water. Lay on a turkish towel, then roll up lightly to absorb moisture. When of proper dampness, iron with a warm iron.

Rayons are tricky to iron and your guide is the manufacturer's label. Set the dial for rayon and press on the wrong side. Iron the hems first, then iron lengthwise, following the threads. Do not iron across the curtain. Silk curtains should not be too wet when ironed or they will be papery. Use a warm iron and work on the reverse side of the curtain, ironing the hems, then lengthwise.

Dacron, Orlon, and nylon curtains should be washed by hand unless the directions say they are machine washable. Shake out the dust and pour a little detergent on badly soiled areas. Fold them into lukewarm suds made with a heavy-duty detergent. (Wash white curtains separately; any bleach can be used.) Rinse thoroughly but do not wring. Drip dry.

If the label says the curtains are machine washable, use the synthetic setting and remove them before the final spin-dry cycle for drip drying. Or tumble-dry them in modern equipment on the wash-and-wear setting.

If the curtains have become limp and you want to stiffen them, use an instant laundry starch such as Perma Starch or Niagara, following the directions on the package. For best results iron with a steam iron at the rayon or synthetic setting, sponging lightly with a damp sponge areas that have become dry.

Cotton lace and net curtains should be measured carefully before they are laundered. Since they are very delicate and the threads are easily broken or stretched, such curtains often are washed in a muslin bag. Otherwise follow the directions given for cotton curtains. Ecru and cream-colored curtains can be retinted by adding a strong solution of tea or coffee (or both) slowly to hot water until the desired shade has been produced on a sample of muslin. Brown dyes, made for cotton materials, also can be used in a weak solution. Test a sample, as before. Immerse the curtains and remove them when the proper shade has been attained. Lace curtains of natural fibers look best if they are stiffened with gelatin or gum arabic, and these finishes are preferred by some for sheer cottons, such as organdy and batiste. See "Starch and Special Finishes."

Dry cotton or linen lace and net curtains on stretchers, made for this purpose, and set them to measure one-half inch shorter than the measurements taken before laundering. This is to allow for the fact that such curtains stretch slightly while hanging. Lace and net curtains may also be dry-cleaned.

Paper curtains are cheap enough to be used as throwaways. Look for cleaning instructions when you buy them. Some can be cleaned by wiping with a damp cloth; others are treated like wallpaper.

Plastic curtains are washed with mild soap or detergent and warm water. Rinse in warm water. Do not iron.

See also "Glass Cloth" and "Shower Curtains."

Cushion See "Furniture—*Uphol-stered*," "Pillows," "Rug Cushions."

Cut Glass Crystal, or flint, glass that has been ornamented with designs that have been cut or ground into it with polishing wheels. See "Glass."

Cutlery Whether made of carbon steel, stainless steel or chrome-plated, knives should not be allowed to soak in water because this damages and loosens the handles. Clean the blades promptly after each use and scour carbon steel blades if they need it. Wash and rinse the handles and blades. Always dry thoroughly.

If you have invested in fine, forged blades, have them sharpened occasionally by a professional grinder. You can then keep them keen by whetting them as required on a carving steel or sharpening stone. Cheap cutlery requires frequent sharpening and will not keep an edge long enough to make professional treatment worth while. In sharpening knives on a steel or

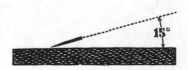

stone, hold the blade at an angle of about 15° for best results. If using a rotary grinder (the kind that has little sharpening wheels), pull the blade through repeatedly. Do not push it back and forth.

Knives with serrated edges, increasingly popular, depend upon notches for their cutting ability. They are never sharpened.

Store your knives in a cutlery rack or on a magnetic wall rack to safeguard their points and edges and as a safety precaution.

Do not use a good knife as a cooking fork or pancake turner because heat damages some blades. And don't let your fine knives be used to cut paper or string, or to sharpen pencils. Do not put knives with plastic or wooden handles in an automatic dishwasher.

Dacron Dacron is the trade name for a polyester fiber by du Pont, engineered for stiffness and resilience. It is spun from a condensation product of ethylene glycol and terephthalic acid.

Dacron fabrics and blends resist wrinkles, are comfortable to wear, dry quickly, and do not require ironing. They range from suitings and knitwear to a variety of dress materials, and sheers for blouses, lingerie, and curtains.

Dacron is heat sensitive; hot cigarette ashes will burn holes in it. It tends to accumulate static electricity. Special rinses will minimize the static. Blends with other fibers decrease its sensitivity to heat.

When dealing with clothing made of 100 percent Dacron, high-percentage blends, and durable-press Dacrons, follow any special directions given by the manufacturer. Dacron can be dry-cleaned

by standard processes or washed according to the directions given under "Wash and Wear." If touch-up ironing is needed, use a low temperature setting (rayon). Here are some tips from du Pont on special problems.

The occasional use of bleach will help keep white Dacron white. Any kind can be used unless the directions warn against chlorine bleach. Durable-press materials and those containing spandex yellow when chlorine bleach is used; use a peroxy bleach instead.

Graying or yellowing of white Dacron can be caused by: an insufficient amount of soap or detergent during laundering, the use of soap and hard water without a water softener, washing colored articles with white, overloading the washer, inadequate rinsing, or the use of chlorine bleach on a chlorine-sensitive finish. Before attempting to correct the condition, try to identify the cause.

To restore whiteness, try first an especially vigorous wash. Treat one item at a time, or a load of not more than 4 pounds. The water selector level should be set to cover the clothes for at least 2 inches to permit them to move freely during the washing cycle. If the agitator is adjustable, set it for maximum agitation. Use hot water (145° to 160° F.). Fill the washer and add 1 cup of heavy-duty detergent and 1 cup of nonprecipitating water softener (Calgon, Spring Rain, Tex). Add the garments, set the timer for a 15-minute wash, and start the machine. Add 1 cup of water softener to a hot deep rinse. Complete the cycle. Repeat the treatment, if necessary. (The article will probably require ironing after this treatment.) If the results are still not satisfactory, try the alkali soak described under "Wash and Wear."

If the discoloration is due to insufficient rinsing or the use of soap in hard water, try this reconditioning method: Fill the washer with hot water (140° F.) and add 1 to 2 cups of a nonprecipitating water softener. (Do not add soap, detergent, bleach, or any other washing aid.) Add the clothes and run them through the complete wash and rinse cycles. Suds which may occur on the surface of the water are evidence that soap film is being removed from the fibers. It may be necessary to repeat this procedure several times before suds cease to form, indicating that the soap or detergent film has been removed completely.

For white fabrics that have yellowed because chlorine bleach has been used on a resin finish, or because they have picked up dyes from colored clothing, try this: To 1 gallon of hot water in a glass or enameled container add 1 tablespoon of a packaged color remover (Rit, Tintex). Soak the garment in this solution for 5 to 10 minutes, rinse thoroughly, and wash. (Do not use color remover in your washer. Follow instructions on the package.)

See also "Wash and Wear," "Pillows," "Comforters," "Curtains," "Sweaters—*Synthetic*," "Antistatic," "Polyester."

Dandelion Stains See "Grass, Flowers, Foliage" in "Stains," p. 229.

Decanter See "Glass."

Deep Freeze See "Electric Freezer."

Delft See "Pottery."

Deodorants Formerly, room deodorants often just covered unpleasant odors with others that were less objectionable, or temporarily dulled the sense of smell. Today there are deodorants that react chemically with odors to destroy them. These are especially useful when circumstances do not permit a room to be thoroughly aired.

The deodorant is distributed as an aerosol mist. One chemical in it combines with the nitrogenous and sulfur compounds in which most unpleasant odors originate, and another takes care of odors caused by stale tobacco, paint, alcohol, etc.

Deodorants (Personal) See "Antiperspirant" in "Stains," p. 225.

Detergent This is a word that was shoved to the foreground with the debut of soapless suds and other chemical cleaners. It means an agent used for cleaning, or purging, but is commonly applied to synthetic substitutes for soap.

See "Synthetic Detergents."

Diamond The diamond, hardest of known substances, "consists of pure carbon, crystallized in regular octahedrons and allied forms, either pure white or variously tinted." It is brother to graphite (in your "lead" pencil) and to charcoal. Sheer geological chance produced it and endowed it with lasting beauty; an artful craftsman cut and polished it to flash fire.

But, if your diamond is to flash fire, it must be kept scrupulously clean so that light, striking at every facet, breaks down into rainbow

65

colors. If your diamond is dirty and gummed up with soap, you might as well be wearing glass. A diamond that is worn every day needs a special cleaning at least once a month.

Diamond-cleaning preparations sold by jewelers and druggists are good for a quick cleanup. Slip your ring onto a bobby pin and dip it into the liquid, then use an eyebrow brush to loosen the dirt at the back of the setting. A synthetic detergent or soap and water, plus a little ammonia, also will clean a diamond nicely. Use your little brush, rinse thoroughly and dry with soft tissue.

For a professional cleaning, as given by jewelers, boil your diamond jewelry in soapsuds. Use mild white flakes (not too many) and a few drops of ammonia. When the solution has come to a boil, place your diamond jewelry in a wire tea strainer and dip it into the suds for a moment or two. Let it cool, then rinse it carefully. Next dip it into a small bowl of alcohol, to cut any remaining film, and lay it in jeweler's sawdust, or on tissue paper, to dry. The alcohol evaporates in an instant, leaving your diamond sparkling like new love.

These directions have been confirmed by one of New York's leading jewelry firms. They are for diamonds only. Do not boil diamond jewelry if it contains any other precious or semi-precious stones.

Diapers You can have your choice of do-it-yourself home-laundered diapers, a diaper service, or disposable paper ones. If you decide to have your own, you will save money but spend time and energy.

You will need from 3 to 6 dozen cloth diapers if you decide to do them at home. Launder them with the baby's other clothing, using mild soap, and rinse thoroughly. Unless the baby develops a rash and the doctor recommends it, boiling is unnecessary.

Disposable paper diapers are the easiest to use. Some have press-together tapes that make safety pins unnecessary. Use them, at any rate, when you are travelling with your baby.

Dishes If you wash your dishes by hand, you might as well do them right. The first step is to scrape off food, using a paper towel or a rubber scraper, and rinse. Cold water for milk, egg, flour, oatmeal and other starches; warm for other foods. This will keep your dishwater from becoming too, too repulsive.

Now make a nice hot suds with a synthetic detergent or mild soap and go to it with mop, cloth or cellulose sponge, according to your preference. If you use soap, a little ammonia will help with greasy things, but avoid it if you are using your best china, especially if it is ornamented with gold or silver. (Ammonia will soften the trim.) The rule is: glassware first, silver second, china third, pots and pans last. Rinse in hot water and wipe, or allow them to dry in a rack. Wipe the glassware and silver, if you used soap, or it will look streaky. You won't need to dry

glassware if you use a detergent.
See also "China," "Glass," "Electric Dishwasher," etc.

Dish Towels Because they will mildew if tossed, damp, into the clothes hamper, dry dish towels thoroughly before consigning them to the laundry, or wash them out daily. Use hot suds and a mild bleach, if needed.

Linen towels are best for drying dishes and glassware, as they are highly absorbent and leave no lint. Less expensive are cotton and linen mixtures. Choose a kind that is at least 25 percent linen. Knitted and gauze cotton tea towels rate high for absorbency and dry fast.

Dishwasher See "Electric Dishwasher."

Disinfectant Solutions of quaternary ammonium compounds (Co-Op, Roccal, etc.) are highly effective, nontoxic disinfectants, which have largely displaced chemicals formerly used. They can be used to treat dishes, utensils, clothing, and contaminated areas such as beds and floors.

Another very effective household disinfectant consists of specially prepared iodine in a detergent. This too is sold under trade names (such as CN). These disinfectants are for general cleaning use, such as floors and sickroom equipment. They are not for clothing or dishes.

The periodic use of disinfectants in washing machines is recommended by the Department of Agriculture because, even when very hot water is used, harmful bacteria remain on the wash. Four types of disinfectant have been found safe and effective, provided they are used correctly. In addition

to the quaternary preparations already mentioned are liquid chlorine bleaches, pine-oil mixtures (Fyne-Pine, Fyne-Tex, King Pine, etc.), and phenolics (Alpine, Pine-Sol), available at groceries.

Quaternary and chlorine bleach disinfectants are effective sanitizers in hot, warm, and cold water. Pine oil and phenolic disinfectants are effective in warm or hot water. Follow the directions on the labels.

Liquid chlorine bleaches are used in the wash water. They are not safe for some fabrics. (See "Chlorine Bleach.") Preferably, add the bleach to the water before putting it in the clothes. Otherwise dilute it with about a quart of water. Usually 1 cup is recommended for a top-loading machine, ½ cup for a front-loading washer.

Pine-oil disinfectants go into the wash water, preferably before the clothes are added. Use ¾ cup for a top-loading machine, ½ cup for a front-loading washer. Phenolics can be used in either the wash or rinse water. For a brand containing about 3 percent of the active ingredient, use 1 cup for a top-loading machine and 10 tablespoons for a front-loading washer.

To destroy bacteria living on the surface of the washer, pour disinfectant into the empty machine and let it run for 15 minutes at a hot water setting.

Small articles not harmed by boiling can be washed and disinfected by boiling them for ten minutes.

Disposable Clothing It is made of specially prepared paper and when it is soiled you throw it away. Diapers came first, then shifts, swimming trunks, and baby clothes. Coming up are football jerseys, men's underwear, doctors' hospital jackets, graduation dresses, beach ponchos, and sheets.

Disposer, Electric See "Electric Garbage Grinder."

Drains Flush drains after use with plenty of hot water. This helps keep them free of grease and leaves the trap (that little S-shaped bend under the sink) filled with clean, fresh water. Drains in hand basins and bathtubs should be kept free of hair and lint. If yours have those pipelike stoppers that will lift out, clean them once a week thoroughly. On other types, hair, etc., often can be removed by means of a wire bent into a hook. A little washing soda down the kitchen drain once a month helps prevent it from becoming sluggish, because it cuts grease.

Sometimes very hot soapy water will suffice to open a sluggish drain. Pour it down, then run in plenty of hot water. If this doesn't work, a thorough treatment with washing soda may turn the trick. Dissolve one pound of soda in three gallons of boiling water and pour it down the drain. This treatment is usually sufficient for a bathroom drain. If, however, the drain is clogged with a solid object you will have to unscrew the "gooseneck," that curved section of pipe under the sink, which serves as a trap. Turn the water off (those knobs under the

sink), cover your wrench with a cloth to prevent it from scratching the finish, and unscrew first the cap at the base of the U-shaped section of pipe, allowing the water to drain into a basin or pan placed underneath. If the object does not come through with the water, unscrew the gooseneck and clean it.

Lye is a last resort for a grease-clogged kitchen drain. It is poisonous and corrosive and must be used with the utmost caution. Lye must not touch porcelain enamel, which it damages instantly upon contact, and it must not touch your skin, as it can cause severe burns. Commercial drain cleaners may contain lye in an especially prepared form. They are available at hardware stores in easy-to-use containers.

Mechanical aids to open drains include the rubber-cupped gadget on a stick, called "the plumber's friend," a suction implement, and the flexible steel clean-out auger, which the plumbers call a "snake." If you reach the stage where you need a "snake" you had better call for help.

Irrelevant note: Plumbers have an especially vicious oversized "snake" for larger pipes, which they call "the cobra."

Draperies Dust heavy drapes when you clean the room, using a hand vacuum or the upholstery attachment of your vacuum cleaner. Lacking these, use a brush of medium stiffness. Work always from the top of the drape down. Regular dusting will stretch the time between cleaning and keep your house from smelling like a sneeze.

Lined drapes, even when made of sheer material, are difficult to wash at home. However, if you know they are washable and want

to do them yourself, snip the lining loose on all but one side to avoid uneven shrinking. Heavy drapes and those of doubtful washing ability should be sent to a dry cleaner.

Cretonnes and colored cottons and linens, if colorfast, can be washed at home if care is used. If you are uncertain about the dyes, test them first by squeezing out a sample, or inconspicuous corner, in a basin of lukewarm water. The water will become discolored if the dyes are not completely fast. This does not mean that the material will not wash; it does mean, though, that care must be used. Wash each piece separately in lukewarm suds and, after rinsing, spread it flat on a large turkish towel and roll it up to extract as much moisture as possible. Unroll immediately and hang it to dry, making sure that the surfaces do not touch, in a place where it will dry as quickly as possible . . . but not in the sun.

Fabrics known to be colorfast can be washed with assurance in a good stiff suds made with lukewarm water. Rinse well and hang straight on the line, or indoors, avoiding direct sunlight.

Iron drapes lengthwise of the material, on the wrong side, except glazed chintz, which looks best if ironed on the right side.

See also "Cotton," "Rayon," "Chintz," "Glass Cloth," etc., for special instructions.

Drudge What you will be if you do your housework without interest, knowledge or a good working schedule.

Dry Cleaning Dry cleaning at home is not recommended because of the hazards involved. Flammable, or explosive, cleaning fluids are dangerous when used in large amounts. See "Cleaning Fluids."

Dryer See "Automatic Dryer."

Dry Spotter Dry spotter is made by mixing 1 part of coconut oil and 8 parts of dry-cleaning solvent, any kind. It is used to remove many kinds of stains. Keep it in a tightly stoppered container to prevent evaporation of the dry-cleaning fluid. If you cannot get coconut oil, use mineral oil (same amount), which is just as good.

Caution: Dry-cleaning fluid is poisonous and may be flammable. Take precautions.

Durable Press Durable-press clothing goes a step beyond wash and wear. In wash and wear, the textile (synthetic and blends) is said to have a "built-in" memory that enables it to return to its original wrinkle-free state when properly washed and drip dried. In durable press, the garment also "remembers" the shape that was "locked in" when it was sewn and pressed. This is accomplished by treating fabrics (of synthetic and natural fibers and blends) with finishing agents which are "cured" or "set" by heat after the garment has been made.

Durable-press techniques are being improved constantly and the result is an ever-increasing range of garments and household accessories which do not require ironing. Proper laundering will enable you to get the best possible results. If full instructions have not been provided by the manufacturer, follow these directions from the Department of Agriculture.

69

Launder durable-press items promptly and before they are heavily soiled. Some synthetic fibers included in them tend to absorb and hold oily soil.

Pretreat spots on moderately soiled clothing by rubbing them with liquid detergent or a paste made of powdered detergent and water. If doubtful of color fastness, first test an inconspicuous area. Should fading result, remove oily stains with cleaning fluid and launder by hand with a mild detergent or soap. Rinse, roll loosely in a towel to remove excess water, then hang to dry. If the clothing is heavily soiled, measure out the amount of detergent for an entire load and apply it full strength to the most soiled areas. Add hot water and let the clothes soak until the water is cool.

Wash in small loads, preferably with cool water. Use the wash-and-wear or durable-press cycle if it is provided. Otherwise adjust the controls by hand to short wash, rinse, and spin cycles. If warm or hot water is needed to remove the soil, rinse in cool water.

Dry also in small loads, about half of the dryer's capacity. This minimizes wrinkling. Again use the wash-and-wear or durable-press cycle, if available, or set the dryer for low or medium heat. At the end of the drying cycle, turn off the heat and let the clothes continue to tumble for a 10-minute cool-down period. Remove them as soon as the dryer stops and hang or fold them.

The heat and tumbling action of an automatic dryer relaxes fibers and removes wrinkles that appear during washing and wearing. If an automatic dryer is not available, shorten the final rinse spin in the washer by advancing the dial, or remove the garments while dripping wet and place them on rust-proof hangers to dry.

Water and fabric softeners can be used as desired. If a bleach is needed, a peroxy type is suggested because chlorine bleaches yellow some durable-press cottons. Stain removal is the same as for other fabrics but quick action is desirable because grease and other stains are harder to remove from some treated cottons. For touch-up pressing use the low setting on your iron.

If you wash by hand, drip dry. Durable-press clothing can also be dry cleaned.

See also "Pleats."

Duragold A tarnishproof alloy that resembles gold. Rub with chamois or a soft cloth.

Duralumin An alloy of aluminum containing 3 to 4 percent of copper and fractional percentages of manganese and magnesium. Duralumin has a satiny finish, does not tarnish or stain and can be washed with soap and water. Rinse and polish with a soft cloth. Duralumin is equal to soft steel in strength and hardness. It is used for bowls, trays, candlesticks, etc.

Dust Brush A dust brush should

be washed occasionally in luke-warm, mild suds, rinsed and hung in the fresh air to dry. Always hang it up when storing it, to protect the bristles.

Dustcloth A solid, gritty dustcloth does more damage than good, because it engraves fine scratches on polished surfaces. Make a habit of whisking it through hot suds occasionally. Rinse it thoroughly and hang it to dry outdoors, if possible.

If you like an oiled duster put a few drops of lemon oil on it. For a "dustless" duster add a little kerosene.

Do not use an oiled duster on a waxed surface. For safety from fire, store in a can with a top.

Dust Mop See "Mop (Dry)."

Dustpan Give it a bath now and then with soap and warm water. Hang it with the edge toward the wall to discourage denting. If the edge does get bent, take time to straighten it out, or you will find yourself chasing dirt halfway across the room every time you use it. Tantalizing.

A dustpan (as well as brush) for stout or lazy sisters has a long handle which makes it unnecessary to stoop.

Dye Stains See "Stains," p. 228.

Dynel Dynel, a Union Carbide textile fiber, is spun from the chemical compounds acrylonitrile and vinyl chloride, and is classified as a modacrylic. It is used for blankets, draperies, pile fabrics, men's socks, infants' wear, suiting blends, shoe fabrics, rainwear, ski suits, shirtings, and carpets.

Dynel fibers are woollike, warm to the touch, and capable of producing a wide variety of textures, ranging from cashmere-soft fabrics to harsh "wools" and "mohair." This versatility is accomplished by varying the size of the filament. Dynel is quick-drying, resilient, warm, fire-resistant, practically shrinkproof, and insects would rather die than eat the stuff. Mildew and fungus leave it unharmed.

Dynel can be washed by hand or in the washing machine. If desired, it can be dry-cleaned by standard methods. Follow instructions inside the garment. There are no limitations on soaps or detergents that can be used, but washing with a mild soap, as for other fine fabrics, is suggested. Keep the water temperature below 170° F. This is quite hot—hotter than the hands will stand. Bleaches do not harm it, but do not use acetone as a spot remover.

The only limitation in finishing 100 percent Dynel articles is that drying, pressing or ironing temperatures should not exceed 170° F. Generally, if articles of 100 percent Dynel are hung out while damp, wrinkles will fall out and no ironing or pressing will be necessary. If you do want to press it, use a dry cover cloth over the fabric and set the temperature control low.

When Dynel is blended with 50 percent or more of another fiber, such as rayon, cotton or wool, in apparel, it is generally recommended that a cool iron be used and that pressing should be on the reverse side.

If Dynel garments are sent to the laundry or dry cleaner, tell them they are Dynel and require their special instructions. See "Blanket (Synthetic)," and "Synthetic Textiles."

Earthenware The term earthenware is applied to nonvitrified, opaque dinnerware and to partially glazed French- and Mexican-type cookingware, more appropriately called pottery.

Modern earthenware table services are not translucent like china but are often a high-class product, beautifully designed and decorated, and finely glazed. Some of it is ovenproof. Treat it as you would good china.

Partially glazed earthenware intended for cooking requires careful handling because it chips easily and breaks if exposed to sudden temperature changes. Do not place it in cool water when it is hot or in hot water when it is cold. Do not let it soak very long in water.

Good cookingware of this type can be used on surface burners as well as in the oven, provided the heat is turned low at the start and increased gradually. It should never be placed on the fire empty. When the vessel and its contents have been warmed thoroughly, full heat may be used. If used for frying, put the butter or other fat in the pan while it is cold and heat it slowly to the proper temperature.

Egg Stains See "Stains," p. 228.

Electric Appliances These are general instructions for electric equipment, as each item is treated separately on the pages that follow. If you are buying new equipment, look for the U. L. (Underwriters Laboratories) seal of approval.

The two most common causes of trouble with electric equipment are faulty plugs and worn cords. Tighten loose prongs in plugs by turning the little screws that hold the wires. If a prong is broken, discard the plug and get a new one. Replace cords as soon as they begin to show wear.

Always disconnect appliances before attempting to clean them, and never immerse them in water or other fluids unless the directions say it is safe. Disconnect toasters, heaters, and other equipment when not in use and before putting on or taking off parts. Do not use indoor equipment outdoors; you *could* get an electric shock. Do not operate any appliance with a damaged cord or plug, or after it has been damaged in any manner. Return it to the nearest authorized service center for repairs or adjustment. Don't use on one appliance parts made for a different model; they may cause trouble. Do not let the cord hang over the edge of the table or touch a hot surface. If children are around or operating the appliance, supervise them closely.

Always use the cord that belongs to a particular piece of equipment. Cords differ in the amount of voltage they carry, and if a circuit is overloaded, you can get a blown fuse. (See "Fuse.") Attach the plug first to the appliance, then plug it into the wall outlet. To disconnect, turn control to "off," then remove the plug from the wall outlet.

"And," says my favorite electrician, "please say to oil 'em." Sealed motors do not require oiling, but failure to oil the kind that do require it sends more electrical equipment back to the factory than any other cause. Always use the amount and kind of oil specified by the manufacturer. Too much oil is as bad as too little. If you are in doubt about when, where, and how to oil, ask your dealer's advice.

Electric Broom The electric broom is a simplified vacuum cleaner, designed for cleaning rugs and smooth-surfaced floors. It is light in weight, easy to use and to store, and much less expensive than the usual vacuum cleaner. The dust is collected in a plastic container which is simply emptied.

Electric Bulbs Dust your electric bulbs as regularly as you dust your room. Wash them about once a month if you want to get full watt value. To do this, disconnect the lamp, then wipe the bulbs carefully with a cloth wrung out of warm suds, taking care not to get the metal part wet. Wipe dry. Wash reflecting bowls at the same time.

Electric light bulbs blackened by use burn 20 percent less efficiently than new ones. Better replace. Dusty shades, reflectors, and glass fixtures can absorb as much as one fourth of a bulb's light.

Electric Cords Electric cords should be replaced promptly if they are damaged. This insures against short circuits and electric shock. Inspect your cords regularly for wear and tear.

Before connecting, or disconnecting, a cord from an outlet controlled by a switch, turn the switch to the off position. If the appliance itself is controlled by a switch, turn it off before connecting or disconnecting. This prevents sparking and eventual wearing away of the contacts.

In disconnecting a cord from a wall socket, pull on the plug, not the cord. Jerking plugs out by the cord strains and loosens the copper wires inside and is likely to break or bend the prongs of the plug. Always be sure your hands are dry when you are handling "live" cords.

Do not switch cords indiscriminately from one appliance to another, but use the one that belongs to it. Keep cords clean by wiping them with a soft, dry cloth. If a cord becomes greasy, disconnect it and wash it with soap and water. Be sure a washed cord is thoroughly dry before you use it again.

Heat also can injure both cord and insulation. Never wrap the cord around an electric iron or a heater while the appliance is still warm. Store your electric cords loosely coiled in a box or drawer or hang them, coiled, over a round peg.

Electric Dishwasher An electric dishwasher does not normally require much attention because after washing and rinsing the dishes it thoroughly rinses itself. The exterior is easy to clean; it is baked-on synthetic enamel, sometimes with a wooden top.

Use a high-grade wax cleaner on the synthetic enamel finish. Avoid harsh gritty cleaners or scouring pads. If your dishwasher has a wooden top, give it the following treatment before using it. First wipe the top with a dry cloth to remove any dust. Saturate a clean cloth with pure mineral oil and polish all exposed wooden surfaces until they shine. Let the wooden top stand overnight to absorb the oil, then repeat the treatment. Let it stand for 4 to 6 hours and then wipe off the excess oil with a dry soft cloth. (If your machine is old and the top has been badly neglected, sand it with #ooo or #oooo sandpaper, then wipe it with a cloth saturated with mineral oil.)

Wooden tops should not be used as a place for thawing food, even when protected by aluminum foil. Water should never be allowed to stand on the wooden top. To remove water stains, rub them with a cloth dipped in mineral oil.

The interior of the dishwasher is largely self-cleaning. Avoid harsh cleansers and scouring pads which may scar it. If a powder is needed use one that doesn't scratch, such as whiting, or Bon Ami.

In operating your dishwasher use hot water (140° to 150° F.) and a standard dishwashing detergent, such as Cascade, Dishwasher All, Electra Sol, Calgonite. Try several kinds until you get the best results for your particular type of water. Too much detergent blankets the water with suds so that the dishes are not cleaned effectively, and sometimes builds up on dinnerware an unsightly chalky deposit that masks the decoration and is difficult to remove.

Dishes and pans should be free of all insoluble matter before being placed in the trays. If they are not, food bits may lodge in the drain and flood the dishwasher. Arrange plates, glassware, silver, and pans according to your model. Heat-sensitive plastics and woodenware, including kitchenware with wooden handles, high-gloss aluminumware, colored aluminum, and lacquered metals, insulated cups and glasses, expensive glassware, and ironware should not be put in a dishwasher. And think twice before you use it for very fine or delicate china. An American manufacturer of high-quality china warns that detergents for dishwashers vary in harshness and that some of them remove platinum and gilt decorations, and occasionally even the glaze. Those with metal baskets unprotected with plastic coatings remove gold and platinum bands by abrasion. Ask your dealer if he can replace the baskets.

To remove chalky deposits left on dinnerware and glasses (but *not* silver and pans), place the affected pieces in the dishwasher. Place a cup filled with chlorine bleach (Clorox, Purex) on the bottom rack. Operate the machine for five minutes. Stop the machine and empty the cup which is now filled with water. Fill the cup with vinegar, replace it in the dishwasher, and finish the cycle. Repeat the vinegar cycle. Finish with a complete cycle, using plain hot water. The deposit is loosened by the bleach and removed by the

vinegar. Some manufacturers recommend using 2 cups filled with vinegar for this operation (without the bleach), followed by a complete cycle with dishwasher detergent.

Electric Fan Most new electric fans are lubricated at the factory. Ask about this when you are buying one. If it needs oiling, plan to oil it about once a year. A few drops are all you need.

To clean an electric fan, first disconnect it. Then wipe the blades and motor casing with a damp cloth. If the casing is very dirty, use a cloth wrung out of soapsuds, taking great care not to let any moisture get inside the casing. Rinse and dry.

When storing your electric fan, cover it completely with paper or cloth (an old pillowcase is fine) to prevent dust from settling on the motor casing and blades.

Electric Freezer The routine care of a home freezer is slight. For the outside of enameled cabinets manufacturers recommend an emulsified cleaning wax. Or you can use mild soap or a detergent and warm water. Do not use abrasives.

Defrosting is called for when the accumulation in the cabinet be-

comes thick enough to interfere with the proper closing of the lid. Too much frost slows down the freezing operation and the general efficiency of the unit. The electric current need not be shut off for routine defrosting. If desirable, remove the food packages to your refrigerator, or place them, well wrapped in newspaper, on a nearby table. (If it is necessary to remove the food, turn the control to the coldest position 12 hours in advance so that the packages will be less likely to thaw.) Scrape down the frost with a wooden paddle or plastic scraper and scoop it out with a piece of cardboard. Do not use any sharp instrument which might damage the cabinet.

The finned condenser of the freezer, behind the louvered panel at the base of the freezer in the front, should be cleaned once a year to maintain highest efficiency. Remove the panel and clean the fins with a stiff brush or vacuum cleaner attachment. May is a good time for this operation, just before hot weather begins.

If, through neglect or any other reason, the frost has turned to ice, or if a food odor has developed, a thorough cleaning is indicated. To do this, first remove all food packages to a large box, thickly insulated with newspapers, and cover

the box with a thick blanket. If the weather is extremely hot, add dry ice, obtained from a frozen-food or ice-cream store.

After all the food has been removed, turn the current off and leave the top partially open to facilitate thawing. If necessary, run cold water over refrigerated surfaces to hasten melting. Finish with your scraper. Wash the inside carefully with lukewarm water containing about a tablespoon of baking soda per quart. Rinse with clear, lukewarm water and wipe dry with soft cloths. Turn the current on, let the freezer run for about half an hour, then replace the food.

If you are going on a long vacation and wish the freezer to remain off, clean the unit thoroughly, as described, and leave the lid open.

Should the electric current be interrupted, keep the lid closed as much as possible to conserve refrigeration. Remember that it takes forty-four hours for foods in a fully loaded freezer to begin to thaw, according to the Bureau of Human Nutrition and Home Economics of the United States Department of Agriculture. In partially loaded freezers, the foods thaw a little faster.

It is considered safe by experts to refreeze foods if the temperature rises no higher than 40° F. In a serious emergency try to get about twenty-five pounds of dry ice from a nearby frozen-food or ice-cream store and sprinkle it over the frozen-food packages. If you cannot obtain the dry ice, contact a frozen-food locker and try to obtain temporary storage there.

Freezers differ in construction and the arrangement of parts. If yours puzzles you in any way, send your model number (stamped on the machine) to the company and ask for the proper booklet.

Electric Fruit Extractor Disconnect after using. Wipe the housing of the motor with a cloth wrung out of soapsuds and rinse with a cloth wrung out of clear water. Wipe dry. Wash the removable parts in the dishpan along with other things, dry, and replace. Apply oil according to the manufacturer's directions. Do not immerse your extractor in water.

Electric Frypan Turn the switch to "off." Disconnect the cord from the outlet, then from the frypan. Let it cool. Never pour cold water into a hot pan; this could cause warping. Do not immerse the heating element in water unless it is water-sealed. Wash the removable parts and the pan in hot sudsy water and dry immediately.

If soaking fails to remove some spots from a plain aluminum surface, use a soap-filled steel-wool pad or an aluminum cleaner. (See "Aluminum.") But do not use them on the terminal-pin area of the skillet. Clean this area with a brush and make sure it is dry before inserting the temperature control for another use. Pans of cast aluminum may be darkened by alkaline foods, strong detergents, or very hard water. To remove this discoloration, fill the pan with water containing cream of tartar

(1 tablespoon of cream of tartar to 1 quart of water) and boil for 15–20 minutes. Wash in soapsuds, rinse, and dry. Washing in an electric dishwasher is not recommended.

Pans with colored exteriors and nonsticking cooking surfaces should be cleaned only with a nonabrasive plastic brush or nylon-mesh scouring pad. The nonstick surface may be darkened after continual use and lose its nonstick quality. You can restore it by using one of the special commercial cleaners available in groceries and hardware stores. Follow the directions on the label when using them. Before using any nonstick cleaner, remember these precautions. Do not cover the skillet with a lid while using the cleaning solution, avoid spilling when handling the solution, and don't let it boil over the sides. This can cause discoloration. See "Silicones" and "Teflon."

Electric Garbage Grinder An electric garbage grinder eliminates muss and fuss in the kitchen by shredding waste foods into fine particles and washing them down the drain. There are several makes and, in operating a grinder, you should follow the directions for your model.

A garbage grinder will dispose of vegetable refuse, fruit pits and rinds, egg shells, and soft foods. It even gnaws small bones to bits. General Electric says ground bones act as an abrasive cleaner on their Disposall. Not on its bill of fare are: metal, including tin foil; glass; plastics; and ceramics. Leather, cloth, string, rubber, seafood shells, artichoke leaves, and corn husks can cause nuisance tripping of the motor overload control. Lye or other drain-cleaning chemicals should not be used. They can damage the mechanism.

The opening, or top, of the garbage grinder replaces the usual sink drain and the rest of the compact unit is underneath the sink. The top of the grinder, turned to the various positions indicated on the dial, acts as a sink stopper or as a strainer, without causing the machine to go into action. When turned to the operating position, the top is locked in place and the motor is ready to be started by turning on the cold water. Cold water is always used because it hardens grease so that it can be ground and floated away. A rapid flow of cold water assists grinding, cleans the disposer, carries food waste through the drain lines, and keeps the pipes clean.

An electric garbage grinder requires little care. No oiling is necessary because the motor is permanently lubricated. The interior never has to be cleaned because the unit scours itself each time it is used. About once a week it should be flushed out thoroughly. To do this, close the opening, run two or three inches of cold water into the sink, and (with the cold water still running) turn the top to the on position. Let the unit operate until the sink has been emptied.

If a forbidden item, such as a bottle cap or piece of broken china, accidentally gets into your garbage grinder, the motor will protest by becoming unusually noisy. When this happens, turn the motor off, remove the top, and take out the foreign material with tongs or a wooden spoon.

Should an odor develop in the sink, run lemon or orange rinds through the machine. This will rout unpleasant odors and leave a clean sweet smell. Grinding a dozen or more ice cubes generously sprinkled with household scouring powder also has a cleaning, deodorizing effect. When grinding ice cubes do not use water.

An electric garbage grinder can be installed in practically any sink with a three-and-a-half to four-inch drain opening that connects with a municipal sewage system or septic tank of the proper capacity. It cannot be used in connection with a cesspool system. If you are thinking of installing one, check the building laws in your community first. The sewer systems of some cities are not adequate and garbage grinders are therefore not allowed.

Electric Grill See "Electric Sandwich Grill."

Electric Heater Dust and dirt cut down the efficiency of electric room heaters just as dirty bulbs and reflectors cut down light. Always disconnect the cord when dusting, cleaning or polishing. If your heater has a fan, oil it at least once a year. The reflectors of sun bowl lamps should be kept brightly polished for maximum efficiency. Slip off the guard and polish it with a suitable fine polish. Sometimes, when this type of heater fails to function, the heating element is loose. Before running to an electrician try tightening it. It twists into a socket just like a light bulb.

Keep your electric heater away from swinging draperies, papers, clothing, small children. Never let it get wet and never touch it when your hands are damp. Use special care in bathrooms and under no circumstances touch it while you are in the bathtub. Always disconnect a heater when it is not in use, even if it has a switch.

When storing, cover with cloth or paper and select a cool, dry place.

Electric Heating Pad Directions vary slightly for different brands of heating pads but here are the general rules for their care:

Inside the pad is a network of fine wires, and if one of these is broken the whole thing will go out of gear. To avoid breaking these wires do not crush or fold the pad and do not carry it by the cord. Grasp it by the pad instead. Let your pad cool before you put it away. Then coil the cord loosely and store it in a cool, dark, dry place.

Pins and metallic clips must not be used to secure the pad. If it is to be applied directly to the body, baste it into the little muslin cover provided with it, or improvise one yourself. This will keep it clean. Unless your model is moistureproof you cannot use it in connection with a wet dressing except when inserted in a moistureproof casing. The casing should be examined each time it is used to make certain it has not developed holes, cracks or blisters. If the casing has deteriorated it should be replaced by a new one.

Electric Iron Most electric irons are chromium-plated and therefore rust- and tarnishproof. Always disconnect the iron as soon as you have finished your work and allow it to cool. If the bottom, called the sole plate, has become stained with starch, wipe it with a cloth wrung out of hot soap suds. To remove melted nylon, heat the iron until the nylon is softened, then scrape it off with a wooden spatula. If necessary, a mild abrasive, such as whiting or silver polish, may be used to clean the sole plate, but be cautious as the chromium plating is damaged easily. Rinse afterward with a cloth wrung out of clear water. On irons with aluminum sole plates fine steel wool can be used to remove stains. Stroke lightly, lengthwise of the iron. Use a soapy sponge or nylon mesh pad on Teflon-coated sole plates.

Never scrape the sole plate with a knife to remove starch and avoid ironing over zippers, hooks or buttons which might scratch the plating. About once a month rub the sole plate with paraffin or beeswax, being careful to wipe off the surplus on a piece of old cloth or paper. This will keep the iron slick and retard stains from starch.

If the plating on the sole plate of your iron has been damaged, you can have it replated (or replaced) at the factory.

Except for the special care required for their steam fixtures, the care of a steam iron is the same as for a dry one. Do not overfill the reservoir, and use the type of water —tap or distilled—recommended for your particular iron. If the opening of the sprinkler nozzle becomes stopped, insert a fine needle in the center hole to clean it. When the ironing is finished, disconnect the iron, and while it is still hot, empty the water reservoir and let the iron rest in an upright position on its heel rest. (Hold self-cleaning models over the sink; they cause a minor explosion when the button is pressed, releasing water and steam.) Wrap the cord around the handle when the iron has cooled and store it in the same position.

Precautions: Do not store your iron, or wrap the cord around it, while it is still warm. Try not to drop it. Dropping causes more casualties to electric irons than any other accident. Replace worn cords promptly. In ironing, don't press too hard. It's the contact of heat with the damp cloth that removes the wrinkles, so why wear yourself out?

Electric Ironer See "Rotary Ironer" and "Flatplate Ironer."

Electric Kettle General Electric's chromium-plated electric kettle should be freshened for first use by having a quart of water boiled in it and discarded. After being in use a while, the inside should be cleaned by boiling in it a quart of water containing ½ cup of white vinegar. Bring to a rolling boil, then unplug the unit and let it stand for half an hour. Pour the solution out. Now fill the kettle to maximum (2 quarts) of fresh tap water and bring again to a rolling boil. Unplug from the wall outlet and pour the water off. For spots on the chromium exterior use a nonabrasive liquid cleaner made for glass or chrome, or use baking soda on a clean damp cloth.

Electric Lamp See "Lamp—Electric" and "Sun Lamp."

Electric Mixer After using your electric mixer, disconnect it from the wall outlet. Remove beaters or other attachments, wash them in hot suds, and dry them. (A dishwasher may be used for these items, but not for stainless steel bowls.)

Wash the bowls by hand as soon as possible and dry them to prevent spotting. Do not use them to soak spoons and other appliances; this could cause corrosive action, damaging to the bowl. Letting the bowl sit around wet may cause it to be spotted. Wipe the power head and other parts of the mixer with a damp cloth. To remove stubborn spots, rub them briskly with a cloth dipped in suds or in a nonabrasive powder such as silver polish. Rinse. Wipe dry with a soft cloth. Do not wind the cord around the mixer for storage. Wrap it in large loops and lay it away.

The newest mixers are factory lubricated and do not require oiling.

Electric Percolator See "Coffee Maker."

Electric Plugs If the prongs holding the wires are loose, tighten the two little screws that hold them in place. If the prongs are broken or bent, get a new plug at your hardware store and have them put it on if you can't do it yourself. Remove plugs from their outlets after switching off the controls (if any) and by grasping the plug rather than the cord. Yanking out the cord is likely to break the little copper wires inside the casing or to pull the wires away from the screws which fasten them to the plug.

Electric Range Clean the outside enameled surfaces, after the range has cooled, with a cloth wrung out of warm water and soap or a detergent. Rinse with a cloth wrung out of clear water. Wipe dry. If food has stuck to the surface, use a soapy plastic sponge or nylon

mesh pad. If spilled foods are wiped up promptly, you won't often have the problem of burned-on food. Use a dry cloth if the surface is hot. To forestall a variety of problems try to avoid overheating, spatters and spills, sudden sharp blows, acids and alkalies.

Be sure the switch is in the off position before attempting to clean the heating units. After each meal, when the stove has cooled, wipe the rims of the units with a damp cloth, being careful not to pull or twist the wires. Spilled foods should be burned off open units. Place a pan of water on the burner, turn the switch to high, and heat until the food remnants have been completely charred. When the unit has cooled, lift it out with a table knife and brush off the charred bits. Clean the rim on which the unit rests, using a mild cleanser. Wipe with a cloth wrung out of detergent suds, rinse and dry. Wash the surfaces of enclosed units in the same way.

Reflector pans under the units usually are removable and can be washed with other utensils. It is important that they be kept shining because they aid in the heat output of the units. Wash them frequently. If the burner handles are removable, pull them off and wash them too. Spills, boil-overs, and grease spatters should be removed as soon as the burner has cooled. Soaking the pans for a few minutes in hot detergent suds will remove most of the deposits. Rub stubborn spots with a plastic sponge or nylon mesh pad. Well cookers and pressure cookers should be washed after each use. Do not leave food in them.

The oven is vented through a duct under a rear surface unit. This vent should be cleaned frequently. If removable, lift the rear surface unit, remove the reflector pan, and take out the duct. Clean it with soap and water, rinse, and replace. If not removable, wash it in place. Never cover the hole in the oven vent track with aluminum foil or any other material—this prevents the vent from functioning properly during cooking.

The broiler and the broiler rack should be removed and cleaned carefully after use, and grease spatters should be wiped off to keep them from burning onto the enamel the next time the broiler is used.

Clean a lightly soiled, old-fashioned oven with soap or detergent and water, or hot water containing washing soda or ammonia. Or place a half cup of ammonia in the oven the night before the oven is to be cleaned. Heavy-duty oven cleaners, such as Easy-Off, also can be used. Follow exactly the manufacturer's directions on the container. Silicone spray, applied to the clean oven, will make it easier to clean next time. Cover the floor around the stove with newspapers when you apply the spray because, if it falls onto the floor, the floor will be dangerously slippery.

In a self-cleaning electric oven the soil is burned off. To clean it, first remove shelves, pans, racks and other oven fittings for manual cleaning. Do not use any cleaner on the oven proper. To do so will damage the porous lining used in such ovens. Simply close the oven door, set the heat at 400° F., and let it burn for at least 4 hours, or until clean.

Electric stoves differ in materials and in the arrangement of their parts. If there is anything you do not understand about your stove, write to the manufacturer, enclosing the serial number, for a booklet.

Electric Refrigerator See "Refrigerator."

Electric Roaster Disconnect the roaster, remove the large inset pans, racks and small utensils and wash them like other pans of the same material. Usually these pans are made of enameled steel, so avoid sudden temperature changes or the surface will crack. Wipe the shell, inside and out, with a damp cloth and polish it with a dry one. Do not put it in water, because the electrical element and controls are built into the outside shell. Be careful not to let drops of water seep into the electric connections or coils of the broiler units. Store in a place easy to reach, with the lid ajar to prevent musty odors from developing.

When using your roaster, be careful not to plug it into a circuit powering other appliances or you may blow a fuse.

Electric Sander Electric sanders for floors and hand sanders for woodwork can be rented from hardware stores and paint shops. They save the home decorator much time and effort, provided the home decorator is competent to use them.

Electric Sandwich Grill Disconnect the cord of your sandwich grill as soon as you have finished cooking and allow it to cool with the grids open. This prevents the grease film from burning. Wipe off crumbs with a damp cloth and clean the grids with a spatula or fine steel wool. Badly stained or greasy grids should be removed, washed, and scoured if necessary. Rinse and dry. Wipe the outside with a damp cloth and polish with a dry one. If very greasy, wash with a cloth wrung out of hot soapsuds. Rub burned-in grease spatters with a little whiting or silver polish. Never put the entire grill into water to clean it. Accessory waffle iron grids should receive the same care given other waffle iron grids. See "Electric Waffle Iron."

Electric Slicing Knife When possible, use a wooden board under the meat to be carved. Like any sharp knife, your slicer can scratch china and metal.

When you have finished carving, unplug the cord from the outlet, then from the knife. Remove the blades and wash them in hot soapsuds, rinse and wipe dry. Wipe the handle and cord with a damp cloth. Never immerse the handle in water; it contains the unsealed motor unit. (Blades, however, may be so washed.) Do not attempt to sharpen the blades since a conventional sharpener will destroy the cutting edge. Replacement blades can be obtained from the manufacturer or a service center.

Electric Smoke Alarm Check your electric smoke alarm frequently to see if the signal indicator lamp is functioning. This is usually located, off-center, in the cover. Once a week check the entire system by depressing the red alarm button in the center of the cover. A loud sound will be produced, as if smoke were present.

Do not paint your smoke alarm or tamper with it in any way. Do not operate it in places where the

temperature exceeds 100° F. or drops below 40° F.

The cover may be removed from the smoke alarm and hand-cleaned with soap and warm water. Dust or grease inside the unit may cause it to sound when no fire exists. To keep down the dust in the smoke alarm system, vacuum the outside of the perforated chamber in the center of the unit, using the soft round brush of your vacuum cleaner.

There are many kinds of smoke alarms made by various companies. If you are in doubt about the operation of yours, get in touch with its service center.

Electric Toaster Disconnect the cord and let the toaster cool. If there is a crumb tray, remove it and brush off the crumbs. Turn other types upside down and shake them gently. Most toasters that do not have trays have a removable base and this should be taken off occasionally for a thorough cleaning and, if required, oiling. Clean the crumbs from around the wires and sides with a soft brush. Do not attempt to wash the inside of your toaster and do not put it into water. The heating unit cleans itself. Don't pry toast out with a fork or the heating unit may be injured. And you may also be injured by shock.

Pop-up toasters that eject their product with undue enthusiasm

can be toned down by adjusting a little spring inside. You don't have to stand there, poised to catch it.

Most electric toasters are plated with chromium, which is rust- and tarnishproof. Wipe the outside with a damp cloth and polish with a dry one. Burned-on spatters of butter can be removed with a damp cloth and a little whiting, baking soda, or silver polish.

A half-inch paintbrush is dandy for removing crumbs from the interior of a toaster.

Electric Toaster-Oven Toaster ovens of various types are similar in construction and operation. Always unplug the cord from the wall socket after using the oven, and let it cool.

Clean the exterior surfaces with a damp cloth wrung out of soapsuds, rinse, and wipe dry. Stubborn spots can be removed from chromium plating by rubbing them with bicarbonate of soda on a damp cloth or with a glass or chromium cleaner.

Pull out the crumb tray (if removable) and brush off the crumbs with a damp cloth. Use nylon or plastic soap-filled pads to remove stubborn spots. Rinse and dry completely before closing the oven. Always be sure to latch the crumb tray shut before operating the toaster.

To clean the interior, remove the racks by lifting them up and out. Wash the racks in soapsuds, rinse, and dry thoroughly. Do not bend the frame or individual wires of the rack. To replace the lower rack, place the rear (sometimes marked R) on the lower backpins. Lower the front of the rack (some-

times marked F) onto the front-pins. When this has been done correctly, the rack will be level and will move forward when the oven door is opened.

The interior walls and glass door should be cleaned frequently with a sponge or cloth wrung as dry as possible out of soapsuds. Rub spots with a plastic (not metallic) sponge and, if this doesn't remove them, try baking soda. Rinse with a clean damp cloth and dry thoroughly. Do not use spray-on or other oven cleaners. They can damage electrical parts.

To insure thorough drying, plug the toaster in a middle-toast setting, and let it run for one cycle.

Electric Waffle Iron Instructions for breaking in a new waffle iron usually say to brush the grids with an unsalted cooking oil (Wesson, Mazola), heat it until the grids begin to smoke, bake a waffle, and discard it. Excess oil is absorbed by this first waffle and the grids are conditioned. If properly used, no further greasing should ever be necessary.

To clean the waffle iron after use, disconnect it, let it cool, wipe the edges of the grids with a clean dry cloth, brush out the crumbs, and wipe the grids with a damp cloth. Do not wash the grids. If batter has spattered on the chromium plating and a damp cloth will not remove it, try detergent on a damp cloth or use silver polish.

Should your waffles stick, owing to faulty pretreating or insufficient shortening in your batter, clean the grids with your brush and pretreat as for a new iron. To remove grease and discoloration from grids, apply

83

with a brush a paste made by mixing baking soda with water. Allow it to remain for a time, then brush or wipe it off and pretreat the grids.

Waffle makers with silicone-treated grids (aluminum colored) can be retreated at home with a silicone spray, available at hardware and department stores. (See "Silicones.") Damaged Teflon-coated grids can be restored by a professional.

Electric Washer See "Washing Machine."

Electric Water Heater See "Water Heater."

Electric Waxer You are not supposed to bear down on the handle when operating an electric floor waxer. You are supposed to remember to oil it, according to the manufacturer's instructions . . . probably once a month. Use only on the voltage indicated.

For best results let the wax dry for at least thirty minutes before you start polishing. If you don't own an electric waxer you can usually rent one by the hour from any first-class paint or hardware store. Get the floors cleaned and put the wax down before you pick up the waxer and you will save cash.

The newest waxers are contrived to remove the old wax, put on new, and finally to polish it.

Emerald The emerald, a variety of the mineral beryl, is a deep, clear green in color and, if of gem quality, transparent. It is believed that the peculiar shade of green which characterizes the emerald is due to the presence of small amounts of chromium. The finest emeralds come from the region of Muzo, in Colombia, South America. Large crystals, which are less valuable, are found in North Carolina and in Siberia.

See "Jewelry."

Emery A variety of the mineral corundum, which is finely granular in structure. In color it is deep gray to bluish or blackish gray . . . sometimes even brownish.

Emery is used in polishing metals and hard stones and, sometimes, in reconditioning furniture. It may be had in various degrees of fineness and the very finest should be used for furniture work.

Emery cloth is prepared by dusting powdered emery on glue-covered cloth. Emery cloth can be purchased at hardware stores in handy household packets, graded from coarse to fine. Emery also is used to stuff that little strawberry in your sewing kit, used to sharpen needles.

Enamelware Enamelware is made by fusing a special kind of glass on a steel base. It must be handled carefully to avoid chipping and cracking. Sudden changes of temperature (cold water poured into a hot vessel, or scalding water into a cold one) will also cause the enamel to crack. When using enamelware pots or pans heat them slowly. Enamelware absorbs heat quickly but spreads it unevenly. If the heat is too great, foods will scorch and heat stains will be caused on the bottom of the vessel.

Ordinary cleaning calls for soap and warm water, rinsing and drying. Do not use metal pot scrapers or sponges, scouring powders, or steel wool. To remove stuck food, put cold water in the pan and let it remain until the food is soft enough to wash off. If food has burned, let the pan cool, then run water into it. Add baking soda (about 2 teaspoons per quart), and boil. This will loosen the burned food so that it can be removed easily with a rubber scraper or plastic sponge.

Light stains can often be removed from enamelware by rubbing them with a damp cloth dipped in baking soda. For stubborn stains use chlorine bleach. If the stain is in the bottom of the pan, let the bleach stand in the pan until it disappears. If elsewhere, cover the stain with a cloth saturated with the bleach.

Acids should not be allowed to stand on an enameled surface because they damage the finish, leaving a rough spot. Acid foods, such as tomatoes, rhubarb and citrus fruits, should never be stored in an enameled vessel. Antimony, a toxic metal, sometimes is used in its manufacture and the acids could break it down to form poisonous compounds. There is no record of food poisoning traceable to food cooked in enamelware vessels, but cases have been traced to acid foods prepared and allowed to stand in them over an extended period.

Enamelware is varied to meet specific requirements: ordinary ware, stain-resistant, acidproof, etc. Kitchen enamelware should not be used by home photographers.

Encron See "Polyester."

Enzyme Product Enzyme presoaks or enzyme-containing laundry detergents can be used in washing clothes. They can be stored as purchased but become inactive if stored after they have been made into a solution.

Ethyl Cellulose A plastic. See "Cellulosics."

Experiment An experiment, like a botch, can prove costly. But experiments are lots of fun. Use reasonable care to safeguard yourself and perform your experiments on objects you do not value highly.

Eyeglasses Opticians recommend washing eyeglasses periodically with warm water and soap to remove the accumulation of oil from the skin. Use a soft brush to clean around the rims. Rinse and polish with a soft lintless cloth, or tissue paper.

Fabric Softeners Fabric softeners (Nusoft, Final Touch, Downy) make textiles soft and fluffy, minimize wrinkling, and reduce the static electricity that accumulates in some synthetics. Follow the directions on the label. If too much is used, fabrics may be less absorbent. The effect of a softener is lost with the next washing.

Faïence See "Pottery."

Fan See "Electric Fan."

Faucet Look up the metal of which the faucet is made: chromium, nickel, etc. Drippy faucets waste water and cause brown and green stains on porcelain enamel bowls and bathtubs. Get the plumber to install a new washer or, if you are smart, put a new one in yourself. You can buy faucet washers in assorted sizes on a little card at your hardware store. To install a washer, first close the valve that shuts off the water

85

(under the sink), take off the handle, then unscrew the nut around the faucet. Put a wad of cloth around the nut so you won't scratch it with your monkey wrench. Now loosen the screw that holds the washer and screw in your new one.

Put the handle back on, being careful to get it in its original position.

(Maybe you can pretend dumb and get your husband to handle this job. A man likes to think that only he can manage a hammer or wrench, and I sometimes think it is a mistake for a woman ever to admit that she can hit a nail.)

Feathers See "Pillows."

Felt A fabric made of wool, fur or other materials, matted . . . not woven. You can keep felt hats neatly brushed and you can remove surface dirt with a clean rubber sponge. For a special beauty treatment steam the hat gently, using the tip of your steam iron or the spout of a teakettle. Steam the crown first, turning the hat slowly until the surface has been covered, then brush it lightly in the direction of the nap. Steam the brim and brush it. Do not get the hat too wet or it will shrink.

Felt Base Floor Covering A floor covering made of paper felt and

asphalt, coated with oil paint. It is cared for like linoleum. See "Linoleum."

Fiberglas Trade-mark for a variety of products made from glass fibers. See "Glass Fibers," "Glass Cloth."

Fingernail Polish See "Lacquer" in "Stains," p. 232.

Finishes for Fabrics Chemists have developed more than 5,000 specialty chemicals and finishing agents for the versatile textiles designed for today's living. Finishes are applied to both man-made and natural cloth to give them desired qualities not inherent in their fibers.

Millions of yards of cottons are treated each year with synthetic resins to give the cloth resilience and to enable garments to keep their shape. These are "wash-and-wear" cottons. For woolens there are finishes that provide moth protection for extended periods, spot resistance, lasting creases or pleats, and machine washability.

Still other finishes make cloth softer, or stiffer, and provide resistance to shrinkage, mildew, stains, spots, and perspiration damage. There are finishes for water repellence, wrinkle resistance, slip resistance (to hold threads in place), and resistance to fire, static, odors, and germs.

Resin finishes disappear if water used for laundering them is too hot. Other finishes wear off after a period of use and can, or cannot, be restored. Most of them require no special treatment on the part of the consumer.

Firebrats See "Silverfish and Firebrats."

Fireplace Ever since the days of the cave man, an open fire has been a comfort and pleasure to the human race. The fireplace in your room is the focus of attention and deserves special care so that it may be attractive in appearance. While it is an almost irresistible impulse, probably also dating to cave man days, to toss scraps of paper and other waste objects into it, do try to resist that urge. Otherwise your fireplace will be as charming as a trash can.

The home economics sisters agree that the ashes from last night's fire should be removed in the morning and a new fire laid. The hearth should be brushed carefully and the damper closed to prevent dust from blowing about the room. In the country, of course, we do no such thing. The next day's fire is much easier to light and burns better if the ashes stay there. Let the flames burn down before you retire and cover the embers with ashes as a fire precaution.

Occasionally your hearth will require special cleaning, and the method will be determined by the type of material which composes it. Soot stains can be removed from stone fireplaces by the following method.

Make a soft soap by adding about a quart of hot water to four ounces of yellow laundry soap and heating the mixture until the soap is dissolved completely. When the mixture has cooled add a half pound of powdered pumice and a half cup of household ammonia. Mix well. After brushing off as much of the soot as possible, apply a coating of your mixture to the stone with a clean brush. Let it remain for about half an hour, then scrub it off with a stiff brush and warm water. Rinse thoroughly with warm water.

For the cleaning of other types of facings, see "Brick Floors," "Slate," and "Marble." See also "Andirons and Fire Tools."

Gas Logs Gas fire logs are made of asbestos. They can be dusted with a cloth or with the dusting attachment of your vacuum cleaner.

Fireproof Finish A label which states that a material is "fireproof" gives the manufacturer's assurance that it has total resistance to destruction by fire. "Flameproof" means that it may change its physical form but will not support combustion. "Flame-resistant" and "fire-retardant" mean that the material will not burn readily.

Fish Oil See "Cod-Liver Oil" in "Stains," p. 227.

Fish Slime See "Stains," p. 228.

Flatplate Ironer Follow the manufacturer's instructions in using your flatplate ironer. The care and cleaning of it is comparatively simple, but make it routine for best results.

A moisture cup, located under the lapboard, catches moisture as it is pressed out of clothes on this type of electric ironer. Empty it after each ironing, oftener if needed.

Wax the aluminum shoe occasionally to keep it slick. When necessary, clean it with a cloth wrung out of warm suds. After drying, rewax the shoe, using paraffin or beeswax.

Every now and then shake out and fluff up the padding. This freshens it and makes it last longer.

To insure even wear, reverse the position of the padding after fluffing it.

Keep the muslin cover clean by laundering it frequently. Liquid wax, applied occasionally to the exterior of the ironer, will keep the finish clean and provide it with a protective coating. Use a kind recommended for such equipment by your dealer.

Protect your ironer from dust by keeping it covered when not in use.

Fleas Escapees from dogs and cats sometimes cause flea infestations of homes. From the shelter of rugs and upholstered furniture they extend their attention to man. To correct the situation, first vacuum the room thoroughly and destroy the dust, then apply spray to the floor. A spray containing methoxychlor, malathion, or ronnel is best.

Apply a 5 percent methoxychlor spray, or a 2 percent malathion spray, to floors and baseboards and to walls to a height of about 1 foot. Apply a light mist to rugs, upholstery, and other materials which might be stained. Treat especially the places where your pet likes to rest.

Sprays for use in the home can be prepared as follows: Mix 6¼ tablespoons of 25 percent methoxychlor emulsifiable concentrate, or 3¾ tablespoons of 50- to 55-percent malathion emulsifiable concentrate, in 1 pint of water. Ronnel sprays for home use are so labeled. Follow the directions given on the label.

Treat your pet too. For dogs and cats, malathion, methoxychlor, rotenone, and pyrethrum (pyrethrins) are sold ready-mixed for use as flea powders or sprays. Select a powder that contains no more than 5 percent of malathion, 5 percent of methoxychlor, 1 percent of rotenone, or 1 percent of pyrethrins. (Sprays for dogs and cats often contain several of these insecticides combined, each at a lower concentration than those listed.) If you are using a spray, select one that has no more than 0.5 percent of malathion or methoxychlor.

In using insecticides follow the directions given on the label exactly. If your dog or cat seems uncomfortable for a few minutes following application of the powder or spray, do not be alarmed. Dying fleas show extra activity. Check your pet during the next few weeks to be sure you have gotten all the fleas. See also "Insecticides."

Floors If you are planning to do a thorough job on a floor, move the furniture out, clean the rugs on both sides and roll them up, then go to it according to the type of floor with which you are dealing. The appearance of the floor affects the appearance of the entire room, and it is not too difficult to keep a floor nice if you follow the correct cleaning procedure.

Word of warning: If you are washing a floor, plot your exit before you start so you won't be stranded in a corner. Otherwise you will either have to shout for newspapers or walk right across the area of your strenuous endeavor. This advice is even more important if you are doing a paint or varnish job.

For cleaning procedure look up the floor according to the finish:

"Wooden Floors," "Linoleum," "Terrazzo," etc. If you don't know what it is, ask someone who does.

Fluorocarbon This is the generic name for one of the man-made textile fibers, better known by the trade names Teflon and Gore-Tex. Fluorocarbons are highly resistant to heat and chemicals, abrasion, and adhesion. Their uses are mainly scientific. See "Teflon."

Flush Flushing a stain means applying water or stain remover to it in sufficient amounts to remove all traces of the staining material.

To do this, place clean absorbent material under the stain, then add the stain remover in small amounts with an eye dropper or syringe. Do not add the stain remover faster than it can be absorbed by the stain. Change the absorbent several times.

When flushing with water on a washable fabric, the article can be dipped up and down in a bowl of warm water. Change the water at least twice. Or launder the article.

Fly See "House Fly."

Flypaper See "Stains," p. 228.

Foam Rubber Foam rubber is produced from latex, the liquid exudation of rubber trees. The liquid latex is beaten to a froth by means of machines that resemble giant egg beaters. It is then poured into molds and heat-treated to set its shape. The result is a very fine-textured material that is moist to the touch, mildew-proof, nonallergenic, light, soft, and porous. It is used for pillows, mattresses, cushioning for chairs, as a nonskid

backing for rugs, etc. Usually, it is used in a continuous piece. Shredded foam rubber is made from scraps, sometimes mixed with adhesives and pressed; it is less desirable.

Being porous, foam rubber permits free circulation of air through it, a sort of breathing action, which keeps it clean and dustfree, cool and comfortable. Foam rubber pillows do not lump or mat and foam rubber mattresses do not have to be turned. They can be cleaned with the dusting attachment of the vacuum cleaner, either in or out of their casings. They should never need washing.

If a foam-rubber pillow has to be washed, preferably hand wash it in its zippered casing. These emergency directions are from the Latex Foam Rubber Council:

Use cool or lukewarm water and a mild detergent and handle the pillow carefully because it is weak when wet. If you use a machine, set it for the lowest possible agitator speed and wash no longer than 10 minutes. Rinse at the same slow speed. Put it in a pillow case and hang it to dry, away from sunlight and any source of heat. If you use a tumble dryer, first squeeze out excess water and, using no heat, let it tumble in the air cycle.

Preferably, shampoo rugs backed with foam rubber. Hang them pile-side down to dry, out of the sun and away from any source of heat. If you must wash a small rug, follow the directions given for pillows.

Foam rubber is slow drying. Use an electric fan to hasten the process.

To clean upholstery covering

over foam-rubber cushioning, use a dry-foam cleaner and try not to get the cushioning wet. Zippered seat covers can be removed for cleaning. Never use mineral spirit solvents (lighter fluid, naphtha, benzine, etc.) or strong chlorine solutions on fabrics encasing foam rubber.

Foliage See "Grass, Flowers, Foliage" in "Stains," p. 229.

Formica A tradename for laminated plastics, made of synthetic resins and cloth or paper. Clean with soap or cleanser, but *not* steel wool. Porcelain cleaners may be used for stubborn stains.

Fortrel See "Polyester."

Foundation Garment See "Girdles."

Fountain Pen Every time a fountain pen is filled it should be flushed out several times with ink to clear it of dried or clotted particles of ink. In other words, fill it and empty it three times before you fill it with ink for use.

To fill a pen properly dip the point into clean ink deep enough to cover the crevice above the point. It is through this crevice, not the point, that the ink enters. Let the pen stay in the ink for about ten seconds to give the ink sac time to fill. Shake the pen hard as you remove it from the bottle to rid it of surplus ink. Wipe the outside carefully with a clean cloth or paper handkerchief, paying particular attention to the crevice and point. Do not use a blotter around the point as particles from it may clog the pen.

If a pen has been neglected badly, or has not been used for some time, flush it repeatedly with warm water to remove dried or clotted ink. If water is not effective, flush the pen with ammonia, then flush it thoroughly with warm water. Shake the water out carefully. Fill the pen as directed above.

Freezer See "Electric Freezer."

French Chalk Soapstone, or steatite, a soft magnesium mineral. Tailors use it to mark cloth. Powdered, it is often used as an absorbent for removing fresh grease stains from fabrics. French chalk is harmless to all materials and leaves no ring. See also "Absorbent."

Fringe On washable materials, such as bedspreads, comb out fringe while it is still wet and it will be comparatively easy. Straighten rug fringes by flipping them out with your hand, then manipulating your vacuum cleaner carefully.

Fruit Stains See "Fruit and Berry" in "Stains," p. 228.

Frying Pan Clean it according to the material of which it is made. See "Iron," "Glass," "Copper," "Electric Frypan," "Pots and Pans."

Furniture No matter what the material, furniture eventually reaches a point where it needs more than dusting and polishing to make it look clean and gleaming. Different materials call for different cleaning methods. Let's begin with furniture of finished wood, then tackle the others alphabetically.

Wooden furniture usually is finished with varnish or lacquer, sometimes with shellac, and rubbed to a high polish. *To dust* use a clean, dry, hemmed duster and give each piece a little extra rub to keep it lustrous. Dirty cloths damage the finish. Unhemmed ones leave more lint. Oiled and treated dusters should be used only on furniture polished with an oil polish. Do not use them on waxed surfaces if you want to rewax them. Oil will gum up the finish.

Even the finest furniture, which receives regular care, accumulates a scum of dirt after a while and needs to be cleaned. De luxe lacquered pieces call for special treatment. (See "Piano.") For the usual finishes use an emulsified oil cleaner-polish, soap and water, or furniture wash.

To clean finished furniture with soap, make rich suds, using pure, white soap or soap flakes and warm water. Dip a soft cloth into the suds, squeeze it as dry as you can and wash a small area. Rinse promptly with a second cloth, wrung out of clear, warm water. Wipe dry. Move to an adjoining area and repeat this routine until the entire piece has been thoroughly cleaned. Use a soft brush on carved pieces. If your suds go flat, mix a fresh, clean batch. When thoroughly dry, polish. (*Caution:* Never let water stand on the surface.) Work carefully, but quickly. Polish.

If the furniture has been finished with a cheap grade of shellac or varnish, it may look whitish after the washing process. If the finish is varnish, go over it with a soft cloth dampened with pure, raw linseed oil. If shellacked, use a cloth very slightly dampened with alcohol and apply it lightly. Too much alcohol will damage the shellac.

To prepare a soapless furniture wash add three tablespoons of raw, or boiled, linseed oil and two tablespoons of gum turpentine to one quart of hot water. Mix it around and allow it to cool. Apply the wash with a soft cloth, well wrung out, covering a small area at a time. Wipe each part dry as you proceed. Polish afterward.

If the piece of furniture under special surveillance has been badly neglected and looks as if refinishing may be the only solution, try this procedure first.

Wash the piece as described above. If using the wash, add a little more turpentine, but test to be sure the finish will stand it. Next dip a cloth in linseed oil (either boiled or raw), then in powdered rottenstone or fine pumice, and rub it over a small area in the direction of the grain. Wipe with a cloth moistened with plain linseed oil. Proceed in this manner until the entire surface has been cleaned, then polish with a flannel cloth. Make minor repairs, then give the whole thing a final polishing. Either oil or wax polishes may be used over the linseed.

Polishing furniture is not a task to be undertaken lightly, if you want to do a good job and not have to repeat it for at least a season. After cleaning the furniture as described, apply the polish of your choice sparingly (too much polish, whether oil or wax, makes the whole job harder), following exactly the manufacturer's directions for polishing. Rub with the grain, using a soft cloth, until a clean finger will leave no mark on the finish. Rub finally with a soft cotton flannel polisher. There is no substitute for hard, thorough rubbing.

For a really good job on chests and desks with drawers, unscrew and remove the handles before cleaning and polishing. On carved legs, etc., apply the polish with a brush wrapped inside the cloth and give it a rub the same way before wielding your final polisher.

There are many shades of opinion on the merits of different furniture polishes and you will have to make your own choice. If using a commercial stand-by, follow the directions on the container. Lemon oil, liquid and paste waxes, all are good if used properly. Use a light-colored wax on blond furniture, dark on mahogany. Blond furniture darkens with time, even if light wax is used, and there apparently is no solution to the problem.

Some women prefer to mix their own polish. Raw linseed oil and turpentine in equal parts is an old recipe. Another mixture consists of equal parts of boiled linseed oil (see "Linseed Oil"), turpentine and vinegar. The chief thing to remember in using any polish is to apply a very thin coating and a lot of elbow grease. Otherwise you will get a gummy, dust-catching surface.

Minor blemishes on furniture can sometimes be corrected, or the appearance of the piece improved, without help from a professional furniture patcher. Your success will depend upon how deeply the surface has been damaged and the care and skill you can muster for the job. Tackling the problem alphabetically, let's begin with alcohol stains. And, while we are

here, how is your supply of coasters?

Alcohol stains are caused by spilled drinks, medicines, skin lotions, and perfumes. Since alcohol dissolves many finishes, you have a real problem. When accidents occur, wipe up the spilled liquid instantly and rub the spot vigorously with the palm of your hand or with a cloth moistened with an oil polish. For old stains use rottenstone or powdered pumice, mixed to a thin paste with raw or boiled linseed oil. Rub lightly in the direction of the grain. Wipe with a cloth dampened with plain linseed oil. Repeat as many times as necessary, then polish. Sometimes refinishing is necessary.

Bloom, the gray discoloration that sometimes appears on highly polished furniture, often disappears when the furniture is wiped with a soft cloth that has been wrung out of warm water containing a little vinegar. (One tablespoon of vinegar to one quart of water.) Wipe dry with a clean, soft cloth. An application of liquid wax often will accomplish the same result. Polish afterward.

Burns, if very light, sometimes disappear when rubbed with your usual polish. If not, use rottenstone or finely powdered pumice, mixed to a thin paste with raw or boiled linseed oil. Rub in the direction of the grain. Wipe with another cloth moistened with plain linseed. Repeat a number of times, if necessary. Polish. If the burn is too deep to be corrected by this method, the furniture will have to be treated professionally. However, the treatment described for deep scratches may improve the appearance of the burn.

Candle wax Scrape away as much of the wax as you can, using a stiff card, smooth stick or your fingernail. Wash off the remainder with a cloth wrung out of mild, warm soapsuds, or wipe with a cloth moistened with cleaning fluid. Polish.

Checked varnish (fine, criss-crossed lines caused by excessive heat or a poor grade of finish) cannot be corrected. The surface must be refinished. Careful polishing will make it look a litle better.

Grease spots Wipe with a cloth moistened with cleaning fluid. Polish.

Heat marks A cloth dampened with camphor oil, peppermint oil or turpentine often will remove white marks caused by hot dishes, etc. Rub lightly. Another method is to use finely powdered rottenstone or pumice, mixed to a light paste with lemon oil or linseed oil. If you do not have rottenstone or pumice on hand, try cigar ash. Rub lightly in the direction of the grain, wipe with a cloth dipped in plain linseed oil, then polish.

Ink After quickly blotting up as much as you can, apply a dampened cloth to the spot and press it down firmly. Turn the cloth to a clean place and again press it against the stain. Repeat as many times as necessary. Do not rub the ink in. Ink washes off some surfaces easily. Old inkstains that have penetrated the wood call for professional treatment, though you might try the rottenstone-linseed-oil treatment described for burns and heat marks.

Paint Wipe off fresh paint spatters with a cloth dampened with liquid wax or turpentine, or use soap and water. Polish. Soften old spots first with linseed oil. Daub it on and let it stay a while. Scrape away the softened paint carefully, then rub off remaining traces with a cloth moistened with linseed oil and rottenstone, mixed to a thin paste. Wipe with plain linseed oil and polish.

Scratches, if light, often disappear when the furniture is carefully waxed or polished. Using your usual mixture, rub an extra amount into the scratch. If the scratch still shows, try rubbing it with a piece of walnut (the kernel, little goose, cut sharply). This will darken the stain. Be careful to rub the walnut meat directly into the scratch so as not to darken the surrounding wood excessively. Another method is to rub, or brush, a little turpentine into the scratch. Let it dry, then polish. A quality of turpentine is that it can penetrate the finish and restore the color of the original stain. Don't use too much; it might soften the finish.

Deep scratches must be filled in carefully, a job that usually calls for a professional furniture man. If you want to try it yourself, this is how it is done. Wrap very fine (size o) steel wool around the pointed end of a manicure stick and smooth the scratch carefully. Brush away all the particles, then apply turpentine, or a matching stain, very carefully, using a fine-tipped water color brush. When this has dried thoroughly, apply a thin coating of white shellac to the

93

scratch, being careful not to spill it over. Let this dry completely and apply a second coating. Repeat the coatings, letting each one dry thoroughly, until the scratch has been filled. Polish carefully.

Water marks A well-waxed surface is a safeguard against water marks. Should a waxed surface show marks from a misplaced water glass or vase, remove the old wax by wiping the surface generously with liquid wax. Wipe with a dry cloth and polish. Apply extra coatings of wax, if desired, to build up protection.

On other surfaces a little peppermint oil or camphor oil on a damp cloth, or a cloth wrung out of warm water containing a few drops of ammonia, often will remove such marks. If not, rub the stain carefully but lightly, in the direction of the grain, with rottenstone or finely powdered pumice, mixed to a thin paste with raw or boiled linseed oil. Wipe with a cloth moistened with plain linseed oil. Polish.

Bamboo, cane, reed, wicker and rattan furniture should be dusted with an untreated cloth or with a cloth dampened with water. Or you can use the dusting attachment of your vacuum cleaner, which is ideal for crevices. To prevent drying out and splitting, this type of furniture should be wet thoroughly about once a year. Put it outside and treat it to fine spray from the garden hose or place it under the bathroom shower. (Do not use water if the finish on the furniture is damaged by it.) If such furniture needs washing use mild pure suds containing a little ammonia. Rinse with clear water. Dry thoroughly. Once a year treat it to a coat of

94

shellac. If painted, follow the directions for painted furniture.

Leather-upholstered furniture should be dry-dusted with an untreated cloth and cleaned, as required, with saddle soap or with a thick suds made of mild, pure soap. Use as little water as possible. If using saddle soap, obtained at a hardware store or shoe shop, follow the directions on the container. Wipe off soap traces with a clean, damp cloth and, when thoroughly dry, polish briskly with a soft, dry cloth.

To prevent leather from drying out and cracking, rub it occasionally (once or twice a year) with castor oil, neat's-foot oil or a good commercial leather conditioner. On light-colored leathers use a white conditioner or white vaseline, since most oils tend to darken leather. After rubbing the oil in thoroughly with your finger tips or with a clean, soft cloth, wipe off every trace with another cloth. If oil remains on the leather, clothing will be soiled.

If using neat's-foot oil, remember that, while it is an excellent leather conditioner and is readily absorbed, it leaves a dull, rather than a glossy, finish. Do *not* use mineral (paraffin) oil. It is not good for leather. Do *not* wax leather furniture.

See also "Leather Goods."

Marble furniture See "Marble."

Metal furniture should be dusted routinely and cleaned according to the particular metal of which it is made. It seldom requires more than dusting. See "Aluminum," "Chromium," "Magnesium," "Iron," etc.

Painted furniture is more easily cleaned if it is kept waxed. For cleaning instructions see "Walls and Ceilings" and "Paint Cleaners."

Plastic furniture should be dusted regularly. A damp cloth usually is all that is needed to remove spilled foods. It can be washed with lukewarm water and a mild soap or detergent. Rinse with a cloth wrung out of clear warm water and wipe dry. Do not use chemical cleaners or chemical aids, such as ammonia, on plastic furniture or table tops with plastic finishes. See "Plastics," "Acrylic Plastics," etc.

Reed furniture. See "Bamboo," above.

Rustic furniture should be given an annual coating of spar varnish to safeguard it against damage from weather and insects.

Upholstered furniture attracts as much dust as your mahogany table-top. Don't neglect it just because the dust is less visible. On cleaning days remove the cushions and clean all surfaces with the upholstery attachment of your vacuum cleaner, or with a good stiff brush. Pay special attention to seams and tufts. After dusting, fluff up the cushions and replace them. An occasional airing out-of-doors gives feather cushions a new lease on life and benefits all types. *Caution:* If your cushions are stuffed with down, don't use your vacuum cleaner on them. It will pull the feathers through and you will spend the afternoon plucking them.

Spots should be removed from upholstery as soon as possible after being made. Follow the directions given for the particular stain in Section II of this book. Always test an inconspicuous portion, or sample, first for colorfastness if using water and for any possible reaction to the chemicals called for.

There are reliable professional cleaning services that will do an all-over cleaning of upholstered furniture. Some will do it right in the home. However, you can do a pretty good job yourself on most materials, except pile fabrics like velvet and plush. Use a good upholstery shampoo or soap lather, which you can whip up yourself. A dry-cleaning fluid can be used on materials that won't stand water.

Should you choose upholstery shampoo, get the kind that makes a thick soapless lather. To make your own, dissolve about six tablespoons of pure, white soap flakes in a pint of boiling water, adding two teaspoons of ammonia or two tablespoons of borax as a softener, if desired. Let the mixture stand until it jells, then whip it like mad with an egg beater. Whether you are using a chemical shampoo or soap, remember that it is the lather you want for this job. The fabric must absorb as little moisture as possible.

Using a small, soft brush, clean an area about eight inches square, applying the lather until that portion is clean. Now wipe it with a

95

clean cloth or sponge, squeezed out of clear warm water. Proceed to an adjoining area and work in this manner until the entire surface has been cleaned. Do not use the cleaned furniture until it is absolutely dry. Do not dry it in the sun; colors may be damaged. An electric fan will speed drying.

For vinyl upholstery see "Vinyl."

See "Foam Rubber" for special instructions.

Wicker furniture. See "Bamboo," p. 94.

Furs Furs represent a considerable investment and are best stored and cleaned by a professional who operates under a guarantee. If they must be stored at home during the summer months, place them in a container with paradichlorobenzene (para) crystals, or naphthalene flakes or balls, and seal all openings. Sprays recommended for mothproofing woolens should *not* be used on furs.

Fuse Many women, who handle electric light bulbs and other equipment without inhibitions, are helpless when confronted with a blown fuse. Provided, of course, that you know where the fuse box is and that someone has had the foresight to place a supply nearby, you should have no trouble meeting the emergency. It is no more difficult to install a fuse than to replace a light bulb, and no more dangerous. Disconnect the appli-

Blown fuse   *Sound fuse*

ances you were using when the circuit went out. With dry hands, unscrew the blown fuse and screw in a new one of the same amperage. The amperage is indicated by a number stamped on the fuse. (If your fuse box is in a damp basement, stand on a dry board.)

If you do not know what caused the fuse to blow, or if the new fuse also blows, better call an electrician. You may have a short circuit. Worn cords, malfunctioning appliances, and overloaded circuits are the usual causes of blown fuses.

Newer houses have circuit breakers rather than fuses to cut off electric power in an emergency. If a circuit cuts off, a brush of the hand will make it resume guard after the electric load has been adjusted. No ampere numbers to be matched; no danger of getting the wrong fuse, and no being caught without the proper one.

Galoshes See "Rubber."

Garbage Grinder See "Electric Garbage Grinder."

Garbage Pail You can buy beautiful enameled and chrome pails that are almost as easy to wash as a dish, so there's absolutely no excuse for one that smells. Line it with paper or a waterproof bag made especially for this purpose, put in only well-drained garbage, and empty it often. Or wrap each contribution securely in newspaper. Wash the can frequently with hot suds, using a little chlorine bleach or "controlled iodine" disinfectant if desired, dry and air in the sun. If you are buying a new garbage pail make certain that the inside of the lid is rustproof, as well as the container.

Outdoor garbage containers should be kept clean, too. Treat them to hot suds now and then and add, if you like, a disinfectant and deodorant. Sprays made especially for garbage cans discourage insect breeding, help eliminate odors, and make the cans easier to clean. See also "Disinfectant."

Garden Tools Clean your garden equipment in the fall and put it away carefully if you want to find it in good condition in the spring. Rust and corrosion take a heavy toll of tools that are stored improperly.

Scrape the mud from hand tools, remove rusty spots with steel wool, and coat the metal with lubricating oil. Wash off all traces of fertilizer from spreaders and, when they have dried, rub the metal with oil. (Fertilizers attract moisture and invite rust.) Insecticides left in a sprayer can ruin it in a single season by corroding the metal. Store your sprayer empty, clean, and dry. A neglected hose, containing water, can freeze and spring a leak. Store it on a reel or coiled on a dry flat surface. (Worn sections of a hose can be joined with new couplings.)

Drain leftover fuel from the gas tanks and carburetors of the garden tractor and power mower to prevent gum deposit. With the engine warm, drain off the oil, then refill the crankcase with fresh oil. Remove the spark plug, squirt a teaspoonful of oil into the firing chamber, give the flywheel a few turns to spread the oil, and replace the spark plug. Cover the exhaust pipe to protect it from moisture.

Garnet A mineral species including many varieties. While garnets conform to the same general formula, they differ widely in composition and color. Most garnets are red, but some are white, brown, yellow, green, and black.

The precious garnet, valued as a gem, is a deep, transparent red. A brilliant, bright green garnet, of gem quality, is found in Siberia.

See "Jewelry."

Gas Fading Rayons especially may fade or develop streaks under the bombardment of smoke and gas fumes in industrial cities. An antifume finish is designed to counteract this and is applied at the factory. No special cleaning or washing instructions are required for fabrics with the antifume finish.

See also "Rayon."

Gasoline Though available from other sources, gasoline usually is distilled from petroleum. It is to be found in various cleaning mixtures of the flammable variety. The use of gasoline for home dry cleaning is highly dangerous and not recommended.

Gasoline Stove Gasoline stoves vary in size from collapsible camp models to full-sized kitchen ranges. A gasoline stove of good manufacture is easy to operate and as efficient as gas. It differs from a gas or oil stove in that the fuel is fed to it under compression.

Because of the fire hazard involved in the use of gasoline, most states have established strict laws controlling the manufacture of gasoline stoves. Provided your stove *is* a dependable model and that it is installed properly, it will be entirely safe. Follow the directions exactly for your particular

97

stove and call in an experienced repairman if any difficulty is encountered. It is impossible to lay down general rules because the stoves differ in their method of operation, but one rule for all types is: *Use only plain gasoline as fuel.* Do not use any of the special mixtures sold for automobiles.

Gas Range If you are careful to wipe up spilled foods immediately, you will be able to keep your gas range shining and won't have to give it a thorough scrubbing often. Grease and food that are allowed to burn on resent being removed.

Always let your range cool off before attempting a beauty treatment. Clean the enameled parts with a cloth wrung out of hot suds, made with soap or a detergent. Rinse with clear, hot water and wipe dry. If food has burned on, use a plastic sponge, or nylon mesh pad.

For a thorough cleaning remove the pans beneath the burners and grates and wash them in hot detergent suds. Rinse with clear water and dry. Now for the burners. Use soap, a heavy-duty detergent, or washing soda, and a stiff brush. A good soak in a very hot solution of any of these cleaners loosens grease and makes its removal easier. Or put them in a pan (not aluminum) with water and soda and boil them. Use 2 tablespoons of soda to a gallon of water.

Whatever method you select, pay particular attention to the gas orifices in the end of the gas cock, through which gas flows to the burners. Clean out the ports (little holes) in the burners with a wire or hairpin if they fail to light. Rinse thoroughly and dry, open

side down, in the oven or in the open air.

Return the drip tray, burners and grates to position and light each burner to be sure it is operating correctly. If you have a model without a drip tray, try lining the surface with aluminum foil.

The broiler should be removed with the steak to prevent additional spattering and should be cleaned carefully each time it is used. Wipe up spattered grease with a paper towel; then, when the surfaces have cooled, wash the inside of the broiler compartment with a cloth wrung from hot detergent suds or hot water containing ammonia or washing soda.

The oven will be easier to clean if you set half a cup of ammonia in it the night before you plan to clean it. The ammonia will soften the burned-on grease and make it easier to remove. (Do not use this method if your oven is equipped with a pilot light; the pilot might ignite the ammonia fumes.) If the build-up of grease is too much for this method you will have to use an oven cleaner. Follow the directions on the container.

A blue, even flame is maintained when gas and air reach the burner in the correct mixture. Too little air will make the flame burn yellow. Such a flame is inefficient and blackens the bottoms of pots and pans. Clean the ports in the burner (little holes) and make sure the air shutter (located at the turn-on end of the burner's arm) is opened slightly to admit air.

If the pilot light on your range goes out, lift off the top and clean the pilot with a fine wire, as dust or soot probably has clogged it. Relight. To increase the flame, turn the little screw to the left. To decrease, turn it to the right.

The flue outlet of your range should be kept open at all times. If it is clogged it will not only cause your oven burners to operate inefficiently but will be dangerous.

It is a good idea to have your range inspected periodically by a reliable serviceman. He can check whether it is sitting level, whether the oven control is operating accurately and whether the burners and pilot light are adjusted for maximum efficiency. Ask your dealer or fuel company about this service.

Gas Water Heater See "Water Heater."

Gelatin Gelatin is an odorless, colorless and tasteless substance obtained by boiling connective tissues of animals, including cartilages, bones and horns. It dissolves in hot water and forms a jelly.

As a food, gelatin is an incomplete protein of low caloric value. It is the principal ingredient of size and glue and makes a nice finish for organdy and other sheer cottons.

See "Starch and Special Finishes."

Gems See "Diamond," "Pearl," "Quartz," etc., and "Jewelry."

Gilding This term describes the golden surface created by covering a substance with a thin layer of gold leaf, or with a thin coating of gold in powder or liquid form. The cleaning method depends upon the kind of gilding and, since it is impossible for anyone but a professional to determine the type, it is best not to experiment.

Regular dusting is the best way to keep gilded objects clean. If more than dusting is needed, a dry-cleaning fluid is safer than one containing water, I have been advised by a museum expert.

If the gilding still looks impossible after cleaning fluid has been used, have it redone by an expert or, if it isn't worth that, get some gilding and do it yourself.

Gilt Gilt is the same as gilding.

Girdles Before washing a girdle, close the zipper and be sure the clasps are open. Pretreat spots, then wash by hand or machine with a mild soap or detergent in cool to lukewarm water. If a bleach is needed, use a peroxy type. Chlorine bleach yellows spandex. After rinsing, roll the garment in a towel to extract water and hang it to dry in an airy place. Do not place it near a source of heat or in the sun. Use of a dryer is not recommended, but if pressed for time tumble dry it at a moderate temperature, usually indicated by a medium or wash-and-wear setting.

Wash latex rubber girdles by hand. Pat them dry with a towel and dust them generously with talcum powder.

For personal daintiness and to insure satisfactory wear, wash girdles frequently. Oily soil and perspiration reduce their elasticity.

Glass Glass is made by fusing silica with alkalies, metal oxides, and salts. Clean it according to the article into which it is made. To wit:

99

Table glass The rule in washing dishes is glassware first, silver second, dishes third and pans last. This gives you clean hot suds for your table glass. Use a synthetic detergent. Rinse in clear hot water and let it drain dry. Or, if you wish, polish glass with a lintless cloth. If a detergent is used, drying is not necessary. (Drain your choice glassware on a soft cloth to avoid chipping.)

Stemware Always lift it by the stem, rather than the cup; it is less likely to be broken. Do not jumble it in the dishpan but dip each piece carefully to avoid broken stems and chipped edges.

Gilt and silver ornamentation will soak off if the water is too hot or if the glassware remains too long in warm suds. Use a synthetic detergent. Do *not* use ammonia, washing soda or harsh soaps. Do not wash glassware with metallic trim in an automatic dishwasher.

Stains or cloudiness in glass vases, carafes, cruets, etc., will yield to ammonia. Fill them with water containing a teaspoon or two of ammonia and let them stand for several hours, or overnight. Wash and rinse. This method works almost as well for mineral deposit. Or you can try shaking tea leaves, plus vinegar, around in the vessel.

Cut glass is flint, or crystal, glass that has been ornamented with designs cut or ground into it with polishing wheels. It is cleaned like other glassware, but a soft brush helps greatly. Rinse carefully.

Regrinding Expensive crystal goblets that have been chipped at the edges can receive first aid from a good glazier. Ask your favorite store where this can be done.

Heat-resistant cooking glass is not unbreakable. Handle it with care. Avoid sharp blows and sudden exposure to heat and cold. Its day-by-day care is exceptionally easy. When it has cooled, put it in the dishwasher (unless it has metallic trim) or wash it by hand in hot detergent suds.

The Corning Glass Company, makers of Pyrex, offer these solutions for special problems. For burned-on or scorched-on food, soak in warm detergent water and loosen with a plastic pad, rubber scraper, or wooden spoon. Next use Bon Ami or baking soda on a wet cloth, sponge, or paper towel. Add ammonia to the water if the spot is greasy. If the burned-on food contains sugar or starch, use baking soda as a cleaner. Soak it in a solution made by adding 3 tablespoons of baking soda to 1 quart of warm water. Gray marks made by spoons, metallic sponges and steel wool pads can be removed by Zud or Delete. Follow the directions on the container.

Precautions: Heat-resistant glass ovenware and bakeware should never be used on top of the range, even if the burner is only on warm or has just been turned off. Ovenware of heat-resistant glass should never be used under a broiler. Cookware designed for the top of the stove is weakened if it boils dry. It should be discarded because breakage is imminent. A special wire grid, supplied with range-top products, must be used to separate the glass from direct contact with the heating element. Be sure it is place on the electric unit before the ware is used with heat.

Glass-ceramic wares, made of various combinations of heat-resistant glass and ceramics, differ in the amount of heat they can stand. (Some can go straight from the freezer to the microwave oven.) They are usually white in color, opaque, and have a shining surface. Glass-ceramic can be glazed or unglazed, depending upon how it is to be used. The glazed kind is used for dinnerware.

The care of glass-ceramic ware is essentially the same as for heat-resistant cooking glass. Use a plastic or nylon pad to remove stuck-on food. Avoid harsh abrasives, steel wool pads, or metal scouring pads. Use wooden spoons, nylon utensils, or rubber spatulas for stirring. Soak burned spots with baking powder and water.

See also "Windows," "Mirrors," "Crystal," "Glass Cloth," and "Glass Fibers."

Glass Cloth The silky superstrong fibers which compose glass cloth are obtained mainly by melting glass marbles of special composition in an electric furnace and letting the melted glass flow through numerous tiny holes in the bottom. The filament is stretched to the desired fineness as it is reeled. One marble three quarters of an inch in diameter spins about 95 miles of filament.

Glass cloth has many industrial uses, being fireproof and practically unaffected by chemicals. It will stand high heat, does not transmit electricity, and is not attacked by mildew, rot, or insects. Aging has little effect on it. All of these qualities recommend it also for its main home use—curtains and draperies. Curtains made of glass do not shrink, stretch, sag, or wrinkle. They absorb little water and can be washed and rehung in a matter of minutes.

Treatment under very high heat and a special finishing bath make today's glass cloth very different from that used in the dress which so intrigued the visiting Queen of Spain at the Chicago World's Fair in '93. For curtains it appears in a range of colors as dainty marquisettes and casement cloth, and for draperies there is a variety of weights and weaves, piece-dyed or printed in attractive patterns.

Hand-washing is recommended for glass curtains and they are very easy to do since the fiber cannot absorb soil. Use hot suds made with any mild soap or detergent. Squeeze the cloth through the suds and through two rinses. (Never machine-wash, rub, twist, or mangle glass materials.) Roll the curtains gently in a turkish towel to remove excess water, then rehang them while they are still damp. Smooth the hems with your fingers. Instructions for washing glass draperies are practically the same, but be sure to remove first any hooks or fastenings that might snag the material. Since glass draperies do not absorb water, they are very light to handle. After washing in hot suds and thorough rinsing, the draperies can be rolled in a towel or hung over a shower curtain rod to remove excess water. Hang them while they are damp. Straighten the hems. They will dry wrinkle free. Sometimes wiping with a damp cloth is all that

101

is needed to remove soil from glass draperies.

Caution: Although glass cloth has high tensile strength, it will not stand excessive rubbing or abrasion. Never wring or twist curtains or draperies during washing. Do not hang them on a line with clothespins. Do not let them flap against window sills, floors, or chairs. Hang them just short of the floor or window sill and slightly away from protruding window ledges. Cover the tip of the curtain rod with cloth before slipping the curtain onto it. *Never iron glass cloth. Never send it to a dry cleaner.* See also "Glass Fibers."

Glasses See "Glass" and "Eyeglasses."

Glass Fibers Glass fibers, of which glass cloth is woven, are used also for stuffing pillows and crib comforters. Such articles are light in weight, will not wad up and will not burn. They are nonallergenic and warm. Provided the covering used on the pillows or comforters is not harmed by water, they are hand washable in lukewarm to cool water. Squeeze the suds through the material repeatedly and rinse. Do not rub or twist.

Fiber-glass lamp shades diffuse light in a close approximation of sunlight. To make them, soft, glittering fiber-glass mat is compressed into a fire-resistant sheet with millions of tiny facets to reflect and diffuse light. They are made in different sizes and colors, with a variety of trim, and can be cleaned by wiping with a damp cloth.

See also "Glass Cloth."

Glazed Finish A finish which gives a shiny appearance to cotton, rayon, acetate, and nylon. Some of these finishes are lost in the first washing. Others last for some time. Look for the label "permanent." Follow any laundering instructions given.

Gloves *Fabric* gloves are washed off the hands in mild, warm soapsuds. Squeeze the suds through the fabric repeatedly. Do not rub, wring or twist. Use a little brush on bad spots. Rinse thoroughly, ease into shape, and dry either flat on a towel or over a rod.

Leather gloves not stamped washable should be dry-cleaned. Washable gloves should be handled according to the manufacturer's instructions. Generally speaking, they are best washed in mild, warm soapsuds while they are on the hands, except for chamois and doeskin, which tear easily when wet. Avoid rubbing. Instead squeeze and press the suds through the leather, using a soft brush on spots. When clean, let a little water run inside the gloves and slip them off the hands. Rinse several times in lukewarm water.

Place the gloves in the fold of a turkish towel and pat them gently to remove excess water. Puff them out by blowing into them, stretch them gently lengthwise and allow them to dry flat on a towel, away from sunlight and artificial heat. When they are nearly dry, stretch them gently this way and that in order to soften the leather, or put them on your hands and rub them carefully. Should your leather gloves dry stiff, fold them in a damp towel and gently finger-press them until they are soft.

Glue See "Stains," p. 228.

Glycerine An ingredient used in making "wet spotter," which is used to remove many kinds of stain. It can be bought at drug stores. See "Wet Spotter."

Gnats See "House Fly."

Gold Gold is one of the earth's most precious metals. It cannot be injured by exposure to the air and is the most ductile and malleable of all metals. Gold can be beaten so thin that one gram will cover fifty-six square inches. In jewelry parlance, pure gold is termed 24 K. The term "carat" is used in all countries and in the United States the common qualities are 10 K, 14 K and 18 K. Twelve carat means that the article is half pure gold, the rest consisting of baser metals such as nickel, copper or silver. Commercial jewelry is not made of pure gold as it is considered too soft to be practical.

"Gold-filled" means that gold has been affixed by soldering or welding, etc., to a surface of base metal. "Rolled gold plate" is another term for the same sort of thing. "Gold-plated" articles contain the least amount of gold, the article being merely dipped into a solution containing gold and lightly coated by an electrolytic process.

Since gold does not tarnish it requires little care other than washing and drying as for other jewelry. Go easy on gold plate or it will soon lose its coating. Gold-plated jewelry that is worn regularly needs replating about once a year. See also "Jewelry."

Grape Stains See "Fruit and Berry" in "Stains," p. 228.

Graphite See "Pencil" in "Stains," p. 235.

Grass Stains See "Grass, Flowers, Foliage" in "Stains," p. 229.

Gravy Stains See "Stains," p. 229.

Grease Stains See "Grease and Oil" in "Stains," p. 229. See also "Furniture" and "Wallpaper."

Gum See "Chewing Gum," p. 226, and "Resins," p. 236, in "Stains."

Gum Arabic A material obtained from plants, which is used to stiffen laces, veils, etc. For directions see "Starch and Special Finishes."

Gum Tragacanth Another material from plants, used instead of starch for finishing certain materials. See "Starch and Special Finishes."

Handkerchief Paper handkerchiefs are sanitary only when disposed of in a sanitary fashion. Pin a paper bag to the side of the bed, or secure it to the bed table with cellulose tape, when Junior has a cold, and have him drop used hankies into it. If possible, burn bag and all.

Hats See "Straw Hats," "Felt," "Velvet."

Hearth See "Fireplace."

Heater See "Electric Heater" and "Water Heater."

Heating System Whether your heating system uses coal, oil or gas, it is a good idea to have it checked and the furnace cleaned

103

once a year. The end of the heating season is a good time to have this done. Your fuel company probably can handle the job or, in lieu of that, recommend an expert. Have your hot-water unit checked at the same time.

Heat Marks See "Furniture."

Home Freezer See "Electric Freezer."

Horn Horn is often used as handles for carving sets, etc. Such sets should go in and out of the dish suds quickly, be rinsed promptly, and dried. Never let them soak in water as this tends to loosen the cement used to hold the handles. Do not place cutlery with horn handles in an automatic dishwasher.

Hornets See "Wasps and Hornets."

Hot-Water Heater See "Water Heater."

House Fly House flies breed in filth and spread the germs of a dozen or more diseases to animals and people. The first line of defense against them is sanitation—the elimination of their breeding places.

Keep garbage and other refuse tightly covered—never let it accumulate in the open. Insist on frequent pickups or get rid of it promptly yourself, by burning if necessary. On the farm, dispose of manure promptly.

Screen doors and windows should be kept in good repair. (Doors should swing outward.) Screens with 14 meshes to the inch are adequate for flies; 16-mesh screens will keep out additonal pests. Galvanized wire screens are good for dry climates; for humid climates use copper, aluminum, bronze, plastic, or a rust-resistant alloy.

To kill flies quickly inside the house, use an insecticide in a space spray or aerosol bomb. Outside the house use a surface or residual spray. Apply it to porches, door and window frames and other places where flies gather, being careful not to spray pans used for pets.

Space and aerosol sprays can be bought ready-mixed for use inside the home. Buy the best grade from a reliable dealer. The following types are available: those containing 0.1 to 0.25 percent pyrethrins plus 1 to 2 percent of a synergist to increase their effectiveness; aerosol sprays whose labels say they are good for flying insects; and space sprays and aerosols containing 2 percent malathion or 0.25 percent ronnel. To kill the flies in a room, release a mist for a few seconds from a hand or power sprayer or from an aerosol bomb. Keep the room closed for an hour.

To treat outdoor surfaces, use a surface or residual spray containing malathion or ronnel, and spray until the surface is damp but without runoff. They leave a killing film that can last for several weeks. See also "Insecticides."

Household Bleach See "Chlorine Bleach."

Household Cement See "Glue, Mucilage, Adhesives" in "Stains," p. 228.

Huckleberry See "Fruit and Berry" in "Stains," p. 228.

Hydrogen Peroxide Hydrogen peroxide is a good bleach, safe for all fibers, which is available at drugstores. As sold, it is a dilute solution, about 3 percent. In very concentrated form hydrogen peroxide has been used to power guided missiles, such as V-2 bombs.

When used as a laundry bleach, peroxide is diluted with water, the concentration depending upon the amount of bleaching to be done. Add one pint to one gallon of water, or use one part of peroxide to eight parts of water. A teaspoon of sodium perborate or borax (or a few drops of ammonia) added to a gallon of this mixture makes the action stronger. These directions are for white fabrics. Test colors before using hydrogen peroxide as a bleach or stain remover.

As a stain remover peroxide is applied with a medicine dropper or glass rod directly to the stain, a pad of clean cloth being placed under the fabric to absorb any excess. For a mild treatment, moisten the stain with a few drops of hydrogen peroxide and place it in the sun. Add more bleach, as needed, to keep the stain moist until it disappears. (This bleach acts slowly.) If the stain is not removed, add several drops of ammonia to about a tablespoon of hydrogen peroxide and moisten the stain immediately with this mixture. Then cover it with a pad of cotton dampened with the same solution. Keep the cotton damp until the stain is gone. (This may take several hours.) Rinse thoroughly.

For a stronger treatment, dampen a cloth with undiluted hydrogen peroxide, cover this with a dry cloth and press it with an iron as hot as the fabric will stand. Rinse with water afterward.

Section II on "Stains" will tell you when to use hydrogen peroxide.

Caution: Once you have removed peroxide from the bottle, never put it back. Wash it down the drain instead. Peroxide is very allergic to impurities and strange things happen when it contacts some of them.

Hypochlorites See "Chlorine Bleach."

Icebox Old-fashioned refrigerators, using ice, are still in use in many rural areas of the United States. The ice compartment requires special attention during cleaning. Remove the ice, the ice rack and the drainpipe. Wash the compartment thoroughly with a cloth or sponge wrung out of warm water containing a tablespoon of baking soda per quart. Rinse and dry. Scrub the inside of the drainpipe with a long-handled stiff-bristled brush and hot water containing soda. Scrub the trap thoroughly, then pour boiling water through the drainpipe and trap to flush it. Replace the parts and the ice promptly.

Remove the food from the food compartment and take out the shelves, if they are removable. Clean the interior and the shelves thoroughly with fresh warm water and soda. Rinse with a cloth wrung out of clear water; wipe dry. Replace the food.

Ice-Cream Stains See "Combination Stains," p. 223.

Indelible Pencil See "Pencil" in "Stains," p. 235.

Ink See "Stains," p. 230. See also "Furniture" and "Wallpaper."

Insects Cleanliness is the first line of defense against household pests. Insects thrive on food spilled on pantry shelves and in the cracks and crevices of cabinets, walls, and floor boards. Out-of-the-way places—behind refrigerators, stoves, washers, and around pipes and toilets—serve as hideouts for breeding. Scrub these places regularly with hot water and soap or detergent.

Store all foods in tightly closed containers and avoid buying dry foods in packages that have breaks in them. Do not leave cardboard cartons used for food or other materials in the kitchen or basement; hitchhiking insects such as cockroaches and silverfish may lurk in their crevices. Dispose of garbage promptly. Do not let waste materials of any sort accumulate; they provide hiding places for insects.

To frustrate prospective invaders, seal cracks and openings where insects could enter your home—around washbasins, toilets, pipes, electric conduits, baseboards, and floorboards.

When an insecticide is needed, first scrub all the areas to be treated. Some insecticides are better than others for specific insects and for that reason instructions are given under separate headings, such as "Ants," "Moths," "Crickets." If you cannot identify the insect that is plaguing you, take or send a sample to the nearest extension office of the Department of Agriculture or to your local farm bureau.

Insecticides recommended for home use contain such substances as diazinon, lindane, malathion, methoxychlor, perthane, propoxur, ronnel, and strobane. All are poisonous. Nontoxic preparations are based on formulations of pyrethrum (flowers of pyrethrum plants) and piperonyl butoxide. Ready-mixed preparations in pressurized cans are the easiest to use. Insecticides should be bought thoughtfully, used carefully, and stored safely.

Buying Read the labels carefully when selecting an insecticide to make sure that it contains the ingredient recommended for the insect that is troubling you. And remember that there are two types of spray, surface and aerosol. If the label says "surface spray" or "residual spray," the insecticide is intended to be sprayed on surfaces to kill crawling insects. Sprayed surfaces retain their lethal power for weeks or even months. Such sprays are usually oil-based but sometimes they are emulsified water solutions. Aerosols, which may be labeled "air spray," or "space spray," are for flying insects. They are excellent for clearing the air of flies, gnats, or mosquitoes. They do not leave a lasting residue and that is why they can be used safely in the air.

Using Always read (or reread) the directions given on the container before using an insecticide; do not depend on your memory. Follow the instructions exactly. The following precautions apply to all insecticides:

Remove all pets, including fish in aquariums, from a room that is to be sprayed or dusted. Also remove their food and water dishes. Keep children away. If the label warns against inhaling pesticidal mists or dusts, leave the windows open while applying them. Remove food and utensils from shelves, drawers, and cabinets and scrub them thoroughly before applying sprays and dusts.

When you finish the job, wash all

exposed skin surfaces with soap and water, and change your clothes if the insecticide has come in contact with them.

Do not smoke while applying insecticides, even if they are not flammable. Traces of insecticide can be carried from the hand to the mouth by a cigarette, and oil-based sprays could be ignited. Do not use oil-based sprays near any open flame (including a pilot light) or near an electric circuit.

Do not combine different insecticides.

Storing Store insecticides with their labels intact in a place where children and pets cannot reach them. Those in pressurized cans should not be stored near any source of heat. Do not store an insecticide near food, under the sink, or in a medicine cabinet. If a container has lost its label, do not guess at its contents; get rid of it safely.

Empty containers Never reuse an empty insecticide container. Rinse it with water. Rinse the outside of pressurized cans. Wrap all empty containers with thick layers of newspaper, put them in the trash can, and make sure the lid is on tight. Do not put pressurized cans in a fire or incinerator; they will explode. Do not burn cardboard containers or paper bags that have contained insecticides. Wrap them with newspapers too and put them in the trash can.

Housekeeping precautions for the use of oil-based insecticides include the following: Do not spray them on silk, rayon, or other fabrics that stain easily. Do not apply them to floors of asphalt tile: they dissolve asphalt. If treating cracks in a parquet floor apply the spray lightly; too much may soften the black cement under the wood and produce a stain. Oil sprays damage some linoleums and plastic materials. If you are in doubt about a surface, test it first in an inconspicuous place. Do not walk on carpets or rugs or sit in upholstered chairs that have been sprayed until they are completely dry, and avoid placing heavy objects on them. Weight or pressure on the damp pile will mat it and the disfigurement may last for several days.

Emergency Action If a pesticide is swallowed accidentally, or if someone becomes ill after using it, consult the label. The more toxic insecticides are labeled poison and an antidote is listed. Administer it, then call your doctor or a hospital immediately.

Insect Repellent. When you go canoeing or on a picnic most insects will find you repulsive if you apply an insect repellent to your skin. Sold as lotions and sprays under various trade names, insect repellents may contain such chemicals as ethylhexanediol, diethyl carbate, or diethyl toluamide. They are harmless to the skin and to most clothing, though some plasticize rayon and Dynel. Read the directions on the label and follow them exactly.

Iodine A chemical element used as an antiseptic and to remove silver nitrate stains.

Iodine Stains See "Stains," p. 231.

IRC See "Polyester."

Iridium A metal allied to platinum and sometimes alloyed with it. Iridium enhances the value of platinum in an alloy, being a more expensive metal. See "Jewelry."

Iron Iron is the most abundant and useful of metals. Rarely found native, it usually is obtained from its ores, the oxides and salts of the element. Pure iron is a soft, silverwhite metal that is scarcely known. As used commercially, iron has an admixture of carbon and varies in color from tin white to dark gray. There are three kinds, differing in the amount of carbon present: one, malleable (or wrought) iron, fusible at very high temperatures, malleable and comparatively soft; two, cast iron, which is hard, brittle and fusible at a lower temperature; and three, steel, which shares the qualities of the other two.

Pots and pans made of cast iron require "seasoning" before they are used to prevent rusting. Sometimes this is done at the factory. If you purchase a pot or Dutch oven that is tagged "preseasoned" you simply scour it, then wash it thoroughly in hot soapsuds, rinse and dry it. Grease the inside and the lid lightly with an unsalted fat and store. Grease it again lightly before putting food on to cook. This procedure, followed for the first month, will put your new pot in Grade-A working condition.

If your iron pot has not been "pretreated" it probably has been given a thin coating of lacquer to prevent rust. This must be scoured off with scouring powder and a stiff brush. Then wash it in hot soapsuds, rinse and dry thoroughly. You are now ready to "season" it. Coat the inside of the pot and cover generously with unsalted fat (lard,

108

vegetable oils, or what have you) and heat it in a slow oven (or over a low fire) for several hours. During the heating process apply more fat now and then. Wipe off excess fat when the seasoning has been completed and you shouldn't have to scour it again. But grease it before and after using for the first few weeks.

Ordinary care from now on will call for soap and hot water, careful rinsing and drying. For a thorough cleaning (as when food has burned) boil it up with hot water to which a little washing soda has been added, or wash it in a soda solution. Afterward wash in hot suds, rinse, and dry carefully. Should rust occur, remove every trace with steel wool or scouring powder, wash, rinse, dry and reseason. If you are using a synthetic detergent, do not soak your ironware in it or the seasoning will be removed.

Don't put an iron pot away with its lid on. It will develop a musty odor if you do and is likely to accumulate moisture and rust. If storing iron utensils for a long period coat them with an unsalted oil, wrap them with paper and put them in a dry place. Or you can give them a coating of paraffin.

Wrought iron, used for lamp stands and other ornamental pieces, is a purer form of iron than cast iron and resists rust. It can be polished with liquid wax to increase its rust resistance and make dusting easier, or you can keep it painted with a good paint, made especially for iron. Such paint is available in both flat and glossy finish and sometimes is called "andiron paint."

Should rust appear on wrought iron, remove it with steel wool and

kerosene. If very badly rusted, soak it for a time in kerosene, then rub it with steel wool.

Iron *furniture* for outdoor use must be kept well painted to prevent rust. If you are beginning at scratch, coat it first with red lead or aluminum paint, after removing every trace of rust with a wire brush, steel wool or emery cloth. If rust remains under the paint it will go on spreading. Apply two or more coats of ornamental paint.

Iron See "Electric Iron."

Ironer See "Rotary Ironer" and "Flatplate Ironer."

Ironing Wash-and-wear clothing, synthetic and durable-press curtains and bed linens, paper napkins and kitchen towels, and place mats that can be wiped clean with a damp cloth have taken a big bite out of the ironing load. You can reduce it further by being fussy about the way you hang up the wash. (If you don't have a dryer, that is.)

Many articles which some women insist should be ironed need not be if they are hung straight or put on hangers and stretchers. These include cotton knitwear, turkish towels, dungarees, and sheets.

Fold the hems of sheets together, right side out, and pin them by the hems straight on the line; straighten the selvages. Put terry cloth robes, seersucker dresses, and corduroy shirts on rustproof coat hangers.

Untreated cotton curtains can be folded lengthwise and ironed double. Other articles that can be ironed folded include everyday napkins and tablecloths, linen and cotton huck towels, sheets and pillowcases. And I should say that the number of times you fold them, before reaching for the iron, is strictly your own business.

As a matter of fact, some women say they don't like sheets ironed. Others say frankly that they don't like to iron them. Fold them meticulously as you take them from the line, smooth them with your hands and place them on the shelf. The same goes for tea towels. Who's to know?

General rules Now that we have disposed of most of the wash in our own way, it may be well to look into some general rules for the successful ironing of the things we are particular about.

Rule One is to have the clothes dampened uniformly and of proper dampness for the particular material. If you can snatch them from the line or dryer when just right to iron, you will find that they iron better and you will be spared the entire operation of sprinkling.

Rule Two is to iron first those articles which require the least heat . . . in this order: nylons and other synthetics, acetate, rayon, silk, wool, cotton and linen. If you plan it that way you won't have to wait for the iron to cool, or risk scorching something nice because you thought the thing had cooled enough.

Ironing instructions are sometimes given in degrees of heat. The

109

range on most irons is 180° to 550° F.

Here are other rules, mainly applicable to linens and cottons. Other materials require special directions, so look up the ones about which you are doubtful. Each is listed separately as "Wool," "Rayon," "Nylon," etc.

Iron clothes in straight strokes with the thread of the material.

Iron clothes on the right side except when it is desired to bring out the pattern of the fabric.

Iron embroidery and cotton lace on the wrong side, on a thick soft pad, to bring out the pattern.

Iron crepe weaves, such as seersuckers, when dry.

Iron first those parts of the garment which, while the rest of the garment is being ironed, hang off the board. Place paper under the board to prevent long pieces from picking up dust.

Fold flat pieces to a size convenient for storing. Fold sheets, tablecloths and other large pieces lengthwise first, then crosswise, until the desired size is reached. Fold towels and pillowcases lengthwise in thirds, then crosswise. (If you want to fold them crosswise first, go ahead and do it.) Napkins and handkerchiefs may be folded in squares.

Allow all pieces to dry thoroughly before putting them away. If possible, hang them on a rack to dry out after ironing.

Ironing Accessories A well-planned laundry and proper equipment make ironing a great deal easier. Adjustable ironing boards that enable the worker to stand or sit, plastic sprinkling bottles that can be squeezed to produce a fine, even spray, cord minders, wrinkle erasers,

press mitts and treated press cloths are some of the gadgets now available to you if you browse in the right stores.

Books and pamphlets on the subject of laundering also are to be had. Included in these are diagrams of laundry centers, designed for efficiency, and many timesaving suggestions on ironing techniques.

Ironing Board An ironing board should be mounted firmly and should be correct in height for you. It should be padded neatly and the cover kept clean by frequent laundering.

The height of your ironing board is correct when, if you rest the palms of your hands on the working surface, your arms are bent slightly at the elbows. Some of the new ironing boards are adjustable in this respect, allowing the ironer to stand or sit.

Wash and bleach your cotton ironing board cover like any other white cotton material. Asbestos covers can be washed on the board with a soft brush or cloth and soap and water. A little household bleach can be added to help remove scorch stains. (Do not use on Nomex covers.) Rinse with clear water. If the cover is removed for washing, replace it on the board while it is wet and allow it to dry in place. The tendency of asbestos covers to lint disappears with use.

When ironing, don't clutter your board with things already ironed or ready to be ironed. If you cramp your working space you are more likely to burn yourself or knock over your iron.

Iron Rust Stains See "Rust" and "Bathtub." See also "Stains," p. 231.

Ivory Ivory objects of natural finish (not tinted, gilded or otherwise decorated) can be washed in mild soapsuds. Rinse carefully and wipe dry. Ivory yellows naturally with age and more rapidly if kept in a place where light does not reach it. Very yellowed ivory handles, etc., can be restored to their original white finish by scraping, but your jeweler should be the one to do it. Knives, etc., with ivory handles should not be allowed to soak in water because the cement holding them to the blades may be loosened by such treatment.

See "Piano" for a discussion of the keyboard.

Jade This lovely stone, used by Orientals for vases, lamps and other works of art as well as for jewelry, derives its name from the Spanish *piedra de jada*, meaning "stone of the side." The ancients, who believed that many precious and semiprecious stones had special healing powers, prescribed it for any kind of pain in the side.

Chemically, jade is a silicate of calcium or magnesium. It is tough and compact and has an oily, or resinous, appearance when polished. Although it is best known in luscious shades of green, jade is found also in delicate pink and pure white.

Jade ornaments usually need only to be dusted. However, they may be washed in mild, warm soapsuds. Rinse carefully and wipe dry.

See also "Jewelry."

Jet Jet is sometimes called black amber. It is a hard, compact form of lignite (brown coal), capable of taking a high polish, and once highly in vogue for buttons, pins and other jewelry. If not decorated with materials damaged by water, it can be washed.

See following entry, "Jewelry."

Jewelry To look its best, jewelry should be kept clean. It also should be stored properly. Jumbling it together in a box or jewelry case invites damage. A diamond will easily nick and scratch other gems as well as metal settings. If you haven't a proper box, wrap each piece in tissue paper.

Care should be taken also when you are wearing jewelry. Leave your good rings and your watch at home when you play tennis or golf. Screw earrings in tightly to avoid dropping them, possibly on a cement pavement. Have the settings of valuable stones and the strings of good necklaces checked periodically by your jeweler as a precaution against loss.

The cleaning of jewelry depends upon the materials of which it is made. Valuable jewelry, of precious metals and stones, loses its sparkle if it is not kept clean. Soap and dirt collect quickly on the backs of all stones and around mountings, dimming their brilliance. For cleaning, outstanding jewelers recommend hot sudsy water and a little brush. A little ammonia helps loosen dirt, but should be omitted for pearls. Scrub and pat each piece with the brush so that the bristles get into every part of the setting. Rinse in

111

clear hot water and dry it with a soft bit of cloth or tissue paper.

Gold jewelry can be rubbed up gently with a soft piece of chamois, but go softly on gold-plated articles or the metal will be worn off. Such pieces can be replated at a moderate price when they begin to look shabby. Wash silver jewelry with soap or detergent and hot water, polish it with a good brand of silver polish, wash it again and rinse well or the tarnish will reappear quickly. Polish dry.

Stone bead necklaces (of topaz, amethyst, crystal, etc.) should be restrung frequently, especially if the beads are heavy or have sharp edges. Some experts advise having this done once a year. Investigate having them strung on fine chain.

Costume jewelry is cleaned with soap or detergent and water also, but use lukewarm water instead of hot to avoid cracking rhinestones, tinted glass, etc. Rinse in water of the same temperature. If desired, settings can be given special attention by tipping a toothpick with cotton, moistening this with alcohol and going over the stones. Work quickly. Too hot water or too long a soaking may loosen cement. Sponge plastics with mild lukewarm suds, rinse with a cloth dampened with clear lukewarm water and wipe dry. (No soaking, no hot water, no alcohol or ammonia!)

Wooden jewelry may be wiped with a soft cloth, wrung out of cool water. Polish by rubbing it gently with the palm of your hand.

A tip from a friendly jeweler is to clean stone beads and lightly tarnished metals with dry baking soda on a brush. (This is sometimes sold as jewelry polish.)

Diamonds and pearls, among the

jewels, require special attention and are treated in their own right. See "Diamond," "Pearl." See also "Watch," "Silver," "Gold," "Platinum," etc., for special or additional information.

Junk Houses filled with accumulations of junk are difficult to clean and unattractive in appearance. Get rid of the stuff regularly. If you haven't the heart to toss out your old lamp shades (you *might* recover them) or the back numbers of your favorite magazine, at least store them neatly in a place where you won't be stumbling over them all of the time.

I have read in an article by a famous child psychologist that women have no right to heave out any of their children's possessions. (Rusty skates, Doctor? Sticks, stones, broken toys including the gruesome remnants of dolls and stuffed animals? Birds' nests and comics?) Pay no attention to this theorist, sister, or you soon will be snowed under.

Use judgment, firmness, diplomacy and tact regarding recent acquisitions. Half-forgotten stuff can be spirited away regularly and probably will not be missed except for occasional passing remarks such as:

"Wonder what happened to 'at ole ambulance." Or

"I fought I had sisteen egg boxes."

Confronted by such indirect (or even direct, by golly) accusations, be nonchalant. Dismiss the matter as lightly as possible and switch the subject adroitly. Do not quail or pale, or all will be lost. Surely you can get the best of your four-year-old in an argument over a battered Band-Aid can or spring's first collection of vegetable and mineral matter.

Kapok Kapok consists of the silky coverings of the seeds of the Kapok or *ceiba pentandra* tree found in the East and West Indies. The "silk cotton" or "kapok tree" is related to the cotton plant but the material is unsuitable for textile purposes.

Kapok is sometimes used to stuff cushions, mattresses, pillows, life preservers and jackets. It is very light in weight.

Mattresses and pillows stuffed with kapok need frequent airing and sunning to keep them fluffy and prolong their service. Turn the mattress often. Kapok pillows cannot be washed.

Kerosene A volatile oil distilled from petroleum and other hydrocarbons. It is highly flammable. Kerosene is useful as a cleaning agent in many household tasks and is used for cooking, heating and lighting in many rural areas. It is used in various commercial cleaners, and some women still like to use it as a soap and grease cutter in home cleaning operations.

Kerosene should not be stored in the home in large amounts. It should be kept tightly stoppered in a cool place, away from all sources of heat.

Kerosene Lamp See "Lamp–Kerosene."

Kerosene Range Clean the enameled surfaces when they are cool with a cloth wrung out of mild, warm suds of detergent or soap. Use fine scouring powder on stubborn spots. Rinse with a cloth wrung from clear water and wipe dry.

Clean the metal parts of the burners with a soft cloth to keep oil from collecting on the outside. If wicks are used, they must be kept very clean. To clean them remove the chimney, the outside collar and the flame spreader. Turn the wick level with the top of the wick tube and remove the charred edges by wiping them with a soft cloth from the center toward the outside. Loose threads may be snipped off with scissors, but don't use scissors to trim the wick. Burn it off instead.

To burn off the wick, tip back the reservoir so that oil will not be fed to the wick, then burn off the uneven part. Wipe the charred edges as described above and smooth them with a cloth or with your finger tips.

Reassemble the parts.

The oven of an oil range is cleaned like other ovens. (See "Gas Range.")

About once a week the perforated parts of the burners of an oil stove should be cleaned with a clean, stiff brush. Olive oil rubbed sparingly over the iron or steel portions will help keep them from rusting. Apply the oil with a soft cloth.

Knife See "Cutlery."

Knitted Woolens See "Sweaters" and "Woolens."

Kodel Trade name for a polyester fiber notable for its heat resistance. It can be ironed satisfactorily at a very low temperature and also at a temperature as high as 425° F., the setting for light cottons and rayon. See "Polyester."

Labeling The service, pleasure, and ease of care which today's fabrics give depend to a certain extent upon your knowledge of their particular qualities and their proper treatment. The label on your garment is of paramount importance.

Under the Textile Fibers Labeling Act (1960), labels on yard goods and clothing must give the generic names and percentages by weight of fibers contained. The advantage of this can be seen in the fact that there are more than 700 trade names classifiable under one of the 17 generic groups defined by the Federal Trade Commission. Some of the 17 generic terms for man-made textiles are already familiar to you: rubber, glass, and metallic. Others are rayon, acetate, and nylon. Acrylic, polyester, and saran have been used so often in conjunction with trade marks and trade names that they have a familiar ring. Less familiar are modacrylic, azlon, spandex, olefin, vinyl, nytril, vinyon, and anidex. Each generic group covers a class of fibers differing significantly from those of the other groups in its chemical composition and physical properties.

Thus an "Acrilan" blouse might be labeled 80 percent acrylic fiber, 20 percent rayon, Acrilan being a trade name. Where less than 5 percent is of another fabric, the label must state "other fabric" or "other fabrics." Also the name of the manufacturer, or person marking or handling the product, must be given and, if imported, the name of the country where it was manufactured or processed.

Washing instructions today must be permanent, that is, written on a slip of cloth sewed to the garment, not on a hang tag which can easily be lost. You can consult them each time you clean the garment, and if

114

the clothing is given away the instructions go with it.

Lace Baste flat cotton and linen laces to a piece of muslin and wash in mild lukewarm suds. They will not need to be ironed. Small lace articles can be washed by shaking them up in a fruit jar, partly filled with warm soapy water. Rinse them in the same way and dry them flat on a turkish towel. If necessary, use rustproof pins to hold them in shape.

To restore oomph to laces that have lost their finish dip them in a gum arabic solution. (See "Starch and Special Finishes.") Stretch over a flat surface to dry. They will not require ironing.

If lace is to be ironed put it upside down on the board and press the wrong side. Straight lace edgings are ironed from the center outward. Iron lace ruffles from the outer edge inward.

Lace tablecloths can be dry-cleaned or washed and dried on a stretcher like lace curtains. (See "Curtains.") Or stretch them gently into shape while they are drying. Nylon lace needs no ironing or stretching.

Lacquer See "Stains," p. 232.

Lacquer (**Oriental**) Lacquered trays, boxes, etc., can be cleaned with liquid wax, applied with a clean soft cloth. Polish gently with a second cloth.

Lacquered Furniture See "Piano" and "Furniture."

Lacquered Metals Lacquered metals need only to be dusted. They may be washed, however, with warm water and a mild soap or detergent. If desired, give them a protective coating of wax.

Laminated Fabrics See "Bonded Fabrics."

Lamp—Electric Disconnect the lamp and remove, for cleaning, bulbs, reflector and shade. Dust with the soft brush of your vacuum cleaner or with a cloth. Glass and plastic globes and reflectors may be washed in warm suds. Rinse and dry carefully. Wipe the bulbs with a damp cloth, taking care not to wet the metal base, and replace them.

Metal lamp bases, if not lacquered, may be polished. (See "Brass," "Silver," "Bronze," etc.) Lacquered metals should be dusted and, occasionally, waxed. Lacquered surfaces that have been damaged by harsh cleaning methods and show cracks or spots of corrosion should be redone. Sometimes the factory where they were made will service them. Clean tôle (painted metal) with a soft cloth, either dry or damp.

Crystal bases are best cleaned with a cloth wrung out of clear water or water containing a synthetic detergent. Rinse with a cloth wrung out of clear water and polish softly with a lintless cloth.

Bases of porcelain, glazed pottery and china can be cleaned with a cloth wrung out of warm mild suds. Use a soft little brush to get at nooks and crannies. Rinse with a cloth wrung out of clear water and wipe dry.

Clean marble and alabaster lamp bases according to the directions given under "Marble."

Kerosene If you have been city-bred, a kerosene lamp, encountered perhaps for the first time on a summer vacation, may prove a monster more formidable than a hoot owl. Once you know how to manage the thing, though, it's all very simple.

Keep the oil reservoir well filled (there's a little screw cap) and wiped clean on the outside. Fill it (when unlighted, of course) away from flames and sparks. Be sure the wick is long enough to go into the oil and that it is clean and neatly trimmed. (You don't cut it with a scissors; just trim off the burned fibers.) Light the lamp with the wick turned low and the chimney either off or held straight to avoid smoking up the glass. Turn the flame up cautiously, as needed. When not in use, keep the wick turned low, but not too low or it may disappear altogether into the reservoir. The reservoir should be emptied periodically and washed with a detergent in warm water. Dry thoroughly before refilling.

Clean the lamp chimney, when cool, with warm water and detergent. Rinse and dry carefully. The burner of the lamp and the bases are cleaned according to the materials of which they are made. Shades, too, if any.

Caution: Kerosene lamps present a serious fire hazard if handled carelessly. Do not place them where they can be blown, or tipped, over. Keep them at a safe distance from fluttering curtains and draperies. Train your children not to touch them.

Lamp Shades Dust them regularly as you would other furniture, using the little round brush of your vacuum cleaner or a soft cloth. Dryclean all hand-painted silk, linen and chintz shades. Water will damage a painted pattern on silk and shrink linen and cotton.

Silk, rayon and nylon shades can be washed, provided the shade is sewed, *not glued,* to the frames and the trimmings are colorfast. Dip the shade in and out of a tub of tepid suds, made with mild, pure soap, or synthetic detergent. Rinse twice in clear, tepid water. Let it drip for a few moments, then let it dry in front of an electric fan, if possible, turning the shade frequently around and over. Quick drying is important because the water may rust the metal frame and stain the fabric. Do not dry silk shades in the sun.

Silk and rayon shades that are glued to the frames (sewed shades too, if desired) can be dry-cleaned.

Real parchment shades should be dusted regularly with an untreated duster and conditioned periodically with neat's-foot oil or castor oil to prevent the leather from drying out. Clean imitation parchment occasionally with liquid wax. Shades of metallic paper seldom need more than dusting. Paraffin (mineral) oil mixed with a little turpentine (one tablespoon of turpentine to onehalf cup of paraffin oil) is recommended for an occasional beauty treatment. Wipe away any surplus carefully. Plastic shades can be wiped with a cloth moistened with cool, soapy water. Rinse with a cloth wrung from clear water and dry. Shades made of fiber glass need only to be wiped with a damp cloth.

Lanolin Lanolin is a substance obtained from the natural grease of wool. It is used in certain hair preparations, as a base for ointments

and cosmetics, as a conditioner for leather and in many other products.

Latex Latex is the liquid exudation of rubber trees. The word is often used in the retail trade to indicate pure rubber, rather than synthetic.

Lead For the removal of stains caused by solder, lead foil, etc., see "Metallic" in "Stains," p. 233.

Lead Pencil See "Pencil" in "Stains," p. 235.

Leather Clothing Leather clothing goes to the dry cleaner unless labeled washable. The Department of Agriculture announced in fall 1959 the perfection of a tanning agent called *glutaraldehyde* which makes possible soft, beautiful leather garments that do not shrink, stiffen, lose color, or become stained by washing or perspiration. Glutaraldehyde is used in combination with other tanning ingredients to produce fine garment leather from sheepskin. Repeated washings with soap and lukewarm water do not damage glutaraldehyde-tanned leathers. Follow directions on the label.

Leatherette A type of artificial leather.

Leather Goods Leather luggage, handbags, briefcases, etc., will retain a smart appearance and wear indefinitely if they are given the proper care. The reason leather cracks, peels, and powders is that it dries out. Neat's-foot oil, lanolin, and castor oil are all good leather conditioners. Mineral oil (paraffin oil) and linseed oil should *not* be used.

Before oil is applied the leather

should be cleaned by careful dusting, or by washing with a cloth wrung out of pure soapsuds, or with saddle soap, according to directions given on the container. Oily spots may be removed with a dry-cleaning fluid.

Neat's-foot oil should be applied while the leather is slightly damp and should be rubbed in with the fingers or a pad of soft cloth. Let it stand on the leather. It will soon soak in, leaving it soft and dry. If the leather is extremely dry it is a good idea to repeat the oiling the following day. The only drawback to neat's-foot oil is that the leather is difficult to polish afterward, so use lanolin, castor oil, or a fifty-fifty combination of the two on glossy or polished leathers. Or you can use half lanolin and half neat's-foot oil. Use white vaseline on white and light-colored leather.

Caution: These directions do not apply to suède or patent leather. See "Shoes" and "Suède." See also "Books," "Furniture," "Mildew," "Gloves," "Chamois."

Artificial Artificial leather is made by coating textiles with pyroxylin, rubber, plastics, etc., grained to look like leather. Wipe with a damp sponge or with a sponge wrung out of mild suds. Rinse with a sponge wrung out of clear water. Wipe dry.

Leather Tile Leather tiles, used for floors and walls, are factory-finished with a special lacquer that makes them resistant to stains, scratches, and abrasion. They are maintained with polishing waxes, either liquid or paste, which clean as they are applied.

Leg Lotion See "Cosmetics" in "Stains," p. 227.

Lemon Oil Lemon oil, used for polishing furniture, is paraffin (mineral) oil containing a little oil of lemon.

Lighting Fixtures A woman I know is about to toss out her electric candelabrum and buy a new one, because the old one looks spotty and apparently is peeling.

Such fixtures often present a problem because it is difficult to know what metal they are made of and whether the metal has been lacquered, plated or gilded. But don't toss out a chandelier because it looks shabby until you have consulted a reliable dealer in electric equipment or your favorite hardware man. If hard pressed, you can gild or silver it yourself. And it may need only a new coat of lacquer.

Linen Fibers of the flax plant were woven into fine cloth in Egypt in 4800 B.C. and are still highly prized today. Linen, while extremely durable, lends itself to exquisitely fine weaves and is appropriately cherished by women who take pride in the appearance of their dinner tables. As a general term, "linen" has been extended to include all bed coverings, table coverings and towels.

In laundering untreated linens, follow the directions given for cotton materials. Do not use chlorine bleaches on wrinkle-resistant linen clothing. They are likely to produce a stain and weaken the fibers. Unless more than the usual stiffening is desired, they do not need to be starched. Iron linens when very thoroughly dampened, on the wrong side. Use a reasonably hot iron.

Linens that are to be stored should be washed in soft, or softened, water. Use softened water for rinsing too. (Iron in hard water leaves a residue in linens. Over a long period of time it rusts, leaving little brown dots.) See also "Durable Press."

Linen Closet Keep the door shut when you are cleaning nearby, but try to air your linen closet daily. Linens should be sorted and kept in neat piles, the guest towels and other special linens carefully hidden in a corner where the family won't grab them. Put linens just back from the laundry on the bottom of each pile so that articles will rotate in use and wear uniformly.

During special cleaning, remove all linens to a safe place and clean the walls, shelves, floor and lighting fixtures thoroughly, according to the material. Air the closet for several hours, then reline the shelves with fresh paper and replace your linens. This is a good time to check on possible (probable!) needs.

Linoleum Linoleum is made by applying to a canvas base a coating of hot, oxidized linseed oil, rosin, powdered cork and pigments. Sweep it or dust it with an unoiled mop. Wash with a cloth or mop wrung out of hot water containing an unbuilt synthetic detergent, mild soap, or washing soda. Rinse with a cloth or mop wrung out of clear hot water. Wipe dry. Clean a small area at a time until the floor has been finished. It is important that the cloths used be well wrung out as water rots linoleum. So does oil. Never let either stand on it. Harsh soaps contain alkalies that also are damaging. Scouring powders cut into the sealed surface.

Waxing helps preserve linoleum, enhances its appearance and makes it easier to clean. It is especially important for printed linoleum because the design is on the surface and tends to wear away. To remove old wax, wash the floor with a strong solution of your favorite floor cleaner.

On linoleum you have your choice of self-polishing, liquid or paste wax. If you use liquid or paste wax apply it very sparingly over a small area at a time and rub it in thoroughly. Then polish with a weighted buffer or an electric waxer. Wax looks best when applied in a miserly fashion; it takes a better polish and is less likely to be slippery. A waxed floor often needs only to be damp-mopped. Self-polishing waxes are generally preferred for kitchen linoleum.

Be leery of special finishes for linoleum. Varnish, shellac, and lacquer are not recommended as a finish. They cause cracks, ridges and discoloration. Worn or discolored linoleum can be painted with floor or deck paint.

Imitation Wash with a cloth or mop wrung out of warm, rather than hot, soapy water. Rinse with a cloth wrung out of clear warm water. Wipe dry. Imitation linoleum can be varnished, if desired, to preserve the pattern.

Linseed Oil Linseed oil used in the preparation of oil paints and varnishes and in many furniture polishes, comes from seeds of the common flax, or lint. It is the most

valuable of the drying oils. The finest grade is called "artist's oil."

If you are following directions that call for *boiled* linseed oil, don't think you can cook up a bit of raw linseed oil in a saucepan. The process employed commercially is both complicated and tedious. The stuff is heated in a copper or iron boiler for two hours, then chemical "dryers" are added and it is boiled for several hours more. It is then left in the boiler, covered, for an additional ten hours, after which it spends two or three weeks in settling tanks.

When you buy linseed oil at a paint or hardware store specify whether you want it "raw" or "boiled." And remember that it is flammable.

For stains caused by linseed oil see "Stains," p. 232.

Lipstick See "Cosmetics" in "Stains," p. 227.

Liquor See "Furniture." Also see "Alcoholic Beverages" in "Stains," p. 224.

Lucite Trade name for an acrylic plastic. See "Acrylic Plastics" and "Plastics."

Lye Lye, a very strong alkali, is used in making soap and for various cleaning operations, notably the opening of stopped drains. If you use lye, follow the directions on the container with the utmost care because it is a dangerous, caustic agent and can cause severe external, as well as internal, poisoning. On no account must your skin come in contact with lye or lye water.

Lye will eat through cloth, enameled surfaces, bristle brushes, rubber gloves, etc., and will damage severely certain metals, such as aluminum. It usually does a good job on a stopped drain but you are taking chances if you use it in a very greasy drain. Under the right conditions it can combine with the grease and form hard soap which blocks the pipe completely.

Trade-marked drain openers labeled sodium hydrate are lye.

When using lye, add no other cleaning agent.

Magnesite A flooring made by mixing assorted stones in a substance similar to concrete, cutting it down and polishing it. See "Stone Floors."

Magnesium Magnesium is a bluish white metal, one third lighter than aluminum. It is obtained by intricate processes from sea water and a tubful of ocean will yield about one pound. In thin ribbon strips and in powder form magnesium is highly flammable, emitting a brilliant white light. In this form it is used for flares at airfields, etc. But don't let this worry you if you have a new magnesium pancake griddle. The metal is incombustible *except* when powdered or cut in the thinnest of strips.

Magnesium is used for all sorts of cooking utensils, for piano frames, garden furniture, ladders and other objects. It is valuable because of its light weight and because it does not rust, tarnish, or corrode.

Magnesium furniture requires no particular care, just dusting and ordinary washing. But watch your magnesium ladder and garden furniture when the wind begins to blow!

Magnesium griddles often are

119

given a protective coating of wax at the factory. This should be removed with a cleaning powder and medium hot water before the utensil is used. Dry and coat the entire cooking area with a vegetable shortening or cooking oil before placing it over the heat.

With use, a magnesium griddle loses its bright silver color and takes on a deep, rich, gunmetal luster. It is then giving its best cooking service so do not try to remove it. Just clean your griddle with a light application of cleanser or steel wool.

Mahogany See "Furniture (Wooden)."

Maid While avoirdupois in a prospective cook is, at least, an indication of a healthy interest in food, it is less desirable in a general maid, as you will soon discover that she can neither stoop nor reach. Forget all that about "training" a maid; the odds are that she will train you. Maids at this writing are practically extinct. It is the era of the cleaning lady and the baby sitter.

Majolica A type of glazed pottery made in Italy, etc. See "Pottery."

Mantel Be fussy about your mantel, because a fireplace is always the focal point of a room. Clean it according to the material of which it is made and do not allow it to become cluttered. See "Marble," "Walls and Ceilings (Painted)," "Iron," etc.

Manufacturer Manufacturers of reliable household equipment are anxious to have you derive satisfaction and pleasure from them.

When repairs are needed, or parts are lost, a courteous note addressed even to a giant corporation often will bring surprising results.

The name and address of the company usually is stamped somewhere on the equipment, along with a number indicating the model. Or you can find the address in your booklet of instructions if you saved it. The care and maintenance departments of the different companies often will repair your electric iron, mend your doll, send you a new handle for your teakettle or skillet and replace small parts of other equipment. They will take up as their own the problem of finding a suitable repairman for your refrigerator, sometimes going to a great deal of trouble and expense to please you. And, believe it or not, there will be times when you won't even be billed.

This is called "public relations," which sounds a little formidable. Public relations, however, means the importance of pleasing you, the consumer, and that is very good business. So, before you throw away that nice electric iron or fire extinguisher that the local fellow says isn't worth fixing, send it to the factory and find out. Pack it securely and fasten your stamped letter of explanations to the box with cellulose tape. That makes things easier at the other end. It

may take a little time but, when you get your equipment back, the chances are it will work like new.

Marble Marble is a form of limestone, more or less crystalline, or granular in structure. It is found in many colors and combinations of colors, also in pure white and black and patterned in strange designs. While subdued colors predominate, brilliant reds, yellows, blues and greens also are seen, blended in fantastic patterns.

The rainbow colors in marble are due mainly to the presence of various iron compounds, while the grayish shadings are caused by fossilized organic materials, both plant and animal. Preserved in the stone are the joints and stems of fossilized stone lilies, or feather stars, delicate creatures of the sea. Fragments of sea shells also are found, giving a lovely iridescent play of color.

This is the material marble, gift of the prehistoric past. It is from 500 to 700 million years old, but especially adaptable to modern design and in great demand because of its beauty and easy-care qualities. Treat it as the luxury product it is, using only recommended products to clean it, and it will always be lovely.

Polished marble in good condition needs only to be dusted or wiped with a soft damp cloth. If it has been soiled through neglect or improper maintenance, the situation can usually be corrected by applying suitable cleaners or stain removers. The instructions which follow were provided by the Vermont Marble Company, Proctor, Vermont. Marble-care kits and the various trade-named products mentioned are available from this company and its branches. Similar kits can be found in some hardware and department stores.

For general cleaning and maintenance use the following: Unpolished marble—use a cloth or a fiber brush and scrub with Wyandotte Detergent. (Avoid common abrasive cleaners.) Rinse carefully. On outdoor marble—patios, garden furniture—use the special product Stone Klene. On polished marble, if a damp cloth will not suffice, use a cloth wrung out of suds made with Ivory or Lux soap flakes. Rinse thoroughly and wipe dry with chamois to prevent streaking. A mild detergent solution (Joy, Ivory) can be used as a one-time cleaner on very soiled marble. (Do not use heavy-duty detergents.) Even a mild detergent should not be used repeatedly because yellowing or other surface change may result on some types of marble. After cleaning, apply a sealer—Tri-Seal for dark marbles, Vermarco White Marble Seal for white. Sealers inhibit soiling and staining. Light paste waxes are also used.

Marble furniture is cleaned by the method described for polished marble. Spilled foods, cosmetics, and drinks should be wiped up promptly, a rule which applies to all fine furniture. Fruit juices, carbonated drinks, and foods containing acids produce dull areas that look like stains but are actually etchings, revealing the color of the unpolished marble which is always lighter. Minor etchings and scratches can usually be removed by patient rubbing with powdered tin oxide (putty powder). Sprinkle the powder on the surface and rub vigorously with a moistened felt pad or chamois. When the shine has been restored, rinse the surface with clean water and dry it thoroughly with a soft cloth. Preferably, apply a sealer to the clean marble after the proper interval.

Marble floors are cleaned with Wyandotte Detergent. Wet the floor with clean water, sprinkle it with detergent, then mop or scrub the floor. Clean a small area at a time and remove the soiled water promptly. Rinse with a clean mop. If some areas are badly soiled, give them this special treatment: Mix the detergent with water to the consistency of thick cream and apply it to the soiled marble. Let it dry, then rinse it off thoroughly with clean water. If the floor looks dusty or white when it is dry, too much detergent has been used or the floor has been incompletely rinsed. Rinse it again. Sealed marble floors can be damp-mopped.

Stains on marble, as on other materials, are easier to remove if they are treated promptly. Remove the material that has caused the stain, then apply the proper stain remover. Solvents recommended are alcohol, acetone, lighter fluid, and flammable cleaning fluids. The best bleach is hydrogen peroxide (35 percent). Light stains can sometimes be removed by rubbing them with Wyandotte Detergent. Deep stains may require patient poulticing. A poultice is made by mixing the stain remover with Wyandotte Detergent or whiting.

Oil and grease stains are usually dark in the center, shading to light. For these, use one of the solvents listed, applied in a poultice or on a white blotter covered with glass or plastic film to hold in the moisture. Repeat as often as necessary. Rinse.

For rust stains, sprinkle on Vermarco Crystal Cleaner and dampen it with water. Let it stand no longer than an hour. On vertical surfaces apply it as a poultice. Or you can use a poultice made with a commercial rust remover. Rinse thoroughly.

Organic stains (yellow to rose) from colored paper, foliage, tobacco, tea, coffee, and cosmetics are removed with hydrogen peroxide. Apply it directly to a flat surface, as a poultice to a vertical surface. Add a few drops of ammonia and let it remain until the bubbling stops. Rinse with water.

For ink stains (except those caused by metallic inks) use hydrogen peroxide. Apply it directly to the stain and rinse after a few minutes. For metallic ink stains use Crystal Cleaner.

If the marble is etched slightly by a stain remover, polish it with putty powder, as previously described.

Carved marble, statuary, and badly soiled or yellowed stone, are best treated with an all-over poultice. Add water to Wyandotte Detergent to make a mudlike paste. Apply the paste (about ½ inch thick) to the entire surface by hand or trowel, and retard drying by keeping the application covered with a damp cloth for 24 hours. Let it dry for another 24 hours. Remove the poultice and rinse the marble thoroughly. (Do not get the poultice on wood or metal.) Wyandotte poultices can be saved and reused.

If your marble needs refinishing, consult your local dealer. It is not easy to do it yourself.

Mascara See "Cosmetics" in "Stains," p. 227.

Matting See "Carpets and Rugs."

Mattress Mattresses accumulate dust and should be cleaned periodically with the upholstery attachment of your vacuum cleaner or a good stiff whisk broom. An occasional sun and air bath will help keep them fresh and clean. If badly soiled, clean them with soap foam or upholstery shampoo, following the directions given for "Furniture—Upholstered."

A quilted pad, placed on top of the mattress, contributes to the comfort of the sleeper and provides sanitary protection. Envelope-style dust jackets also are sold as mattress protectors.

To insure long wear and comfortable service, a hair mattress should be turned frequently from side to side and from end to end. Makers of fine mattresses recommend turning them daily; you, however, probably care more for yourself than for the mattress to undertake it. Turn it, though, at least once a week. (Foam-rubber mattresses do not need to be turned.)

If you have a good mattress that has become lumpy or has lost its bounce, think about having it remade. There are firms that specialize in this sort of thing. For a fraction of the cost of a new one, your mattress can be cleaned, sterilized and completely remade. Mattresses and inner springs also can be cut down in size and otherwise remodeled.

See also "Kapok" and "Foam Rubber."

Mattress Pad Soak in cool water, if stained, then wash in rich, hot suds. Rinse three times and hang, folded one third over the line, in the sun, if possible. Hang straight and, after it is dry, smooth it with your hands. Or put it in an automatic dryer. Do not iron.

Mayonnaise See "Combination Stains," p. 223.

Meat Juice See "Combination Stains," p. 223.

Medicine See "Stains," p. 232.

Melamine and Urea Melamine plastic is used for dinnerware, table and counter tops, cutlery handles, buttons, housings for electric shavers, and other appliances. Urea is used for buttons, bottle tops, electric plugs, and wall plates. Both plastics are hard to break but should be protected against sharp or severe blows.

Melamine and urea are odorless, nontoxic, and tasteless. They can be washed with soap or detergent in very hot water, but should not be subjected to oven heat or a direct flame. Freezing does not affect them. Alcohol, cleaning fluids, mild acids, and alkalies do not damage them; but keep abrasives away.

Dinnerware of melamine is in the high-quality bracket, but it can go into the dishwasher and emerge undamaged. Even boiling water will not soften it. Special washing compounds are available to remove stains. These include the following, recommended by a manufacturer of melamine dinnerware: Dip-It, M-E Cleaner and Maid-Easy. Baking soda will often re-

123

move light stains. Sodium perborate is usually effective for heavy stains. Heavy abrasives, including steel wool pads, should not be used. A mild detergent such as Cascade or Finish is suggested for automatic dishwashers. See also "Plastics."

Melmac Trade name for a melamine plastic. See "Melamine and Urea."

Mending The adage has been repeated so often that it is absolutely trite, but for all that, it is as true today as when it was first propounded that "a stitch in time saves nine." Try to take care of small rips and tears before your linens and clothing go into the tub or washing machine.

Mercurochrome See "Stains," p. 233.

Merthiolate See "Mercurochrome" in "Stains," p. 233.

Metallic Paper See "Lamp Shades."

Metallic Stains See "Stains," p. 233.

Metallic Yarn Textiles including metallic yarns are dry-cleaned or washed according to their tags. Ordinary home cleaning fluids and upholstery shampoos do not damage them. Many washable fabrics

can go into the washing machine for laundering with the usual soaps and detergents, but don't use water hotter than 140° F. Better avoid bleaches, which are damaging to some metallic yarns. In ironing, set the dial for rayon. See also "Brocade."

Metals The various metals used about the house are treated individually in this book, so look up "Gold," "Silver," "Monel Metal," "Aluminum," etc., and also "Jewelry." The surface of a metal must be scratched lightly with an appropriate abrasive if it is to shine. If the abrasive selected is too harsh, the scratches will show. If it is too soft, it will not polish the surface. Some metals like acids, others prefer alkalies. Therefore the same polish cannot be used on all metals.

Metaphen See "Mercurochrome" in "Stains," p. 233.

Methoxychlor See "Insecticides."

Metlon See "Metallic Yarn."

Micarta A trade name for a laminated phenolic resin. See "Phenolic" and "Plastics."

Mice Block all entrances; store loose foods in jars and tins; keep garbage and trash closely covered in metal cans. Starve the cat.

Mice enter the house through small holes around pipes, through defective or ill-fitting cellar screens and under loosely hung doors. Autumn is the time to be especially on guard because cold weather drives them from the fields to the shelter and abundant food supply of your home. They eat human food and carry several human diseases. If the infestation is extremely serious, you can call in a professional exterminator. Otherwise, lay in a good supply of spring traps, bait them carefully with mouse delicacies and sit down to listen for them to snap. Set your traps night after night until victory has been achieved.

Peanut butter smeared on the trigger of the trap is one of the best baits. Other good ones are cake, bacon, flour, nut meats, cheese, and soft candies such as gumdrops and milk chocolate. Place the traps at right angles to walls between objects, or near holes and damaged materials, so that the mice will intercept the triggers. Rolled oats or dry cereals, sprinkled around baited traps, sometimes help. Trap-shy characters can sometimes be outwitted by concealing the entire trap with rolled oats, cereal, or flour.

If you prefer to use poisoned baits, buy a kind recommended for this specific purpose and follow the directions on the container exactly. According to the Department of the Interior, the least hazardous are the anticoagulants (Diphacin, fumarin, pival, PMP, and warfarin). These can be bought readymixed or as concentrates which can be mixed at home. Several weeks may be required to achieve control by means of them. Be careful not to let them contaminate food. Safeguard children and pets by placing the bait in protected stations—behind a board nailed to a wall, inside a sealed cigar box with a mouse-sized hole, etc. Dispose of dead mice promptly and safely.

Other rodenticides give faster results than the anticoagulants but they are extremely poisonous and should be used only by a professional exterminator.

Microwave Oven Microwave energy, on which this oven operates, is a type of high-frequency radio energy. It enters at the top of the oven in the form of invisible waves, called microwaves, and is distributed throughout the oven by a "stirrer," located behind the plastic cover at the top. Microwave energy is reflected away from metals, goes through glass, ceramics and paper, and is absorbed by foods. These it penetrates to the center and quickly cooks.

Be sure the power is off and the stove cool before you begin to clean any part of your microwave oven. Spatters and spills on the inner walls of the oven can be removed with a paper towel or damp cloth. Use a cloth dipped in soapsuds for greasy spots. Rinse and dry. Do not ever remove for cleaning the cover over the "stirrer" in the top of the oven. Do not ever use a commercial oven cleaner on any part of a microwave oven.

Use care if it is necessary to remove the glass shelf for cleaning. The glass is breakable. Wash the shelf and the well underneath it with warm soapsuds, rinse, and dry. Or you can wash the shelf in the dishwasher.

The inside of the door can be wiped daily with a cloth wrung out of soapsuds. Rinse and dry thoroughly. To insure a tight seal around the door, all metal and plastic parts of the area must be wiped frequently with a damp cloth to remove soil. A build-up of soil could cause a leakage of microwave energy from the oven. *Do not* use abrasives such as cleaning powders or steel and plastic pads. They will mar the surface of these parts. Finally, remember that cleaning materials used on the door must be rinsed off completely.

The outside of your oven should be cleaned often with soap and water, rinsed, and wiped dry. Stubborn spots can be removed with a mild household cleanser whose label says that it is safe to use on painted surfaces. The outer pane of the window is plastic. Wipe it clean with a damp cloth. Wipe the chrome trim with a damp cloth, then immediately with a dry towel. With this treatment it will stay bright and shining. If it becomes necessary to clean the cord, use a damp cloth. For stubborn spots, a cloth wrung out of soapsuds can be used, but rinse and dry thoroughly.

The light compartment is usually in the upper front of the left-hand interior wall. When replacing a lamp, first remove the lamp compartment cover by removing the screw which holds the cover in place. Follow instructions located inside the lamp cover.

Push the bulb in gently and turn it to the left (counterclockwise), then pull the lamp outward from the socket. Replace the lamp with one that is exactly the same. Lamps can be bought in drug, hardware, and sewing supply stores.

If you have dropped your microwave oven or it does not seem to work properly, call the company's service center.

Mildew Spores of molds, always present in the air, are the cause of mildew. In warm humid weather they flourish on any substance that can provide the simple nutrients they require. They grow on textiles, leather, wood, and paper—especially in places that are poorly ventilated and lighted—causing stains, discoloration, and eventual destruction. A musty unpleasant odor advertises their presence.

To prevent mildew keep your home clean, well ventilated, and dry. Grease and soil provide food for developing molds. Even mildew-resistant fabrics such as synthetics may be attacked if allowed to lie around damp and soiled.

In humid weather ventilate your house when the air outside is drier than the air inside. Cool air holds less moisture than warm air, so take advantage of cool nights for a thorough airing. The moisture will be absorbed and carried outdoors. (An electric fan will help.) Closets and dresser drawers may be left open periodically to discourage the accummulation of moisture and to freshen the air. Make sure that clothing in closets is hung loosely so that air can circulate around it, and put articles especially susceptible to mildew (shoes, luggage) on a shelf instead of on the floor. A small electric light burning continuously in a closet will often provide sufficient heat to prevent mildew.

Sometimes, especially if a house has been closed, a brief heating will be needed to rid it of mildew-inducing dampness. Use the furnace, or an electric heater, then open the doors and windows to let out the moisture-laden air.

Air conditioners and electric dehumidifiers remove moisture from the air and, properly installed, are useful. They draw in the damp air, condensing the moisture it contains on refrigerated coils.

Chemical moisture absorbers also are available. Silica gel, activated alumina, and calcium chloride absorb moisture from the air and are sold for this purpose in drugstores, department stores, and by building supply dealers—often under trade names.

Silica gel and activated alumina granules absorb half their weight of water, feel dry even when saturated, are harmless to fabrics, and can be dried out and used over and over. These chemicals are placed in small cloth bags which are suspended in clothes closets, or placed in a pan on a shelf or on the floor. They may also be sprinkled between layers of clothing in chests or trunks. Keep the doors shut and the chests closed. To dry the granules put them in a pan and heat them for several hours in a vented oven (300° F.). Silica gel is sometimes treated with a color indicator so that it changes from blue to pink as it absorbs moisture.

Calcium chloride is available in granular form and in specialized products consisting of porous clay-like materials soaked with the chemical. The specialized products are placed in cloth bags which are hung in closets or other damp areas. They can be dried in an oven and reused. Granular calcium chloride holds twice its weight in water but gradually liquefies as it absorbs moisture. It damages clothing and household textiles if allowed to contact them, producing holes. To use it place the granulated chemical on a rustproof screen, supported in an enamelware container. Place the container (uncovered) on the floor of the closet and keep the door shut. When the granules liquefy, discard them and add fresh chemical.

Musty odors in a basement or shower stall indicate mold growth. Eliminate the odor and forestall damage. Usually thorough heating and drying will take care of the problem but special treatment may be required.

Sprinkle dirt floors in musty cellars with chloride of lime, available at groceries. Let it remain until the odor is gone, then sweep it up. Scrub cement floors, tiled walls, and tiled floors with a solution of chlorine bleach. Use one half to one cup of bleach to each gallon of water. Rinse with clear water and wipe the surface as dry as possible, leaving the windows open to complete the process. Warning: On plastic and asphalt tile, work quickly to avoid a spotted surface.

Also useful in eliminating musty odors are low-pressure aerosol sprays which contain a fungi-toxic (mildew-inhibiting) chemical. Not all room sprays contain a fungicide, so read the labels carefully when making a selection. In using such sprays follow the manufacturer's directions exactly.

Give special care to some articles. Do not let clothing or linens lie around damp or go into the hamper wet. Wash out dishcloths and hang them to dry. Spread out washcloths and damp towels. Stretch shower curtains to dry; the part wadded against the wall mildews first. In washing garments and linens use plenty of sudsy water, rinse well, and dry quickly and thoroughly. Fabrics dried slowly may get sour and musty smelling, a sign that molds are at work.

127

Draperies, slip covers, golf bags, and outerwear can be treated with water-repellent sprays to make them less susceptible to the growth of molds. Such products are available in low-pressure aerosol containers. Germicidal mothproofing and water-repellent sprays may also give protection against mildew. Read the labels for information and follow the instructions given.

Store only clean things. Soiled clothes and household textiles are more likely to be attacked than clean ones. Have them washed or dry-cleaned before putting them away. And unless you know that your starch contains a mildew inhibitor do not store starched clothing. Mildew thrives on starch.

Occasionally, on warm, dry days, sun and air clothing stored in closets. It pays especially to examine cotton, rayon, wool, and leather clothing put away in garment bags. Unless they are protected by a mildew inhibitor they are likely to be attacked.

Mildew inhibitors that can be used to protect clothing during storage include paradichlorobenzene (para crystals), widely used for moth control. Scatter the crystals through the folds of garments in boxes, bags, and trunks, kept as airtight as possible, to control mildew effectively. Or hang bags of crystals in the tops of garment bags so that heavy vapors settle on the materials being protected. Use about 1 pound of crystals for 100 cubic feet of air space. As the vapor disappears more para crystals must be added to maintain its effectiveness. Para crystals may also be had in spray cans.

128

Warning: Para crystals damage some plastics so avoid using plastic hangers and remove plastic buttons, buckles, and ornaments from clothing.

Leather goods can be protected against mildew by sponging with 1 percent solution of dichlorophene in denatured or rubbing alcohol. Or use hexachlorophene or thymol in the same way (1 percent solution in alcohol). These chemicals can be prepared by your druggist, or your luggage store may have them packaged especially for leather goods. Try a little of the solution on a part of the leather that does not show to be sure it does not change the color. Give the inside and outside a coating and repeat as needed.

A good wax dressing will also protect leather goods from mildew in warm, humid weather. Read the labels when making your selection. Some shoe dressings on the market contain a fungicide (hexachlorophene or paranitrophenol) to prevent the growth of mold, and wax or a silicone resin to protect from perspiration and wet weather. A coating of floor wax applied to shoes, uppers and soles, keeps moisture out and helps prevent mildew. Do not use paranitrophenol on white or light-colored leather.

Protect stored shoes, jackets, luggage, and other leather goods in humid weather by spraying them with paradichlorobenzene or paraformaldehyde. Wrap them in packages and seal them. (Do not use paradichlorobenzene on luggage with plastic fittings.)

Wood mildew, inside the house or out, rarely occurs. It can be controlled by the use of mildew-resistant paint, available at paint stores.

Paper and books should be kept as dry as possible in damp weather to discourage mildew. Burn a small electric light in a closed bookcase. Or use silica gel or calcium chloride in a closed space. Also effective are the volatile mildew inhibitors, paradichlorobenzene and paraformaldehyde. Hang a bag containing one of these in a closed bookcase. Or dust books and papers with paraformaldehyde, then wrap them in tight packages. (This chemical is poisonous and may be irritating to some people.)

How to Remove Mildew Mildew spots on *clothing and household products* should be removed as soon as they are discovered, before they have a chance to weaken or rot the material. Brush them outdoors, if possible, to avoid scattering spores throughout the house, then sun and air them thoroughly. If spots still show, have nonwashables dry-cleaned. Treat washables as follows: Wash the articles at once with soap or detergent and water. Rinse and dry in the sun. If a spot remains use lemon juice or a bleach. See "Mildew" in "Stains," p. 233.

Upholstery, rugs, and mattresses should be taken outside if this is possible and brushed with a broom to remove loose mold. Then run a

vacuum over stained places to remove more of the mold. Dispose of lint so that it is not scattered throughout the house. If possible, sun and air articles outdoors until they are thoroughly dry. Indoors, use an electric fan.

If mildew remains, sponge the article lightly with thick suds made with soap or detergent and rinse with a clean damp cloth. (Take care not to wet the filling of cushions.) Or sponge upholstered furniture with a solution of denatured or rubbing alcohol (1 cup of alcohol to 1 cup of water). Dry thoroughly.

Sponge mildewed rugs and carpets with thick suds or a rug shampoo. Remove the suds with a clean damp cloth and dry in the sun if possible. Use a low-pressure spray containing a fungicide (½ to 1 cup of liquid household bleach to 1 gallon of water) to get rid of the mildew. Repeat spraying frequently in areas where mildew persists.

If mildew has gone inside an article, consult a reliable fungicide service, listed in the Yellow Pages of the telephone directory under "Pest Control," or "Exterminating and Fumigation."

Leather goods infested with mildew should be wiped with a cloth wrung out of dilute alcohol (1 cup of denatured or rubbing alcohol to 1 cup of water). Dry in a current of air. If mildew remains, wash the article with thick suds made of soap or detergent, saddle soap, or soap containing a fungicide or germicide. Rinse with a damp cloth and dry in an airy place. Polish leather shoes and luggage with a good wax dressing.

If mildew has grown on the

129

inside of shoes, there is often an unpleasant odor and molds of various colors appear. This type of mold can be removed with a formaldehyde solution, bought at a drugstore. Apply the solution carefully with a cotton-tipped applicator stick, then wrap the shoes tightly in a paper or plastic bag and let the formaldehyde penetrate for at least an hour. Air the shoes thoroughly outdoors before you wear them.

Warning: Formaldehyde vapors are very irritating. Do not inhale them. Do not get the solution on your skin.

Sprays made especially for freshening shoes can be bought at shoe and department stores. They contain such fungicides as hexachlorophene and dichlorophene. Follow the directions on the box.

Wood badly infested with mildew may need to be replaced with wood that has been treated or is decay resistant. Get help if you cannot decide.

Clean mildewed floors, woodwork, and other wooden parts infected by scrubbing them with a mild alkali such as washing soda or trisodium phosphate (4 to 6 tablespoons to 1 gallon of water), or with disinfectants such as a quaternary disinfectant or pentachlorophenate. Paint stores, grocery stores, and janitors' supply houses sell these products under various trade names. Rinse and allow the wood to dry completely, then apply a mildew-resistant paint.

Paper and books should be wiped with a clean dry cloth to remove loose dry mold. If mildewed paper is damp, dry it first

in an airy place. Dry damp wallpaper slowly, for several days if necessary, to dry the plaster as well as the paper. If too much heat is used the plaster will crack.

If the mildewed paper is washable, wipe it with a cloth wrung out of soapsuds, then with a cloth wrung out of clear water. Pat it (do not rub it) with a soft dry cloth. If a stain remains, treat it with household bleach. Rinse with a cloth wrung out of clear water. Or use ink eradicator.

Spread the pages of books fanwise to dry. If they are very damp, sprinkle cornstarch or talcum between the pages to absorb the moisture. Let it remain for several hours, then brush it off. Use a mildew inhibitor (paradichlorobenzene or paraformaldehyde) to stop the growth of molds.

(This material is taken from a booklet published by the Agricultural Research Service of the United States Department of Agriculture.)

Milk See "Nongreasy Stains," p. 222.

Mimeograph Correction Fluid See "Lacquer" in "Stains," p. 232.

Mineral Oil Mineral (paraffin) oil is a name used for crude petroleum and refined petroleum oil. When properly refined it is a clear, viscous fluid without odor or taste. Mineral oil is useful in the home in certain cleaning operations and is used as the base of some furniture polishes, such as "lemon oil." Do not use it on leather.

Mirrors Mirrors can be cleaned with a soft damp cloth wrung out of plain warm water, or water to which a little vinegar or ammonia has been added. Spray-on window cleaners also can be used. Polish with a lintless cloth or chamois leather. Moistened face or toilet tissue can be used for a quick cleanup of the bathroom mirror. Polish with dry tissue.

In washing mirrors great care must be taken not to wet the backing. Don't let water seep in around the edges, or between the glass and the frame, or the mirror will be damaged.

Good mirrors that have become useless and unsightly through damaged backing can be resilvered. Consult your favorite hardware dealer or furniture repairman about this. If you are frightfully clever you might want to undertake it yourself, but it isn't exactly easy. Clean mirror frames according to directions given under "Picture."

Mites Mites are small, often very minute, arachnids which occasionally become household pests. Those that bite cause swelling, itching, and sometimes fever, but seldom transmit diseases.

Mites that bite include bird and rodent mites, certain food mites, and chiggers, which breed outdoors and enter the home only on clothing. Clover mites, which sometimes invade homes, are harmless but leave bright red spots when crushed.

An insect repellent applied to the body or clothing will prevent mites from biting you. Select one containing deet, ethyl hexanediol, dimethyl carbate, or dimethyl phthalate. Itching caused by the bites can be relieved with an ointment containing benzocaine. These can be bought at hardware and sporting goods stores and at drugstores.

Rodent and bird mites can breed in a home where rats, mice, or pet birds are present. Bird coops and wild birds' nests near a chimney, window, or ventilator are other sources of bird mites. Food mites breed in cheese, grains, etc.

To destroy mites, treat infested areas with a household surface spray containing malathion, then turn your attention to their source. (See "Rats," "Mice.") If the source is birds, destroy nests near house openings and clean up bird cages or chicken coops and spray them with malathion. If food is infested, destroy it. Clean the food shelves carefully, then spray them with an insecticide containing not more than 2 percent malathion. When the spray has dried, cover the shelves with fresh paper or foil. Replace the food and keep it covered.

The clover mite breeds in areas of new lawns and heavily fertilized old ones. From there it often goes a step farther—into the house. Here it becomes a first-class pest. It does not carry disease or damage household supplies, but it simply overruns everything. Crushed, it leaves a red mark which is especially noticeable on a white surface.

Clover mites occur in the northern United States and are most annoying in late fall and early spring. Outdoor sprays seem not to affect them indoors, and indoor sprays do not harm them. Aside from outdoor care, the only weapon seems to be your vacuum cleaner. See "Insecticides" for precautions.

Mixer See "Electric Mixer."

Modacrylic As the name suggests, modacrylic textile fibers are modified acrylics. They contain less than

131

85 percent (but must contain at least 35 percent) of the chemical substance acrylonitrile. Modacrylics are sold under the trade names Dynel, Verel and SEF. Since the fibers differ, each is listed.

Mohair A textile made of wool from the Angora goat. See "Woolens."

Mold See "Mildew."

Monel Metal Monel metal is an alloy of nickel and copper, named for the French scientist who perfected it. Wipe Monel metal with a cloth wrung out of hot soapy water, or water with a detergent, rinse and rub dry. If desired, scour it with a fine cleaning powder.

Monvelle See "Biconstituent."

Mop (Dry) Give it a good shake out-of-doors if you live in the country, to get rid of the dust. If you live in the city, shake it into a big paper bag or clean it with your vacuum cleaner. When dust clings tenaciously to the strings, the mop needs a bath. A mop made of cotton yarn should be soaked overnight in water containing soap or detergent. Wash it by plunging it up and down in the water. Remove hairs and lint. Rinse thoroughly, squeeze out excess water, and untangle the strings by "combing" them with a pencil. Shake the mop to fluff the yarn and hang it to dry in an airy place, preferably outdoors. Some cotton mops, made to fit over metal frames, can be slipped off and washed by machine. Enclose them in a nylon mesh (or muslin) bag, to avoid unraveling the yarn.

Wool mops do not need to be washed often because dust is more easily shaken out of the yarn. Wash your wool mop, without previous soaking, in lukewarm suds made with a mild synthetic detergent. Rinse in lukewarm water, squeeze out excess, shake to fluff, and dry in any airy place away from direct sun or any source of heat.

Mop sprays or conditioners containing deodorized kerosene improve the efficiency of dry mops (and dustcloths) by causing the dust to cling. Used sparingly, according to the directions, they will not damage waxed surfaces.

Mop (Oiled) Wash mops used for oiled floors like other dry mops, but make the suds stronger. When dry, add a few drops of oil polish to the strings and store the mop head in a closed metal can. Oiled mops and dusters sometimes ignite spontaneously and cause fires.

Mop (Wet) Mops used with cleaning compounds, soaps, and detergents usually need only to be rinsed thoroughly after use. Squeeze the water out of string mops and gently separate the strands. Press sponge mops as dry as possible and hang

them in the shade. Cotton yarn mops can dry in the sun. They benefit by a trim now and then. Using sturdy scissors, snip off frayed ends. Mops should never be stored wet in a pail or on the floor. Hang them up to dry and when you store them. If put away damp, they are likely to mildew and develop an unpleasant odor. See "Sponge (Cellulose)."

Mosquito Aside from being an unwelcome pest, mosquitoes sometimes carry diseases such as malaria and encephalitis to man. Who does not know its song in the night?

Adult mosquitoes inside the home can be destroyed by using an aerosol spray designed for flying insects. Such sprays may contain pyrethrum (pyrethrins) plus a synergist such as piperonyl butoxide. An aerosol bomb containing malathion or methoxychlor is also highly effective.

Release of the aerosol for a few seconds will quickly kill all mosquitos in an average-sized room. Close doors and windows during the treatment and keep closed for 5 to 10 minutes afterwards. (Do not spray a room containing people or pets, including fish.)

Sometimes an outdoor cleanup of stagnant water is in order, for it is here that mosquitoes breed. Look for larvae (wigglers) in old tin cans, discarded tires, rain barrels, and clogged rain gutters. Empty birdbaths and scrub them at least once a week. Inside your home, check fish bowls and aquariums (not all kinds of fish destroy mosquito larvae) and saucers under plants.

Sometimes mosquito larvae are found in fishponds and ornamental pools. If you do not have fish in your pool, you can apply a "House and Garden Spray" or an "Indoor-Outdoor Household Spray" to kill mosquito larvae. Use only sprays labeled for mosquito control and treatment of plants. These sprays come in push-button containers. Use them sparingly. For a pool 5 to 6 feet across use the spray for about five seconds. Wait 24 hours, then examine the water. If some of the larvae are still living, spray again. Pupae are not killed by the spray, so watch the pool and get them when they are in the larval stage.

Do not apply insecticides to ponds containing fish. Mosquito breeding can be almost eliminated by keeping the pool clean. Vegetation, particularly the kind that floats, should not be allowed to grow into large mats. If the surface of the water is relatively free of floating plants, the fish will be able to eat most of the larvae. See also "Insect Repellent" and "Insecticides."

Mother-of-Pearl The rainbow substance which lines sea shells: nacre. See "Pearl Handles."

Moths (Clothes) Two important organs of thought, The New Yorker and House and Garden, have, at different times, advanced the fascinating theory that there is some connection between marriage and moths. Correlated with this theory is the vague implication that women bring them, since bachelors apparently do not have them. Right here and now I wish to state that as a bachelor girl I, also, gathered no moths. But let's not go blaming each other. The problem is: What to do? Consider first three circumstances.

1. You have moths and have them bad. The best thing to do is to call in a reliable exterminator.

His services may be expensive, but it will pay you in the end because moth damage can run easily into hundreds of dollars.

2. You think you haven't any, but your sweaters, upholstery and coats seem to be wearing in the darnedest places or sprouting holes beyond all reason. You had better wake up and *do* something, my dear. The larvae are there!

3. You have never had moths that you know of, but you are married and have an accumulation of blankets, sweaters and other impedimenta to store. Don't be lulled by a false sense of security; rather be on guard to defend your woolies against possible invasion.

Your enemy is a small yellowish moth no more than three-eighths of an inch from antenna to tail, and the larva (worm) is white with a brownish head. May and June are the months when the clothes moth flits normally, but we have encouraged him with steam-heated homes until he is practically a year-round foe. Moth larvae like woolens best, especially spotted and soiled woolens. If very hungry they become less particular and even attack cottons. Furs and feathers are ambrosia to them. Rayon and other synthetics are moth-resistant unless mixed with wool or spotted with food.

The moth hazard is minimized by good housekeeping tactics. Rugs that are vacuumed and rotated regularly and clothing that is well cared for and properly stored are not likely to be attacked. Use your vacuum cleaner brushes to keep cracks in the floors and baseboards free of lint and dust where moths can breed. Never let old sweaters or bits of woolen cloth lie around in boxes, corners, drawers, or on

shelves. They are often a source of infestation. Remove spots from clothing and keep woolens well brushed. Store only clean clothing. Either have it dry-cleaned or brush it carefully and hang it in the sun. Hot sunlight destroys moth life, but it must reach every part of the garment and this is difficult to arrange, what with pockets and seams providing ideal hiding places. Dry cleaning also kills moth life. Neither treatment, however, guarantees the fabric against a future invasion. Either have your dry cleaner mothproof your clean woolens for you or do it yourself with a stainless household insecticide containing methoxychlor, Perthane, or Strobane. The insecticide should be packaged and labeled for this use. Follow the directions given on the label.

In treating woolens, hang them on a clothesline and spray them lightly but uniformly until the surface is moist. Do not overspray. Too much spraying will leave a white deposit after the fabric has dried. A slight excess can be brushed off, but a heavy one may require the services of a dry cleaner.

Clothes moths frequently share their food sources with carpet beetles, which often go undetected while the damage they do is blamed on moths. The two pests together are responsible for an estimated damage of 500 million dollars a year in the United States. If you have rugs or carpeting that need protective treatment, get professional help. See "Carpet Beetle" for description.

Surface sprays can be used on all places where insects like to crawl. Use a spray that contains 3 to 5 percent of premium-grade malathion or ronnel, or ½ percent of lindane or diazinon. These insecticides can be bought in ready-to-use pressurized containers that deliver a coarse spray, or you can buy a liquid insecticide and apply it with a household hand sprayer that delivers a continuous spray. When the spray dries, a deposit is left which kills insects that crawl over it.

Spray these areas: Along the edges of wall-to-wall carpeting, behind radiators, along baseboards and moldings, in corners, cracks, and other places that are hard to reach. Before spraying closets, remove all the clothes. Apply the spray to corners and crevices, around shelving, and at the ends of clothes rods. Do not use aerosol sprays. They deliver a fine spray which does not moisten the surface as the coarse sprays do, and they do not give lasting protection.

Clothing and blankets can be mothproofed by spraying them with a stainless insecticide containing methoxychlor, Strobane, or Perthane.

Mothproofing rinses seem to have disappeared from the market, but they are very effective. If you want to mix your own, use this formula from the Department of Agriculture: Mix together 1 ounce of sodium fluorosilicate (from your druggist) and about ⅓ the amount of a mild detergent. Add 1 gallon of lukewarm water and stir thoroughly. Immerse washed articles in this solution and let them soak for 10 or 15 minutes. Squeeze out excess water and allow to dry.

Furniture upholstered in wool or mohair, when threatened by moths, should be brushed or vacuumed thoroughly and sprayed with one of the insecticides recommended for clothing. If slipcovered, be particularly alert. Let the the stuffing of upholstered furniupholstery dry before you use the furniture. If moths have invaded ture, mattresses, or pillows, spraying will not help. You will have to discard the infested furnishings or have them fumigated by a professional. Select a firm that guarantees its work because this treatment is not always successful and a reupholstering job may have to follow.

Frequently overlooked are the felts and hammers of pianos, which are often damaged severely by moths and carpet beetles. The chemicals recommended for clothing can be used to protect them, but let your piano tuner apply them lest other parts of the piano be damaged.

Stored woolens (in boxes, chests, sealed closets) can be protected with paradichlorobenzene (para) crystals or naphthalene flakes or balls. Para crystals act faster than naphthalene, do not attract moisture and liquefy, and the odor disappears quickly. (But do not place clothes on a plastic hanger if you use it. It sometimes softens plastic hangers and buttons of the clear transparent type. If clothing sticks to the hanger some of the plastic may be absorbed, leaving a stiff, shiny stain. To remove it, see "Plastic" in "Stains," p. 235.)

You can use moth crystals by sprinkling them over woolens being stored; by placing them in a shallow container on a shelf, or suspended on a clothes rod or hook in a thin bag or perforated container; by blowing the fumes through

135

them in your storage closet with a special vacuum cleaner attachment. The important thing is to use enough of the crystals and to store them sealed tight.

If you are using the vacuum cleaner method hang the clothes loosely on hangers so that the fumes may reach all parts. Place the vacuum, with the crystal container in place, inside the closet with the switch on. Close the door and seal it with newspaper wadding or with gummed tape (a special kind is made for fumigating). Plug in the vacuum and let it run. The instructions given by the manufacturer of your particular type of vacuum cleaner will tell you how much para to use and how to operate your machine. After removing the vacuum, reseal the closet.

If you use a container, let it be a shallow pan on the top shelf, a perforated plastic or metal box, or a little muslin bag suspended from a hook or rod. The reason for this is that the fumes work downward. Seal the closet tight and keep it sealed for two weeks for a complete kill. Allow 1 pound for each 100 cubic feet of closet space.

If you are storing woolens in boxes or trunks sprinkle each layer generously with crystals, using tissue paper between layers. Use 1 pound of crystals, flakes, or balls in a trunk-size container and seal with tape when filled. Felt hats should be brushed carefully, sprinkled with

crystals and stored in sealed boxes for maximum protection. In handling blankets sprinkle one half the surface with crystals, and fold the other half over. Again sprinkle one half and again fold, until the blanket is of convenient size for storage. Wrap each blanket in paper and seal the flaps with gummed tape. Mothproof boxes and bags are useless if the clothing placed in them has not been cleaned and treated before being placed inside. Any openings or rips should be sealed.

Cedar chests and closets are effective mainly because they can be closed tightly. Play safe and mothproof articles stored in them.

Valuable rugs and furs are best stored professionally by a reliable firm that guarantees against moths, fire, etc. Less important rugs, if stored at home, may be sprinkled generously with crystals, rolled, wrapped in heavy paper and sealed with tape. If you store furs at home, use crystals, flakes, or balls in a tight container. Sprays are not recommended for furs.

Moths (Pantry) See "Pantry Pests."

Mucilage See "Glue, Mucilage, Adhesives" in "Stains," p. 228.

Mucus See "Stains," p. 234.

Mud See "Stains," p. 234.

Muriatic Acid Muriatic acid is a solution of hydrochloric acid in water, used by professionals to clean down newly laid brick and tile work. Its function is to dissolve smears and splashes of mortar. As used, it is diluted with from eight to ten parts of water. The solution is brushed on with a scrubbing brush, then rinsed off with plain water. Muriatic acid is injurious to the skin, to woodwork and to fabrics. It should be applied by a competent worker who is familiar with its properties, not by an amateur.

Mustard Stains See "Stains," p. 234.

Nail Polish See "Lacquer" in "Stains," p. 232.

Naphtha Naphtha is a member of the coal tar family. There are many grades, heavy to light. Naphtha is used for fuel and lighting in some areas, as a solvent for rubber and certain greasy stains and as an ingredient in some paints, varnishes and wax polishes. It is explosive and highly flammable. Large amounts should not be used or stored in the home and it should be kept away from flames and sparks. If possible, work with naptha should be performed out-of-doors. See "Cleaning Fluids."

Neat's-Foot Oil An amber-colored oil obtained from the feet of bovine cattle, such as cows. It is extremely valuable as a leather conditioner. You can buy neat's-foot oil at paint and hardware stores, at shoe shops and drugstores. Neat's-foot oil does not clean leather; it protects it from deterioration due to drying. So use saddle soap or mild soap and water first, then rub the oil in with your finger tips or with a soft pad of cloth.

Neat's-foot oil is not suitable for articles on which a glossy shine is desired. It leaves a dull finish, difficult to polish.

Neckties Washing a necktie sometimes does it more good than dry

cleaning. Make a thick suds with lukewarm water and an unbuilt synthetic detergent. Wash the tie carefully; do not rub or twist it out of shape. Use a soft brush on badly soiled places. Rinse carefully in lukewarm water. Roll and squeeze to extract excess water. Starch the tie lightly, shape it carefully and hang it over a rod to dry.

Press the tie before it is completely dry. To do this, cut a piece of cardboard in the shape and size of the larger half of the tie and slip it inside. Press first on the wrong side, then on the right, using a press cloth. The cardboard keeps the tie from being marked by the seams. When the tie has been pressed carefully on both sides, remove the cardboard and press the edges. A steam iron is excellent for this pressing job.

Nickel Nickel is a hard, silver-white, lustrous metal, usually used around the home as a plating over steel or copper. It also is used in the alloy, Monel metal. "Nickel" is an abbreviation of the German *kupfernickel* (copper mimic). It was first obtained from the copper-colored ore, niccolite, in 1751. The designation implies some annoyance on the part of an early prospector, who thought he had found copper. The value of copper at that time was well known, while that of the new metal was a question mark.

Clean nickel with soap and water, rinse, then polish with a soft

137

cloth. If this treatment is not sufficient, use whiting, or a fine cleaning powder, moistened with alcohol. Rinse and polish. Nickel darkens if it is not cleaned frequently.

Nitrate A plastic. See "Cellulosics."

Nomex See "Aramid."

Nonstick Pans See "Pots and Pans."

Nylon Nylon, spun in a test tube from chemicals found in coal, air, and water, was the first no-iron synthetic to achieve commercial success. It was first produced in 1928 by chemists engaged in basic research for the du Pont Company. Years of experimentation and testing followed.

It made its bow to the public in 1940 in the guise of sheer, quick-drying hosiery and was acclaimed with cheers. Eighteen months later the stockings were unobtainable. Nylon had gone to war. It was making tough ropes for mountain troops, cord for bomber tires, parachutes, military clothing, life rafts.

In 1945, nylon returned to the domestic field and the first wash-and-wear clothing began to appear. The strong silky fibers were woven into gossamer hosiery; dainty lingerie with pleated net, lace, and embroideries that never needed ironing; dresses, blouses, and tough light-weight outdoor gear that could take real punishment. Nylon resists moths, mildew, aging, and most chemicals. When properly heat-set, nylon materials will not stretch, but if stretch is wanted it can be achieved. Nylon textured under heat to resemble minute accordion pleats, coiled springs, loops, and curls, not only retains its new form but springs back to it if pulled straight. This makes possible stretch clothing.

Nylon is easy to care for. Many spots can be sponged off with plain warm water if treated when fresh, and standard cleaning fluids can be used for greasy stains. Provided the dyes are fast, it can be machine laundered with heavy-duty detergents. It is heat-sensitive. White textiles should always be laundered separately because they tend to pick up tints from colored clothing. Qiana is a du Pont trade name for a nylon fiber.

See "Wash and Wear." See also "Antistatic," "Sweaters, Synthetic," "Curtains."

Nylon Coat Read and follow carefully the manufacturer's advice for deep-piled nylon and Orlon acrylic coats. Some of them should be cleaned professionally by the Furrier method. If the coat is washable, follow these directions from the du Pont Company.

Pretreat badly soiled areas thoroughly by rubbing them with a paste made of synthetic detergent and water. On oily stains use dry-cleaning fluid or a spotting agent. Coats may be hand or machine washed. Hand wash the garment in warm (100° F.) water and heavy-duty detergent. Avoid twisting and other rough handling. Rinse carefully in warm water. To machine-wash your coat use warm suds made with a heavy-duty detergent. Use the highest water level available. If you intend to machine-dry your coat, let it go through the complete washing cycle. Otherwise remove it before the spinning, or water extraction, phase begins.

Drip-dry your coat by hanging it soaking wet on a strong rust-proof hanger. Straighten the hem and adjust the collar while they are still wet.

Machine-drying your coat in a tumble-type dryer, after either hand or machine washing, may seem best to you. Because it is difficult for some dryers to handle coats containing too much water, any excess water should be removed before machine-drying is attempted. For a machine-washed coat, simply let it go through the complete washing cycle, including the spinning or water extraction phase. Allow a hand-washed coat to drip on a hanger until it is almost dry before you put it in the dryer.

In drying a coat, set the machine at the lowest setting available and tumble until it is damp dry. Remove the coat immediately after completion of the damp-drying cycle and put it on a strong rust-proof hanger. Shape the collar, cuffs, and seams and let the lines of the coat fall into place.

Nylon Plastic Nylon plastic is translucent or opaque, milky white when uncolored and softly pastel when tinted, with a texture similar to horn. It is light in weight, rigid, yet slightly resilient. Although nylon will stand rough treatment and is not affected by freezing temperatures, it is not intended for continuous outdoor use.

Nylon plastic is used for tumblers that will bounce but not break, for brushes and bristles, combs, funnels, and salad sets. Slide fasteners made of nylon can be ironed with a warm (never hot) iron. Dry-cleaning fluids will not damage them. Brushes with nylon bristles and nylon backs can be sterilized by boiling. (If the handles are transparent they are probably acrylic and cannot be boiled.)

Utensils made of nylon can go into the automatic dishwasher and emerge unscathed. If dishes are piled on top of them they may lose their shape, but prompt rewashing will restore it. Nylon utensils used with coffee, mustard, beets, and other colored foods should be washed quickly to avoid stains.

Nylon plastic is not affected by chemicals. It cannot go into an oven or over a flame. Use no abrasives. See also "Plastics."

Objets d'Art See "Art Objects."

Oilcloth Oilcloth is made by coating a textile with a mixture of linseed oil, whiting and pigment. It should not be folded when wet because of its tendency to crack along the folds and at the corners. Sunlight and strong heat also damage it. Remove food stains quickly, before they become set. Clean oilcloth by wiping it with a damp cloth or a cloth dampened in warm, mild suds. Do not machine-wash it. Do not use harsh cleaning powders and do not set hot dishes on it. Alcohol, acetone and amyl acetate are especially damaging to the finish.

Oiled Floors See "Wooden Floors."

Oil Paintings If your oil painting is at all valuable, leave it strictly alone, except for dusting. Paintings seldom need first-aid treatment in the home. If any doubt exists about the condition of the painting, don't touch it until it can be examined by a professional restorer. The associate curator of a famous art mu-

139

seum reluctantly offers the following advice regarding the care of oil paintings:

"Superficial dust and dirt can be removed from an oil painting in sound condition by a light brushing with absorbent cotton or a soft brush. Either of these can be used dry or moistened with a gasoline-type dry-cleaning fluid (flammable; proper precautions must be taken). The canvas must be firmly and uniformly supported from the reverse while any pressure is being put upon the face of the painting.

"Paintings should not be treated, on front or back, with soap, water, bread crumbs, erasers, raw potato, sliced onion, or oil of any kind. Some of these may improve the appearance of a painting temporarily, but all can be harmful in inexperienced hands.

"A painting whose surface has become dull can frequently be brightened by the use of a good quality prepared wax emulsion cream furniture polish. If the manufacturer's directions for use on fine furniture are carefully followed, no harm should result and the thin film of wax left on the surface is a safe and moderately durable protection.

"No other treatment should be followed by inexperienced persons."

Oil Stains See "Furniture," "Wallpaper." See also "Greasy Stains," p. 222.

Olefin Olefins are high-strength synthetic textile fibers based on polyethylene and polypropylene. They are resistant to stains, sunlight, aging, acids, and alkalies. Mildew does not attack them. An outstanding quality is that they ab-

sorb moisture and thus have a low static level.

These fibers appear in blends with wool, acrylics, cotton, and rayon for clothing. Alone, they are used for knitwear such as socks, sweaters, and sports shirts, and for bathing suits, lingerie, diapers and babies' pants, neckties, and Ban-Lon outer sportswear.

Olefin fibers are extremely light and therefore provide superior bulk and cover. Manufacturers say olefin textiles "breathe" and thus do not become clammy and sticky. Household furnishings (upholstery, rugs) resist stains and spills, which are easily wiped up.

Olefin clothing is machine washable in warm water and can be machine dried at a low temperature setting (140° to 160° F.). It requires little or no ironing. For touch-up, use a low setting. See also "Synthetic Textiles."

Onyx Onyx is a kind of quartz, similar to agate, characterized by a structure in parallel bands of varying color and translucence. In fine specimens the colors are defined sharply, white with black, brown or red. Onyx has been valued since ancient times and many of the finest cameos have been carved from it. See "Jewelry" and "Quartz."

Onyx Marble Onyx marble, sometimes called Oriental alabaster, is a translucent and particularly iridescent variety of carbonate of lime, bearing some resemblance to the stone, onyx. Hence its name. It is a material of great beauty and is used to make cases for clocks, vases, lamps and tabletops.

Ancient quarries in Egypt were rediscovered about 1850 and these furnish a highly prized quality of stone. However, the chief supply comes from Algeria, where a fine quality is obtained abundantly. More recently, a similar stone has been found in Mexico. This is called Mexican onyx or tecali marble. See "Marble."

Opal It has been said that the opal retains in its depths the rainbow tints of long-dead forest fires. Opals are a solidified jelly (hydrated amorphous silica) and their colors are caused by the refraction of light on thin films that fill what once were cracks in the stone. The colors vary with temperature and climate and sometimes disappear altogether. An opal is then said to be dead. Magical qualities, both lucky and unlucky, have been attributed to the opal. One ancient belief was that if you carried an opal wrapped in a bay leaf you would be rendered invisible. Another was that it would make the owner beloved so long as he had faith in its powers. See "Jewelry."

Organdy Cotton organdy should be laundered in warm suds made with a mild, pure soap and handled gently so as not to distort the threads. Rinse carefully. If the organdy has a permanent finish, it will not require starch. After many washings, however, it probably will benefit from a light starch. Limp organdies require regular starching —one part basic mixture and one part water. Gelatin, gum arabic and gum tragacanth are preferred as a stiffening by some women. Organdies may be rolled while wet in a turkish towel to absorb moisture. In this case they can be ironed

almost immediately. If embroidered, iron on the reverse side.

Organza Organza, a sheer dress material similar to organdy but with more body and stiffness, is made of various fibers—silk, rayon, nylon. Follow the instructions on the label for washing or dry cleaning.

Orlon Orlon is the trade name for du Pont's acrylic fiber. It has many of the desirable characteristics of nylon. It is important where strength and low stretch are required. It washes easily, dries quickly, has good heat and moisture resistance, is not attacked by moths or mildew and can be set by heat so that it resumes its original shape and dimensions after washing.

Orlon is almost equal to nylon in tensile strength, withstands heat better, is more absorbent and has better covering, or bulking, ability. Orlon is not affected by the acidic fumes that damage nylon. Most ordinary chemicals and solvents will not harm it. It is practically impervious to moths and other insects, molds, and bacteria.

Orlon continuous filament yarn is silklike, warm, dry and luxurious to the touch. Orlon staple, on the other hand, is like wool, warm and soft. While light in weight, Orlon has the strength and feel of heavier materials and good recovery from wrinkles.

Orlon is used alone and in blends for sports shirts, blouses, sweaters, skirts, blankets, socks, work clothing, service uniforms, pleated materials, and pile coatings. Spots can be sponged off with water or cleaning fluids. It can be washed or dry-cleaned according to the label. See "Acrylic Textiles," "Sweaters," "Blanket." See also "Wash and Wear," "Nylon Coats."

Oxalic Acid The acid of sorrel, a family of plants. Its household use is as a bleach and stain remover, especially effective for ink and iron rust stains. Oxalic crystals may be bought in drugstores. They are very poisonous.

In removing stains from cloth with oxalic acid, follow these directions for a "mild" treatment. Dissolve one tablespoon of crystals in one cup of warm water. Wet the stain with this solution and keep it wet until the stain is gone. Rinse thoroughly with water. For a "strong" treatment, make the water as hot as the fabric will stand or (except on nylon) sprinkle the crystals directly on the dampened stain, then dip it in very hot water.

For copper stains in bathtubs use it straight. See "Bathtub" for directions.

Paint Your procedure in cleaning a painted surface and your selection of a cleaner for the job probably will be influenced by several factors. If the surface is chipped, scuffed and needs redoing anyhow, you will no doubt proceed with scouring powders and strong cleaners and a what-the-heck attitude. If you rent your apartment or home, you probably won't be as particular as if you owned the place. If you own the place, you will be more careful, but, if you did that paint job yourself, you will give the surface tender, loving care.

Some paints are not washable. These include the water washes, such as calcimine and whitewash. Oil paints thinned with water

142

(Kem-tone, etc.) are difficult to clean. Good oil paints, thinned with turpentine, and rubberized and synthetic resin paints can be cleaned satisfactorily if a proper method is selected.

For procedure see "Walls and Ceilings" and "Furniture." For a discussion of various cleaners see "Paint Cleaners." For paint stains on textiles, see "Stains," p. 234.

Paintbrushes See "Brushes—Paint."

Paint Cleaners Paint cleaners are sold commercially in liquid, powder and paste form. The liquid cleaners may be soap solutions, with or without water-softening agents, or non-soap solutions containing trisodium phosphate, washing soda or sodium silicate. The paste cleaners are similar to the liquids, using enough soap to form a paste. Some cleaners consist of wax emulsions, plus soap and an abrasive. The powders are the solid ingredients found in the liquid and paste types. If you are using a commercial paint cleaner, follow the directions on the container exactly and do not use more than advised. What we call "paint cleaners" painters often laughingly call "paint removers."

A good cleaner for flat paint is trisodium phosphate, which you should be able to obtain at a paint store. Commercial paint cleaners often contain trisodium phosphate and Oakite is its grocery store equivalent. If using trisodium phosphate, use one tablespoon to a gallon of warm water, rinse, and wipe dry. Follow the directions in using packaged cleaners.

To clean glossy enamel paint and other paints with a glossy finish in good condition use a cloth wrung out of plain hot water, or hot water containing one teaspoon of washing soda per gallon—more, if desirable. Rub gently. Soapless detergents also may be used. Trisodium phosphate and many of the commercial paint cleaners dull the finish of enamel paints and soap leaves a film. Scuffed paint calls for a fine abrasive, such as whiting.

Paintings See "Oil Paintings" and "Water Color Paintings."

Paint Stains See "Furniture." See also "Stains," p. 234.

Palladium Palladium is a silver-white metal, malleable and ductile, often used instead of platinum and sometimes called platinum. However, it is a much less expensive metal. Clean it like platinum. See "Jewelry," "Platinum."

Pantry Pests If moths are flying around your pantry, a search for contaminated cereals, flour, dried peas, cornstarch, etc. is indicated. Flour moths, beetles, and weevils invade the home front via the packing house and grocery and multiply in the forgotten package on the pantry shelf. Look for lumpy masses in flour and corn meal and little webby threads adhering to the sides of cardboard containers. These indicate that the worms of flour moths are present. Holes in dried peas and beans have been made by beetles or weevils.

Your first step is to locate and destroy all contaminated packages. Your second step is to remove all containers from the shelves and wash the shelves with hot suds, paying particular attention to the ledges on which the shelves rest. The third

step is to spray all surfaces with a household surface spray containing not more than 2 percent of malathion. (Read the label on the insecticide before buying it to be sure it contains the proper amount of active ingredient.) Spray lightly but thoroughly. When the spray has dried, cover the shelves with clean paper or foil. Replace the packages.

Because most dry packaged foods are attractive to pantry pests, it is a good idea to inspect them carefully for breaks when you are buying them. Examine spice packages too, especially red pepper, paprika, and chili powder.

Food that may be infested—but you aren't sure—can be sterilized by placing it in the oven at about 140° F. for half an hour. Small packages may be heated as they are; large packages should be emptied into cake or pie pans. Store them afterward in clean metal or glass containers that have tight-fitting covers.

There is no solution for the problem of two-legged pantry pests!

See "Insecticides" for precautions.

Paraffin Paraffin is a solid, waxy substance obtained from petroleum. Its uses include waterproofing, the prevention of decomposition, etc. The homemaker knows it best as a topping to preserve jellies from mold and a material to make her electric iron slick. For paraffin

spilled on cloth see "Candle Wax" in "Stains," p. 226.

Paraffin Oil Paraffin oil, also called mineral oil, is liquid paraffin. In a pure state it is colorless, odorless, translucent, and tasteless. Paraffin oil is used in some furniture polishes, in cold creams and in hair preparations. Do not use it on leather.

Parchment Parchment is made from skins of goats and sheep, especially dressed so that it may be written on. The skin is scraped with sharp instruments and rubbed with pumice until the desired thickness is obtained. See "Lamp Shades."

Patent Leather Leather dressed so as to have a high gloss. See "Shoes."

Peach Stains See "Fruit and Berry" in "Stains," p. 228.

Pearl The pearl has been called the purest of gems because it requires neither cutting nor polishing. Pearls have been known and prized since ancient times and are found wherever mussels and oysters flourish. Chemically, pearls consist of layers of calcium carbonate and animal tissue, called nacre, which lines the shells. They are formed when an irritating particle, such as a grain of sand, invades the shell. Pearls are usually silvery white, or bluish white, but some are pink, yellow, copper-colored, smoky brown, gray and black. Light-blue, purple, and black pearls are found in the common clam. The finest gray and black pearls come from the Gulf of California. Pink pearls are of two varieties, those from the common conch shells of West Indian seas and those

144

from fresh mussels, found in France, Scotland, Germany, and the United States. Ceylon, the Persian Gulf, Thursday Island, and the west coast of Australia produce the most beautiful white pearls.

Cultured pearls are made by injecting a small bead or similar object into a pearl oyster shell. Imitation pearls are usually made of glass coated with an essence of fish scales.

Pearls in rings and pins can be washed with mild soap or a synthetic detergent and water. Do not use ammonia. Pearl necklaces should be restrung at least once a year, or whenever they are loose on the string. To keep them clean, rub them gently and frequently with a piece of clean, soft chamois leather, taking care to rub between the beads. This will remove the film of dirt that collects on the pearls when they are worn.

Artificial pearls are cleaned in the same way as genuine pearls.

Caution: Acids dissolve pearls; high heat destroys them.

Pearl Handles Pearl handles are made of mother-of-pearl, the nacre that lines sea shells. They need only soap and water. No ammonia. Do not let pearl handles soak in water as this treatment may loosen the cement that holds them in place. Do not put them in your dishwasher.

Pear Stains See "Fruit and Berry" in "Stains," p. 228.

Pen See "Ink" in "Stains," p. 230.

Pencil Marks See "Wallpaper." See also "Stains," p. 235.

Percholorethylene See "Cleaning Fluids."

Percolator See "Coffee Maker."

Perfume See "Furniture." See also "Stains," p. 235.

Permanent Press See "Durable Press."

Peroxide See "Hydrogen Peroxide."

Peroxy Bleach Peroxy bleaches (Snowy, Beads O'Bleach, Dexol) are not as strong as chlorine bleaches, but they are safe for all fabrics. Use them for textiles with durable-press finishes and for silk, wool, and spandex, which are damaged by chlorine. Such bleaches contain sodium perborate or potassium monopersulfate. See also "Bleach" and "Chlorine Bleach."

Perspiration See "Stains," p. 235.

Pests Look them up by name: "Moths," "Mice," "Silver Fish," etc.

Petrolatum See "Petroleum Jelly."

Petroleum Ether This is the same as benzine. See "Benzine" and "Cleaning Fluids."

Petroleum Jelly Petroleum jelly, better known by its trade name, Vaseline, is a soft greasy substance used as a soothing ointment and as a lubricant. It is one of many petroleum derivatives. In household use it is valuable for loosening heavy grease and tar stains to facilitate their removal with solvents, for conditioning leather and for preventing rust. For stains caused by this substance see "Vaseline" in "Stains," p. 238.

Petroleum Naphtha Most used of the flammable grease solvents; sold under its own name and trade names. Use a type with a high flash point (less likely to ignite). See "Cleaning Fluids."

Pewter Pewter is a gray alloy of several metals, usually tin with lead, or tin with copper. It has been made in China for over three thousand years. Since pewter is a soft metal, it should not be subjected to harsh polishes. For a dull finish rub it with rottenstone and olive oil, mixed to a paste. Use a soft cloth. Wash, rinse and wipe dry. For a bright finish use a paste made by mixing whiting and denatured alcohol. Let the paste dry on the pewter, then polish. Wash, rinse, and dry. Special polishes are available for pewter.

Bad spots can be removed from pewter by rubbing them with grade oo steel wool, dipped in olive oil. The oil prevents scratching.

Very old pewter sometimes acquires a brownish scale (museum scale) caused by climatic action on the tin in the alloy. This can be removed by soaking the pieces in a strong solution of lye. (See "Lye" for precautions.) Japanned pieces and those with wooden knobs and handles should not receive this treatment. Be sure the articles are covered completely. After allowing them to soak for about fifteen minutes, remove them with tongs, rinse them carefully, and scrub them with a stiff brush. It may be necessary to repeat this treatment a number of times to remove the scale completely. After it has been removed,

145

the pewter may be polished in the usual way.

Another method is to use a chelating agent (Versine, Permakleer). Ask your druggist.

Phenolic There are two types of phenolic plastic, molded and cast. Molded phenolics are light in weight and very durable. They are hard to break or scratch. Limited in color to blacks and browns, they are found in the home as TV and radio cabinets, pot and iron handles, wall paneling, and other utilitarian furnishings.

Cast phenolic is decorative. It is produced in a full range of translucent, transparent, and opaque colors as well as in marbled effects. Pen desk sets, chessmen, clock cases, jewelry, teething rings, and cutlery handles are made of phenolic.

These plastics are unharmed by chemicals and by heat up to 300° F. They are not damaged by freezing temperatures. Do not subject them to high heat or place them near an open flame. They can be handwashed with very hot water containing soap or detergent, but cannot stand boiling water. Cleaning fluids do not affect them, but do not use abrasives. See also "Plastics."

Phonograph Records Tonal reproduction is impaired if phonograph records become smudged or dusty. Claude Rie, producer of high-quality discs, recommends washing them with a soft cloth moistened

with lukewarm water containing a mild detergent. Rinse them with a cloth squeezed out of clear lukewarm water and wipe dry with a lint-free cotton or linen cloth.

Piano "A fine piano is a work of art. Therefore, to treat it roughly, carelessly or negligently is to commit a crime against a beautiful piece of expensive craftsmanship. To pay a lot of money for a fine piano and then allow it to go to ruin for lack of expert care is not merely aesthetically wrong—it is bad business."

There, my friends, in three potent sentences, is the opinion of an expert on the subject of piano care. The author is Dr. William Braid White, director of acoustic research for the American Steel and Wire Company. Of what does piano care consist? The summary which follows has been compiled from information furnished by Steinway and Sons, makers of fine pianos for nearly a century.

Tuning Proper care of a piano demands at least three, and preferably four, tunings a year, during spring, summer, winter and autumn. Pianos get out of tune, whether used or not, as the result of contraction and expansion due to atmospheric changes. Tuning does not affect the tone of a piano. It simply puts the strings in unison and at the proper pitch.

Regulating In addition to tuning, a piano requires tone and action regulating, and other servicing from time to time. All pianos tend to become more brilliant with use, owing to the constant pounding of the hammer felts against the steel strings. As the felt becomes hard through this pounding, the tone becomes more brilliant. If your piano should become too brilliant, regulating will restore the desired degree of mellowness, provided there is sufficient hammer felt left. Occasional action regulating is also desirable so that the mechanisms may be smooth and responsive to the touch of the player. This is particularly desirable in damp climates, since the felt bushings in the action parts absorb moisture and swell, causing the action to become sluggish.

Location Your piano should be kept in a normal temperature and free from dampness. Dampness will cause rust on the metal parts and swelling of the action. It will also injure the finish of the case, and may raise the softer fibers of the soundboard.

Do not place your piano near steam pipes, registers or stoves, or where one end may be hot and the other cold. Do not open opposite windows of a warm room, permitting cold drafts to blow on the piano. However well the finish may have endured weather testing, it may be seriously affected by rapid changes of temperature.

Interior Have the interior of your piano cleaned from time to time. This helps to prevent damage to the fine wool felts, which are liable to attack from moths. It also prevents corrosion of the strings and pins. Ask your tuner about moth-proofing the felts and hammers.

Exterior and keys Do not use furniture polish or other preparations for polishing purposes, or any coarse fabrics on the case of a new piano. If dull, wipe it with a soft,

damp (not wet) chamois or a soft, dampened cheesecloth. Then remove the moisture with a dry, soft cloth or chamois. (If the chamois is brand-new, soak it in water for twenty-four hours before using it.) If your piano is old, with a waxed or varnished case, clean it according to directions given under "Furniture."

Do not place vases or other objects on your piano. They may leave pressure marks. Close the top when the piano is not in use, but expose the keyboard to light. Ivory turns yellow if continuously kept from the light. If the keys become dusty or dirty, wipe them lengthwise with a soft, slightly dampened cloth and then follow with a soft, dry cloth.

Precaution: If your piano is to be left in an unoccupied house for some time, place camphor where it will not affect the finish of any metal or wooden parts; place quantities of newspapers in the interior to absorb moisture and cover the top with a heavy flannel cover or blankets.

Steinway experts say that when the finish of a piano becomes scarred, checked, etc., it should be sent to the factory. There the finish will be removed down to the raw wood and the case completely refinished. Keys that have become very yellow can be removed and sent to the factory for scraping and repolishing by an ivory expert. However, their true color is not white. The ivory is specially treated and bleached. It will not remain white indefinitely.

Picture On any glass, use an aerosol window spray or any of the cleaning mixtures recommended for windows. Be careful not to let your cleaner seep between the frame and the glass and stain the picture or mat. Polish with paper towels or tissues.

Clean wooden frames by wiping them with a soft cloth wrung out of warm soapy water. Dry. Apply wax or oil polish, if desired.

Soiled gilt frames may be cleaned, if necessary, with a cloth moistened with a little dry-cleaning fluid.

See also "Gilding," "Oil Paintings," and "Water Color Paintings."

Pile Coats See "Nylon Coat."

Pilling Fiber ends of some fabrics tend to roll into little balls, or pills, which cling tightly to the surface. They are especially noticeable on sweaters. Washing and wearing increase the pilling. To minimize pilling, turn the garment inside out before washing. Some advise washing it in a mesh bag.

To remove pills, stretch the fabric snugly over a curved surface so that the pills stand up, and snip them off with a scissors. Or shave them off carefully with a safety razor.

Pillows (Down and Feather) Fluff them daily and air them at least once a month outdoors or on a chair by an open window. Fresh air puffs them up and gives them a new lease on life.

Pillows, often very neglected, are entitled to a bath now and then and this service can be performed by any first-class laundry. Laundry washing service differs from a renovating job. In renovating a pillow the feathers are removed from the ticking and washed separately. New feathers and down are then added if needed. Worn ticking will be replaced. Ask your laundryman about this service.

If you are washing your own pillows, first make sure that there are no ripped seams and that the ticking is in good condition. Loose feathers can cause trouble in a washer or dryer. If the ticking is weak, plan to replace it and wash the feathers separately in a muslin bag. Also wash separately the feathers of heavily stuffed pillows.

To transfer the feathers, rip out the stitching at one end of the pillow, baste the bag securely around the opening, and shake the feathers into the bag. Tightly baste the opening of the filled bag.

If the ticking is sound, rip the stitching in opposite corners for an inch or so, then pin up the openings with a heavy safety pin. These slits provide outlets for air. (Pillows with eyelet ventilators do not require this.)

Fill the washer with warm water, add detergent for a normal load, and agitate to dissolve it. Wash two pillows together, or one at a time with enough bath towels to balance the load. Immerse the pillows in the suds until they are thoroughly wet, then agitate the washer for 10 minutes. Repeat the wash if the pillows are very soiled, using slightly less detergent. Complete the rinsing cycles, then give the pillows an extra rinse.

Before putting the pillows in the dryer, check the corners to make sure the safety pins are secure. Tumble for about an hour at the warmest setting, then reduce the heat and tumble them until they are dry. If you are not using a dryer, hang the pillows outdoors in the shade, using 3 or more clothespins. Fluff them every half hour or so and turn them so that they will dry uniformly. If they are not dry by night, bring them inside. Rehang them outdoors in the morning.

Pillows (Other than Feather) Washing is not recommended for foam-rubber pillows, but see "Foam Rubber" for emergency action. Kapok pillows are not washable.

Polyester filled pillows (Dacron fiberfill) often carry hang tags giving special instructions for their care. Some are washable, others are not. When no instructions are given and the pillow is designed to be washable, follow these instructions.

Wash by hand in lukewarm suds made preferably with a nonsudsing detergent for easier rinsing. Compress the pillow repeatedly to create a flow of washing water through the pillow. Rinse thoroughly. (Do not wring or twist.) Remove remaining water by spinning in an automatic washing machine. Dry in a tumble-type dryer on a low temperature setting or hang it outdoors.

The "Sontique" pillow is re-fluffed after use by holding the diagonal corners and giving them a shake. If the outer ticking becomes soiled, unzip it and remove it for machine washing and drying. If the casing is durable-press, it won't need ironing. Several times a year, re-fluff the pillow batt. Remove the zippered ticking. Place the batt, still encased in its marquisette cover, in the dryer for 20 minutes at maximum temperature. Wash by hand if the pillow batt has become soiled, and machine dry.

An "Adoration" pillow can be washed by machine. Be sure that it is completely wet before you place it in the machine. Use warm water, the wash-and-wear cycle, and machine dry at the maximum temperature setting.

Piqué A white cotton fabric woven in wales or crossbars. Wash like any cotton material, starch as desired and iron on the reverse side.

Pitch See "Tar" in "Stains," p. 237.

Plaster of Paris A plaster made from calcined (dried out by heat) gypsum. When diluted with water to a thin paste it sets rapidly and, at the moment of setting, expands. Most types of earth shrink when they dry.

Plaster of Paris is valuable for filling cracks and cavities in plaster, for making surgical casts, ornaments, etc. "Patching plasters" are plaster of Paris containing retarders to keep it from setting too rapidly. Statues and other ornaments made of plaster of Paris cannot be cleaned by any satisfactory home method. They can only be dusted.

Any material used to cover the plaster may change the color and quality of the surface. However, if the piece is not valuable and it is awfully smudgy, try a very thin spray of the best covering flat white paint you can locate. Spraying paint requires considerable skill so undertake such a project with due forethought.

Plastic Coat Hangers Textile chemists recommend a thorough airing of clothes cleaned in coin-operated dry cleaning establishments. The airing can be done outdoors or in a well-ventilated room. But do not use plastic hangers for this purpose. Enough solvent may be retained in

149

shoulder pads or thick fabrics to soften the plastic. When this happens the garment sticks to the hanger and is difficult to remove without damage. The same warning applies to clothes that are exposed to the fumes of moth preventatives.

Plastic Dishes See "Melamine and Urea."

Plastic Floor Coverings See "Vinyl Floors."

Plastics Plastics is a family name like cloth or metal. Just as there are many kinds of cloth and metal, there are many kinds of plastic, each with its individual characteristics and qualifications for certain jobs.

Plastics are synthetic, or man-made, materials which have been developed by chemists in search of durable and attractive substances to take the place of the more expensive natural materials such as wood and metal. All are made from combinations of carbon with oxygen, hydrogen, nitrogen, chlorine, and sulfur. By varying the combination of these ingredients, the chemist can create a plastic to suit almost any need.

Plastics represent a billion-dollar industry, which is still growing by leaps and bounds. In addition to serving as substitutes for natural products such as wood and metal in a variety of household articles, plastics are spun into textiles and used to form dirt-, stain- and wrinkle-resisting finishes. They are used in making wet-strength paper for grocery sacks, hand towels, money, tea bags, and transparent film for protecting foods, dishes, linens, clothing, and silver. Sometimes they are an ingredient of paints and varnishes.

Plastics are divided into two main groups. Thermoplastic plastics soften when exposed to sufficient heat and harden when cooled. These include the acrylics, cellulosics, nylon, polyethylene, polystyrene and vinyls. Thermosetting plastics are plastics that are set permanently by heat into various shapes during forming. Heat applied later will not soften them. The thermosetting plastics include phenolics, amino plastics (Melamine and urea), cold-molded polyesters, silicones, and casein.

Plastics are easy to care for. All can be cleaned safely with warm water and soap and a very soft cloth. This is preferred to wiping them with a dry, or even a damp, cloth as there is a tendency for dust particles to scratch the surface of fine plastics unless they are lubricated. Soap and water provide that lubrication.

Plastic bibs, aprons, tablecloths, placemats, curtains, and raincoats can be washed by machine. Use the slowest wash and spin action. Wash from 2 to 4 minutes with warm water. Rinse with warm water.

To provide more detailed information about plastics, what they will and will not do and the special care they require, plastics in household use are listed in this book alphabetically and a reference to their family branch is given. Thus, you might look up "Lucite" and find that it is an acrylic plastic. You would then look up "Acrylic Plastics" to learn more about it.

Plastic Sheeting Articles made of washable plastic sheeting (shower curtains, storage bags, covers for furniture and equipment) benefit by a brief machine washing now and then. Warm water helps keep the plastic soft and pliable. If the sheeting has a printed pattern, test it first for color fastness. To do this, wipe a small inconspicuous area with full-strength liquid detergent on a cloth wrung out of hot water. If color comes off, do not put the article in the washer. Just sponge it with luke-warm suds.

For machine-washing colorfast washable sheeting, use warm water and a small amount of detergent. Make the washing cycle short. If the water is hard, a suitable softener (Calgon, Oakite) in the rinse water will prevent water spots. Place small articles in a mesh bag to keep them from being sucked into the pump or drain. Use slow agitation and spin speed if these controls are available. Agitate for 2 or 3 minutes, then spin off water. Do not put plastic articles through the wringer; such treatment can cause permanent creases. Just shake the water out, refill the tub with warm water, and rinse them briefly. Wipe dry with a clean towel, or hang to dry—away from sunlight and any source of heat.

Special note: If a shower curtain is mildewed, brush off as much as possible, then wipe it with a chlorine bleach solution before placing it in the washer. For a soap-filled shower curtain, use only water softener in the washing water and agitate for 5 minutes. The soap film will provide sufficient detergent. Use the softener in the rinse water too. Rehang to dry.

Plastic Stain See "Stains," p. 235.

Plastic Tile See "Polystyrene" and "Vinyl."

Platinum Platinum ranks above gold among the precious metals. It is non-tarnishing and dull silver in color. Platinum is very heavy, easily worked, and is unaffected by all simple acids. It melts only at a very high temperature. These qualities make it extremely useful in chemical and other scientific processes. It also is used for jewelry.

Platinum was first discovered in South America and takes its name from the Spanish word, *plata* (silver), because of its resemblance to that metal. There is nothing tricky about cleaning platinum. If dirty from grease, etc., simply wash it with a detergent or soap and water, rinse and dry with tissues.

See also "Jewelry."

Playing Cards Wipe plastic cards with a damp cloth. To clean paper cards wipe them carefully with a bit of cotton moistened with spirits of camphor. Dry with clean cotton.

Pleats First iron the hem, then iron the pleats from the bottom up. For a fussy job pin each pleat to the ironing pad, taking care to place the pins so that the marks won't show. On wool use a press cloth and a warm iron and set it down gently on the cloth instead of using a gliding motion. Always leave wool slightly damp for best results in pressing.

Unless directions advise a different course, hand wash dresses and skirts with permanent pleats in cool or lukewarm water. Do not scrub or twist them. Remove them sopping wet from the final rinse and place on hangers to drip dry, with zippers or other fasteners closed. Adjust pleats with your fingers.

Separate skirts should be supported in at least three places to keep the bands straight. If quick drying is desired, roll into tubular form with the pleats parallel and, beginning at the waistband, gently

151

squeeze out excess water before hanging to dry.

While hand washing gives the best results, some pleated garments are machine washable. If the label says the garment can be washed by machine, omit the water extraction cycle because it is likely to cause hard-to-remove wrinkles. Use luke-warm water (100° F.) and detergent or soap with a water softener. Rinse thoroughly. Remove the garment dripping wet before the final spin-dry cycle and drip dry as described for hand washing.

If pressing is desirable, use a steam or dry iron on the synthetic setting. Press on the reverse side, after aligning the pleats, using a dampened press cloth. Let each pressed area cool before you lift or move the garment. Dacron polyester and Orlon acrylics can be cleaned and repleated by your dry cleaner.

Plexiglas Trade name for an acrylic plastic that made its debut in World War II as the blister (nose, that is) on bombers. See "Acrylic Plastics."

Plexon Plexon is a trade name for fabrics made of cotton, linen, synthetic and other yarns that have been treated with a fine plastic coating to give them extreme durability and make them immune to moisture, fading, stains, and chemicals. Plexon can be made resistant to almost any chemical, as specified. Similarly the thickness of the coating can be varied, as desired.

Plexon fabrics are nonflammable to self-extinguishing. They are damaged little by age or sunlight and are impervious to mildew and moths. Weak alkalies and acids affect them only slightly. Strong acids and alkalies vary from "no effect" to "decomposition," depending on the coating. Acetone, ethyl acetate, and other lacquer solvents should be avoided.

Plexon is used for draperies, upholstery, handbags, shoes, lamp shades and fashion accessories. Clean it by wiping it with a damp cloth or with a cloth wrung out of warm suds, made with soap or a detergent. Rinse.

Plum See "Fruit and Berry" in "Stains," p. 228.

Plumbing Better leave major repairs to a competent plumber, but do you know how to shut off your main water supply in case of a leak? Nice to know.

See "Sink" and "Drains."

Plush See "Upholstery."

Pokeberry See "Fruit and Berry" in "Stains," p. 228.

Polyester Polyester is a generic term used in classifying synthetic textile fibers according to their composition. In this group the fiber-forming substance is obtained mainly from dihydric alcohol and terephthalic acid.

Polyester textiles and their blends are notable because, correctly laundered, they do not require ironing. Their popularity for suits and dresses is still soaring. Polyester curtains are outstanding for their daintiness and ease of care. Sales of no-iron cotton-polyester sheets and pillow cases are zooming.

Polyester fibers are crisp to the touch, resilient, resistant to moisture and thus to stretching or sagging in damp weather. The first polyester fiber (Terylene) was developed in England. Its American manufacture began in 1951, as Dacron. Polyester textiles are sold under various other trade names such as Avlin, Dacron, Encron, Fortrel, Kodel, Quintess, Spectran, Textura, Trevira, Zefran, Allied Chemical, Beaunit, and IRC.

Polyester textiles are comfortable to wear, dry quickly, and require no ironing. They range from suitings and knitwear to dress materials, and sheers for blouses, lingerie, and curtains. Polyesters are heat sensitive; hot cigarette ashes will burn holes in them. And they tend to accumulate static electricity. Blends with other materials decrease their sensitivity to heat. Antistatics will minimize the static electricity charge.

When dealing with clothing made of 100 percent polyester or with cotton blends, follow any special directions given by the manufacturer. Polyesters can be dry-cleaned by standard processes or washed by directions given under "Wash and Wear"—warm water, no rough handling, and drip dry. If touch-up ironing should be needed, use a low-temperature (rayon) setting. Use any bleach. See also "Curtains."

Polyethylene Versatile polyethylene may be rigid, semi-rigid, a film, or a coating. Semi-rigid polyethylene remains flexible even under refrigeration. It is so light in weight that it will float on water. Polyethylene is unbreakable even when dropped or crushed. In texture it is waxy, except as film, when it has a satiny transparent finish. Colors range the spectrum scale and may be translucent or opaque.

Polyethylene is used to make ice-cube trays that can be twisted to eject the ice, refrigerator food containers and mixing bowls that can be pinched to form pouring spouts, and bottles that can be squeezed. It is also used to make frozen food wraps that can be sealed without heat, refrigerator food bags, storage boxes, flashlights, pipe, and kitchenware.

Qualities which recommend polyethylene for the uses listed are that it resists heat and freezing, that it is impenetrable to water though it allows oxygen to pass through, and that it is not damaged by food acids and common chemicals. It is odorless, tasteless, and nontoxic.

Articles made of polyethylene can be hand-washed with very hot water and soap or detergent. Brief contacts with boiling water during use will not harm such articles, but they should not be subjected to high heat or direct flames. Do not let cleaning fluids contact polyethylene; some cause damage. Do not use abrasives. Can go into the dishwasher. See also "Plastics."

Polystyrene Polystyrene is a rigid plastic, seen in clear, colorless, transparent form and in a full range of transparent, opaque, and translucent colors. An odd characteristic is that it produces a metallic sound when tapped with a spoon. Like the acrylics, polystyrene is able to pick up light and transmit it unseen, even around curves, to an opposite edge or groove.

Polystyrene is light in weight and unaffected by freezing temperatures, but not designed for outdoor use. It does not absorb moisture and is odorless, tasteless, and nontoxic. The usual run of household acids, oils, and alcohol do not harm it, but keep cleaning fluids, gasoline, nail polish and polish remover, turpentine, acetone, and citrus rinds away. (Only the rinds are injurious; the juices cause no harm.)

Like all thermoplastics, polystyrene should not be subjected to high heat. It should never go into an oven or over a flame. Handle it with normal precautions, avoiding sharp knocks and twisting.

Polystyrene is used for rigid refrigerator boxes, canisters, storage boxes, picnicware, toys, refrigerator door liners and bins, lighting fixtures, costume jewelry, and housings for radios, phonographs, and air conditioners.

Hand-wash polystyrene with warm water and mild soap. Do not use abrasives. See also "Plastics."

Pongee In Chinese pongee is called *punki* (our loom). It is a soft washable silk woven from filaments prepared from wild silkworms. The care of pongee is described under "Silk."

Porcelain Porcelain is a term correctly applied to the finest type of ceramic ware (china), having a translucent body and, if glazed, a transparent glaze also. It originated in China, where it is mentioned in books of the Han Dynasty as early as 206 to 220 B.C. Chinese porcelains reached their peak of perfection in the Ming Dynasty during the fourteenth century. The base was a special clay called kaolin. Early European porcelains were attempted imitations of the hard Oriental porcelains so greatly admired in dishes and ornaments imported from the Far East.

The term porcelain is applied loosely today in less glamorous fields. Enamelware pots and pans, as well as kitchen and bathroom fixtures, are frequently called porcelain. So-called porcelain enamel is a clay mixture, molded in casts and baked. Enamelware is enamel, or glass, fused on steel at a high temperature. Vitreous china is made of fine china clay and is prepared like porcelain enamel.

See "China," "Enamelware," "Sink," etc.

Porcelain Cleaners Among cleaners made especially to remove stains from porcelain are Dip-It, M-E Cleaner, and Maid-Easy, sold in department and hardware stores. These can be used on melamine plastic dinnerware as well as on china. Follow the directions on the container. Baking soda, often useful in removing tea and coffee stains from china, is not effective for plastics, but sodium perborate and the commercial products listed do a good job.

Pots and Pans Avoid harsh abrasives, metal scrapers, and rough handling that could cause dents. Do not let gas flames lick up the sides and cause heat stains. Do not store foods in metal or enameled cooking utensils because salt and acids damage some of them. Do not run cold water into a hot pan; such treatment can warp a metal pan and crack glass or earthenware. To remove stuck food, put cold water in the pan and let it stand until the food is soft. If food has burned, boil water in the pan. Add (except for aluminumware, which it darkens) about two teaspoons of baking soda per quart of water. For specific instructions, see "Aluminum," "Copper," "Steel—*Stainless*," etc.

Nonstick cookware is mainly achieved by fluorocarbon resins such as Teflon, discovered at the du Pont laboratories. Sometimes silicones are used. Abrasive materials should

154

not be used on either type. Instructions from du Pont for cookware with Teflon-enamel linings follow:

Pretreatment Wash the new utensil in hot suds, rinse, and wipe dry. Lightly grease the nonstick surfaces of skillets, griddles, and bakeware (except angel-cake pans) with cooking oil.

Use Temperatures over 450° F. cause discoloration; avoid them. Light greasing is recommended for pans used to bake foods containing sugar or fruit. This facilitates the removal of fragile cakes, encourages even browning, and improves flavor.

Washing Wash pans thoroughly after use; do not merely swish them under a faucet. If there is a stubborn spot, use a nylon mesh dish pad or rubber scraper. Never use steel wool, metal sponges, or scouring powder. Thorough cleaning prevents the buildup of a greasy film which could impair the nonstick quality of the pan. Teflon-lined cookware can go into the dishwasher, provided that such treatment will not damage the exterior. Uncoated parts of the pan can be cleaned by the usual method.

Scratches do not impair the nonstick quality of the coating. Hairline scratches will not widen and the coating will not peel off. Only the appearance of the pan is affected. To avoid scratches, use metal accessories with a light touch or, better yet, use Teflon-plastic utensils.

Stains, unless allowed to build up, do not impair the finish. Commercial preparations (Dip-It, S-T Teflon Cleaner) are offered on the market. If you use them, follow the directions on the label. The following home remedy often does the trick. Prepare a solution in these proportions: 1 cup of water, 2 tablespoons of baking soda, and ½

cup of chlorine bleach. Put enough of this solution in the pan to cover the stain and boil it for 5–10 minutes. Wash, rinse, and dry the pan. Before using it again, wipe it with cooking oil. (This solution may lighten the color of the lining. If it boils over, it may stain the outside of the pan.)

Refinishing Damaged Teflon linings should be replaced only by a professional. (See also "Teflon.")

Pottery One of the two main classifications of ceramics. Pottery includes earthenware, stoneware, queensware, salt glaze, etc. The Anglo-Saxon earthenware, a soft pottery covered with glaze, finds its counterpart in delft (The Netherlands), faïence (France) and majolica (Italy).

Glazed and partially glazed pottery can be hand-washed in warm, mild suds, but don't let it soak. Unglazed pottery can be dusted only.

Powder-Post Beetles These beetles tunnel through the frames and floors of houses and through furniture, weakening the wood. Their larvae feed on wood cellulose and increase the damage. Powder-post beetles, which include the old house borer, are of many kinds, varying from ⅛ of an inch to 1 inch in length. Some attack hardwoods, others softwoods, and still others prefer bamboo. Their presence is indicated by holes up to ⅜ of an inch in diameter in the wood, by little piles of borings near the holes or on the floor below ceiling beams, and by the presence of the beetles themselves.

If you think your house is infested with these pests, consult a reliable exterminator. You may be

155

able to take care of a light infestation yourself, if it is easily accessible, by spraying with a surface spray containing lindane. See "Insecticides" for precautions.

Preshrunk If the label says the garment, or yard goods, you are buying is "preshrunk," look further to see how much residual shrinkage is left. If the residual shrinkage is stipulated as 2 percent or less, you are safe. If more than 2 percent, the fit of the garment may be spoiled by washing or pressing. Preshrunk finishes do not harm texture or color. Actually they strengthen textile fibers. Wash according to directions for the fabric, as wool, cotton, linen, etc.

Stores will sometimes shrink woolens bought by the yard, which have not been previously treated. If not, do it yourself by pressing them with a steam iron and a press cloth, or roll them in a damp sheet, allow them to remain until thoroughly moist, then press. Clipping the selvage at intervals makes for even shrinking.

"Sanforized" is a trade-mark of a special type of preshrinking.

Press Cloth See "Woolens."

Pressure Cooker Wash your pressure cooker or canner after each use but do not immerse the cover in water to avoid damaging the dial gauge and possibly clogging the vents. Wipe the cover with a soapy cloth, and rinse it with a clean damp one. To clean the openings in the cover, draw a string or pipe cleaner through them. Carefully wash the gasket. Removable petcocks and safety valves should be washed, dried, and replaced. For an

156

occasional special cleaning, soak these parts in vinegar, then wash and dry them. Ball-and-socket arrangements should be cleaned now and then with silver polish.

If steam escapes from a source other than a weight-type gauge, examine the sealing edges of the vessel and the cover. If they are not smooth, rub them with a fine cleaning powder. Reversing the gasket sometimes helps, but if the gasket is worn or stretched get a new one from your dealer or manufacturer.

Should you remove the gauge from the cover, replace it carefully. A little plumber's paste (preferably with an oil or graphite base) on the threads will prevent steam leakage. Gauges that seem not to register accurately should be checked locally or packed carefully and sent with a letter to the maintenance department of the factory that made the cooker. If the gauge cannot be repaired, you can get a new one.

Canners should be stored clean and dry at the end of the season. Coat the threads of the thumbscrews with petroleum jelly (Vaseline) or salt-free cooking oil to avoid rust. Place crumpled newspaper inside to absorb moisture. Wrap the cover with paper and invert it on the kettle.

Pressurized Cans Pressurized containers with push-button controls dispense their contents as a mist, spray, powder, or foam. They depend for their activity upon compressed gases, which serve as propellants. Such cans should never be punctured, or thrown into a fire or incinerator. They should not be stored in any place where the temperature may reach 125° F.—near radiators, stoves, or in direct sunlight. Keep them out of the reach of children.

Printer's Ink See "Ink" in "Stains," p. 230.

Psocids See "Book Lice."

Pumice A spongy, porous stone tossed out by volcanoes. It is usually a form of obsidian, should you be curious, containing from 60 to 75 percent silica. Pumice is a good scourer and polisher. It can be obtained in powdered form in varying degrees of fineness, at paint and hardware stores. Many commercial scouring powders contain pumice.

Putty Putty is a kind of paste made by mixing whiting, or soft carbonate of lime, with linseed oil. Putty is used to seal windowpanes and to fill cracks in wood that is to be painted.

Putty Powder Powdered tin oxide, a fine powder used for polishing glass, steel and jewels. It is sometimes called jeweler's putty.

Pyrex Trade name for heat-resistant glassware used in cooking. See "Glass."

Qiana Qiana is du Pont's trade name for a luxurious nylon fiber that looks and feels like silk. When combined with nonwashable materials such as silk linings and decorations, it should be dry-cleaned

only. Garments marked washable can be machine-washed in warm water with a detergent. Tumble dry at a low to medium temperature. When the dryer stops, remove the garment immediately. Or use warm water with a detergent. and remove from the final rinse, without spinning, to drip dry. For hand washing, use warm water with a detergent, and drip dry. Press with a steam iron on the wool setting.

Quartz The term quartz covers a range of lovely gems, all forms of native silica. In its crystallized form quartz will scratch glass and will not melt in the flames of a blowtorch.

Quartz may be clear and colorless, or it may be tinted in delicate colors. When colorless it is called "rock crystal" or "Lake George diamonds." Pink quartz is known as rose quartz, purple or bluish violet as amethyst. There are also milk quartz (milk-white), smoky quartz (smoky yellow or brown), yellow (or false topaz), agate, onyx, etc. In Japan beautiful spheres of quartz several inches in diameter are found.

Aside from its value as a jewel, quartz has many uses, varying from making spectrum analyses to manufacturing sandpaper, glass, and porcelain.

See "Jewelry."

Quilt Cotton quilts that are well stitched and made of colorfast fabrics can be washed like blankets and do not require ironing, provided they are hung very straight on a taut line. They are heavy to handle when wet.

If you send them to a commercial laundry be sure that you select

157

a reliable one and that your quilt is marked for special attention. Otherwise you may have a ruined heirloom.

See "Blanket (Woolen)."

Quintess See "Polyester."

Radiator Radiators are difficult to clean thoroughly, but this must be done regularly, especially during the heating season, to avoid soil and stains on the walls behind and above them. Heat carries the dust up and spreads it over paint and wallpaper.

Most vacuum cleaners are provided with a device for cleaning radiators, which does a pretty fair job. The dust is sucked out; or you can reverse the action and blow it out and down onto a newspaper, dampened to make the dust cling. A good radiator brush, however, does the most thoroughgoing job.

Radiators should be cleaned once a week during the heating season, less often during the summer.

Radiator Valve If you have steam heat and want to get the maximum in comfort and value from the fuel you burn, try this on your radiator valves. It is best to do it before the furnace is turned on for the season. Or you can do a few valves at a time.

First ascertain that the wooden

knob on each radiator is turned to the off position. Then unscrew the valves. Place them in an enameled kettle containing a solution of water and washing soda (or water and trisodium phosphate). Use about one tablespoon to each quart of water. Bring to a boil and boil for several minutes. Remove the valves from the kettle; shake the water out of each gently, rinse and return the valves to the radiators. Turn the knobs to on, and sit back to enjoy hearing them whistle and "perk."

Heating experts recommend a boiling up of this sort once a year, but few people seem to have heard of it. Often when you might think you need new valves a cleaning is all that is required.

Petcocks on hot water radiators incidentally, should be opened several times each heating season to draw off air which accumulates at the top. (Newer types do not require this.)

Raincoats Some raincoats are "waterproof," others merely "water-repellent." To be actually waterproof, no water must come through the material, however sopping the rain (rubber, pliofilm). Water-repellent coats resist dampness and consist of a closely woven fabric, which has been treated with Zelan or some other water-resisting formula. Some of these, including Zelan, retain their water-repellent properties in dry cleaning. Others must be reprocessed at the dry-cleaning plant. Unless otherwise specified on the label, always have raincoats dry-cleaned. Rainwear of synthetic materials can often be washed.

General good care includes the following pointers. Keep raincoats away from excessive heat and be sure that they are thoroughly dry and the fabric smooth before putting them away. Hang rubberized coats on a hook by means of the hanger sewed inside, not on a coat hanger. Mend breaks by taking a small piece of fabric from the hem or buckle end of the belt and securing it to the back of the break with rubber cement.

Clean plastic raincoats with a damp cloth and soap or mild detergent. Water repellents in aerosol form are available at department stores. If you use them, follow the directions on the label.

Range See "Gas Range," "Electric Range," etc.

Raspberry See "Fruit and Berry" in "Stains," p. 228.

Rats When old barns or other buildings are torn down, rats which have infested them sometimes invade neighboring homes in large numbers, in search of shelter and food. If you are ever confronted by such a situation, your best course will be to call in a professional exterminator. Cornered, rats will attack people and pets. They also transmit diseases.

For occasional invaders, use spring traps, poisoned baits, or both. Red squill and the anticoagulants listed under "Mice" are relatively safe poisons. Red squill is a single-dose poison for Norway rats only—the ones that tunnel through the ground under floors and foundations. Anticoagulants are multiple-dose poisons that kill all kinds. Sometimes it is a good idea to use both types. The use of anticoagulants and effective baits for rodents are described under "Mice."

Both types of poison can be bought in seed stores and drugstores in ready-to-use form or as powders to be mixed with bait at home. Follow exactly the directions given for the rat killer you buy. Keep it out of reach of children and pets. Dispose of dead rats promptly and safely.

Red squill is usually mixed with freshly ground meat or fish. Anticoagulants are mixed with dry baits such as cornmeal or rolled oats. Other, more virulent, poisons are effective rodenticides but they should be used only by a professional exterminator.

Rats enter homes in search of food, shelter, and water. Do not encourage them by allowing trash to accumulate. Keep garbage in tightly covered metal cans and do not leave food exposed. Close off all holes in the exterior walls of your home and check doors and screens for holes and rips. Leave no space more than ¼ of an inch around windows, doors, and other openings.

If rats are a neighborhood problem ask for help from your local board of health.

Rayon Rayon, the first synthetic textile fiber, emerged from the test tube in Europe and appeared on the market there in 1902. It dates to laboratory attempts, begun as early as the seventeenth century, to create artificial silk. Chardonnet, a French scientist, was finally successful in producing a reasonable facsimile. Rayon today is sometimes called a semisynthetic, in contrast to newer fibers that are completely chemical. It is derived from cellulose, present in nearly all plant life. Wood pulp and cotton linters are mainly used.

Rayon textiles have many advantages. They are water-absorbent, nonstatic, and can be dyed with exceptional colorfastness in a wide variety of shades, from delicate pastels to brilliant hues. While all are derived from cellulose, the methods used to produce them are different and the fibers which result are very different too.

Viscose rayon is the original rayon. To make it, pure cellulose is converted into a thick, viscous solution by chemical treatment. The solution is pumped through a spinneret, a small metal disc with many tiny holes, into a hardening bath where the filaments coagulate. Each minute hole spins a filament. Viscose rayon is a versatile fiber, sturdy, and equal to many tasks. It is soft to the touch, drapes well, and can be dyed in a wide range of colors that are very fast to light. Viscose is used for suitings, carpets, blankets, sports and dress fabrics, voiles, blends, knitted fabrics, velvet, and plush. These rayons absorb and hold moisture, an advantage or disadvantage, depending on their use. They dry slowly, and are attacked by mildew and rot fungi, but not by insects.

Cuprammonium rayon is made from purified cellulose dissolved in a solution containing a copper and ammonia compound. It is similar to viscose, but its fibers are extremely soft, not quite as tough, and less resistant to heat. Cuprammonium rayon is used for lightweight dress fabrics, sheers, crêpes, marquisettes, voiles, gloves, hosiery, and upholstery cloth. All rayon of this type is sold under the trade name Bemberg.

Rayon fabrics can be dry-cleaned or hand-washed, depending upon construction, finish, and dyes. Look inside for the label. If hand-washed,

treat them gently because the fibers tend to be weak when wet. If washing instructions are not given, or are incomplete, follow the directions given for acetates. See "Acetate."

Reed See "Furniture."

Refrigerator Self-defrosting refrigerators, in normal use, need to be cleaned about once a year. Those with ice-freezing compartments need attention when the ice on the coils is from one-quarter to one-half inch thick. At this time it may be cleaned if it needs it. Gas refrigerators need a little special attention.

Not self-defrosting Unplug your refrigerator or set the thermostat in the off position. Remove the food from the shelves and the ice from the trays. Never use a sharp or pointed instrument for the refrigerator; it may result in damage to the cooling coils. Use of a plastic scraper is recommended.

To hurry the defrosting, place pans of hot water in the frozen food storage compartment. This is the quick defrost method. It should be used when ice cream or other perishable foods are in the refrigerator.

Wash the chiller tray in warm soda water (1 tablespoon of baking soda to 1 quart of water). Wipe the frozen food storage compartment with a damp cloth, rinse, and wipe dry. Remove vegetables and wipe up spills in the bottom of the refrigerator.

The overnight defrosting method is used when no frozen foods or ice cream are being stored. Proceed as directed but with the thermostatic control on defrost.

Keep your refrigerator door closed. Moderate refrigeration continues.

The outside of the refrigerator should be cleaned with a liquid or paste wax recommended for use on electric appliances or with mild soap and water. Do not use oily furniture polish, cleaning powders, or alkaline soaps. Raise the condenser at the bottom of the refrigerator and clean with a broom or vacuum cleaner.

Self-defrosting Refrigerator and freezer sections should be cleaned at least once a year. Preferably have the machine disconnected or the thermostat turned off. Use warm water and baking soda (1 tablespoon per quart of water). Rinse with warm water and wipe dry. Clean the door gaskets, vegetable crisper, and all plastic parts the same way. Wash the ice trays and ice-water bucket in lukewarm water only. If there is a drain plug under the vegetable crisper, remove it and flush it out with soda-water solution and a brush.

When moving your refrigerator pull the cabinet straight out and push it straight in. Moving it sideways can cause damage to floor covering by rollers.

The defrost pan, located behind the grille at the bottom of the refrigerator, should be cleaned at least once a year, and oftener if food is spilled in the freezer section. For efficient operation, remove the grille and sweep up or vacuum the dust that is readily accessible behind it. Then pull out the flat tray and pan and clean them.

On **gas refrigerators,** to assure maximum efficiency, the burner compartment (usually at the bottom) should be cleaned occasionally and also the top louver assembly, on the top of the cabinet at the back. Use a vacuum cleaner attachment or a damp cloth. Special attention should be given the top louver since dust tends to accumulate on the underneath side where it is likely not to be noticed. Use a knife blade wrapped in cloth, or, for a really thorough job, remove the screws which hold the louver assembly and lift it out for cleaning. While this is out, clean the finned section underneath with a vacuum cleaner attachment. It is important, in gas refrigerators, that the top louver be unobstructed at all times so that air may flow underneath, through the burner compartment, up the back and out of the top louver. Otherwise, clean like electric refrigerator.

Note: Refrigerator models differ in many respects but these three samples are typical. If there is something that puzzles you about your refrigerator, send its model number to the factory and ask for a booklet.

Registers Hot-air registers are dust catchers and distributors and should be cleaned once a week while the furnace is in operation. Lift out the grating, place it on a dampened newspaper and clean it with a brush or vacuum cleaner attachment. Clean the opening of the shaft also.

Reinforced Polyesters These rugged plastics invite outdoor use. In this group the plastic is combined with other materials which give it great strength.

Reinforced polyesters can be produced in all colors, transparent or opaque. They are very difficult to

161

scratch and can be made as strong as needed. Such plastics resist the penetration of water and are not affected by freezing temperatures.

Reinforced polyesters are used for luggage, awnings, roofing, wall partitions, light panels, lamp shades, fishing rods, and chairs. Since they vary in the chemicals they will stand, it is necessary to check the labels and instruction tags on merchandise.

Wash these plastics, when required, with warm water and soap or detergent. They are not damaged by cleaning fluids, but keep abrasives away. Do not place them near an open flame. See also "Plastics."

Resin For resin stains see "Stains," p. 236.

Rhinestone An artificial stone made of paste (a kind of fine and brilliant glass). Rhinestones were first made at Strasbourg and were named for the River Rhine. See "Jewelry."

Roaches See "Cockroaches."

Roaster See "Electric Roaster."

Rotary Ironer When the ironing has been completed and before the motor has been cut off, release the hot shoe from the roll so that it will not scorch the cover and padding.

The surface of the ironer shoe should be washed with a cloth squeezed out of suds. This will remove any traces of starch. Dry and rewax it, using paraffin or beeswax. Keep the muslin cover clean. To replace it, after laundering, move the shoe away from the roll and heat the shoe to normal ironing temperature. Unroll the undercover

for about six inches and place one edge of the roll under it. Rewind the undercover back over the muslin cover and move the shoe against the roll. Iron the cover on, smoothing it with the palms of the hands. When the cover has been completely ironed on, stop the ironer. Pull up the drawstrings at each end, tie them securely and tuck them under the ends of the roll.

Air the roll padding every three months. To do this remove the muslin roll cover and unwind the undercover back to where it is attached to the padding and let it air for several hours in the open air and sunlight. (Do not loosen the padding from the roll for this operation.)

To avoid scratching the shoe, keep hooks and eyes, buttons, etc., toward the roll as much as possible. In ironing, use the full length of the roll as much as possible and iron small articles alternately at the ends. This tends to keep the padding firm and even and helps prevent the ends of the roll cover from being scorched.

If your ironer has been permanently lubricated at the factory, you will never have to oil it. Consult your dealer if you are uncertain about this.

Rottenstone A soft stone, sometimes called Tripoli after the country from which it was originally obtained. Powdered rottenstone is used for all sorts of finer grinding and polishing in the arts. Mixed with linseed oil (see "Linseed Oil") it will remove white spots and other light blemishes from furniture. The mixture is applied lightly with a soft cloth, following the grain of the wood. See "Furniture."

Rouge Cleaning and polishing rouge is a red powder, consisting of peroxide of iron. It is used to polish gems, metal, glass, etc. Treated cloths, sold for polishing silver, often are impregnated with jeweler's rouge.

Routine A household routine is nice to have because it helps you to finish quickly. It should be sufficiently elastic, however, to enable you to meet emergencies and special occasions.

Rovana Rovana is a textile, which is described as a saran microtape. Combined with Verel and rayon, Rovana provides outstandingly fire-resistant material for hospital and home draperies, and other items. These can be dry-cleaned, but tell your dry cleaner what the material is.

Washable Rovana can be machine-washed with a neutral (mild) soap or detergent and plenty of cool water. Rinse in cool water (high level), stopping the machine during draining and filling. Extract the rinse water by bringing the extractor immediately to full speed, then turning it off. Tumble dry for 20 to 30 minutes at a temperature between 140° to 160° F., and remove the article immediately after drying. If these instructions are followed, Rovana should not need ironing.

Rubber Articles made of natural rubber can be kept clean with soap and water. The addition of a little ammonia helps. Rinse them carefully and be sure they are perfectly dry before you store them. Or you can clean them with alcohol.

Rubber is damaged by heat, light, cleaning fluids, oil, grease, tar, and copper. Heat, including sunlight (unless the rubber has been prepared to resist it), cracks and weakens rubber, making it sticky and inert. Grease, oil, and tar, if left in contact long, are absorbed, causing the rubber to swell and weaken. Standard cleaning fluids can be used to remove grease, oil, and tar, and small articles can be soaked in them, but not for more than 2 or 3 minutes. Rubber gloves, worn to protect the hands while polishing copper or brass, or when using copper filament scouring balls, become soft and sticky at first, then hard and brittle. (Gloves of synthetic rubber stand chemical cleaners and cleaning fluids better and are not damaged by oil or grease.) Wash and powder with talc both types after each use.

Store rubber articles in a cool, dark place. Be sure they are clean and dry and, if they are to be folded, dust the surfaces that will touch with talcum powder or cornstarch. Blow a little air into hot water bottles, ice packs, neck collars, etc., replace the caps, and put them in boxes, preferably the ones they came in. Store rubber tubing loosely coiled and free of kinks.

163

Boots, rubbers, and galoshes should be washed off with water, or soap and water, to remove dirt and mud. Wipe them dry, or dry them in a cool, airy place. When you store them, stuff crumpled newspapers loosely inside to preserve their shape.

Sheets, raincoats, and other articles of rubber-coated cloth can be spread on a table and scrubbed with warm suds and a soft brush. Rinse them with a cloth wrung from plain warm water and hang them to dry in a cool, airy place. Avoid chlorine bleaches.

Cold and hot patches for mending rubber can be bought at department and hardware stores and at service stations. See also "Garden Tools," "Girdles," "Rubber Tile."

Rubber Cement See "Glue, Mucilage, Adhesives" in "Stains," p. 228.

Rubber Tile Floors of rubber tile should be swept or dusted with an untreated mop or vacuum cleaner brush. Wash them with a synthetic detergent or mild soap and lukewarm water plus a little ammonia or other water softener. Proceed as for linoleum, cleaning a small area at a time with a soft cloth, sponge or mop, well wrung out. Rinse with clear, lukewarm water. Continue to an adjoining area until the surface has been cleaned.

For a very soiled floor, use your cleaner in a stronger dilution or use warm water and washing soda or trisodium phosphate. (One to two tablespoons to a pail of water.) Use steel wool or scouring powder on stubborn spots. Rinse well with a cloth, sponge, or mop wrung out of clear warm water.

Paste waxes can be used on high-grade rubber tile, but may damage inexpensive rubber floors. If you are uncertain, use only self-polishing wax. Waxing is optional.

Ruby Strange as it may seem, this clear, rich red, highly prized jewel is a variety of corundum, that humble agent used for grinding and polishing gems. A ruby of good red color ranks above the diamond in value. A fine gem of from one to three carats in weight sells for a price from three to ten times that of a diamond of similar weight and quality. The finest rubies (pigeon's blood) come from Upper Burma.

Synthetic rubies, first produced in 1894 by the French chemist Verneuil, have many of the characteristics of genuine rubies, but the grain runs in curved, rather than straight, lines and the color is more carmine. Such rubies are made by mixing, as a powder, the chemical elements of the true stone, then melting them under very intense heat.

For the care of jewelry starring rubies see "Jewelry."

Rug See "Carpets and Rugs."

Rug Anchor Small rugs can be a safety hazard, especially on waxed floors, if precautions have not been taken to make them skidproof. Manufacturers, recognizing this, often provide them with a rubberized backing.

For rugs not provided with anchorage, products are available which you can apply yourself. These include sprays which are applied to the back of the rug, sprinkle-on powders that are dusted on the floor, and paint-on adhesives.

Also available are rubber or rubberized underlays. These may lose some of their adhesive quality after a while when used on waxed floors. If they seem discouraged and listless, wash them with a synthetic detergent or with warm soapy water containing a little ammonia, rinse them with warm water, and allow them to dry. They will then resume their anchoring duties efficiently.

Rug Cushions Rug cushions give floors a lush feeling and prolong the life of rugs and carpets. They should be cleaned thoroughly twice a year . . . on both sides. Use a vacuum cleaner if you have one. The rug attachment does a thoroughgoing job, but use the brush and that lightly on loosely matted types.

You are smart if you bought mothproof cushions. If not, examine them periodically for signs of moths and other insect pests.

Running Colors See "Dyes" in "Stains," p. 228.

Rust Preparations to prevent the formation of rust on iron and steel can be bought at hardware stores. Rust removers also are available.

Important to remember: If oxidation (rust formation) has begun, no matter how slight the degree, it will continue under any coating. So be sure the surface to be protected is both bright and thoroughly dry before filming it over. To remove oxidation, scour with an abrasive or steel wool. Kerosene helps, too.

Rust stains in bathtubs and sinks can be prevented by eliminating leaky faucets. For the removal of rust stains from plumbing fixtures see "Bathtub." For rust stains on fabrics see "Iron Rust" in "Stains," p. 231.

Salad Dressing See "Combination Stains," p. 223.

Sandwich Grill See "Electric Sandwich Grill."

Sanforized A trade name. See "Preshrunk."

Sanitizer See "Disinfectant."

Sapphire See "Quartz" and "Jewelry."

Saran Saran is a synthetic textile, classified as a vinylidene chloride, which is derived by chemical processes from salt and petroleum. It is a very durable fabric, used for upholstery, seat covers for cars, outdoor furniture, carpets, curtains, shoes, luggage, and handbags. Saran is available in many colors and in a wide array of patterns and weaves.

This fabric is very water-resistant and is not affected by age. Moths and mildew will not attack it. It is highly resistant to acids and alkalies (except ammonia) and to most other chemicals, including acetone and the common solvents. A rugged fabric, saran resists scuffing, tearing and snagging. While it will not stand great heat, it is self-extinguishing if ignited. Its colors are lasting, being built into the material.

Saran is easy to clean. Just wipe it with a damp cloth, or with a cloth wrung out of warm suds. If dirt or other matter has worked down into the weave and left a mark, use a good stiff brush, slightly dampened with soapsuds. Do not use too wet a cloth, or brush, in cleaning saran as the water may seep through the weave

165

and wet the material underneath.

Under very dry atmospheric conditions saran may accumulate a static electrical charge, like fine pile rugs. To eliminate this simply wipe the surface with a cloth thoroughly saturated with a strong solution of a synthetic detergent.

Saran plastic film is useful as a protective wrapping for foods, linens, china, and silver.

Schedule Any woman who wants to have time for special activities and hobbies must have a working schedule. Otherwise she will be continually at loose ends and her work never finished. Hit-or-miss housekeeping results in frazzled nerves, ineffective work, wasted time, cross children and unpleasant husbands. On the other hand, don't make your schedule so detailed and exact that you are hard pressed to follow it. Block in the main things.

Should your schedule hopelessly elude you, do not attempt to catch up with it. Sit tight for a few days and let it come round to you.

The old jingle, incidentally, goes: Wash on Monday, iron on Tuesday, mend on Wednesday, upstairs Thursday, downstairs Friday, bake on Saturday, church on Sunday. Turn it around any way you want, but do have a plan.

Scorch See "Stains," p. 236.

Scorpions Scorpians are arachnids of varying size—lobsterish in appearance—which are found in some parts of the South. Sometimes they enter homes. They live on spiders and insects and do not ordinarily sting people unless they are disturbed. During the day they hide in closets, folded blankets, shoes,

etc.; at night they seek water. Their sting is painful, sometimes fatal.

To keep scorpions out of the home, or to destroy those that have entered it, use a household surface spray containing lindane. Spray baseboards, window and door casings, and the foundation of the house. For added protection, in an infested neighborhood, spray the lower parts of tree trunks, stumps, piles of lumber, and rock walls. For this, use a water-based spray because oil-based sprays are harmful to plants. See "Insecticides" for precautions.

Do not keep a children's sandbox if you live in an area where there are scorpions. Call your doctor instantly if anyone is stung. The first six hours are the most crucial.

Scouring Powder See "Abrasive."

Scratches See "Furniture" and "Floors."

Screens See "Window Screens" and "Andirons and Fire Tools."

Sealers For surface protection and ease of maintenance, modern floors of various types are often finished with special preparations known as sealers. Sealers for wooden floors are more durable than varnish, shellac, and similar finishes because they penetrate the wood and do not tend to crack or peel. Other sealers are made for stone, cement, tile, marble, brick, etc. Such sealers are often applied to floors when they are laid, or they may be applied by home owners when renovating or refinishing floors. It is important to use the right type. For information about sealers consult a top specialist in flooring, or write to the manufacturer of your particular type of floor.

Seersucker Wash untreated seersuckers according to the directions given for white and colored cottons. Ironing is not required, provided the garment is hung carefully. Smooth the hem and seams of dresses and hang them on rustproof coat hangers. Pad the shoulders with tissue paper for a fussy job; otherwise make sure the material is smooth and straight for drying. If you still want to iron it, iron when practically dry and on the wrong side. Seersuckers with resin finishes need no special treatment but don't use a chlorine bleach.

SEF See "Modacrylic."

Septic Tank Septic tanks and cesspools are country arrangements for the disposal of sewage in areas not served by a municipal sewage system. They differ in construction but their basic idea is the same. Both depend, for satisfactory functioning, upon the action of bacteria upon waste matter. The main thing to know about these installations is that they require professional cleaning about every three years. This you had best not forget, or you may find yourself in serious trouble.

Shades See "Window Shades."

Shellac See "Floors" and "Stains," p. 236.

Shoes Your shoes will look better and last longer if you take these precautions: Be sure they fit when you buy them. Use shoe trees or

toe cushions (for sandals). Keep the heels from running over and wear rubbers when it's wet.

Run-over heels not only look sloppy and make your feet ache but throw the whole shoe out of shape so that shoe trees could hardly be expected to remedy the damage. Going without rubbers when it rains makes the leather stretch and the soles bulge at the seams.

Shoes should be kept clean and polished with the proper dressing. Remove any oil or grease spots with cleaning fluid on a soft cloth and brush them well before polishing or dressing.

Wet leather shoes should be stuffed with paper to hold their shape while drying and should not be placed near heat. A little castor oil, rubbed into the uppers and soles of slick leather shoes, after they have dried, will soften and recondition the leather. Castor oil is better than other leather conditioners for this purpose as it does not affect the finish and the shoes can be polished afterward.

Suede shoes are brushed with a bristle, rubber, or wire brush in a circular motion. Use wire brushes lightly or you may destroy the nap. After brushing carefully, smooth the nap in one direction. There are aerosol dressings which raise the nap, and other dressings containing dyes to restore color. If oil or grease stains on suede do not yield to cleaning fluid, try mixing the fluid with fuller's earth or other

absorbent, and letting the paste stand on the spot overnight.

Smooth leather shoes can be cleaned with saddle soap and shined with a polish of the same color, lighter, or neutral. Patent leather is cleaned with a soft damp cloth and a mild soap. No waxes or polishes for patent leather; they tend to crack it.

White, rough leathers are first brushed with a soft, clean bristle brush, then cleaned with white shoe dressing. Brush off excess. Smooth white shoes are cleaned with a white cream dressing and a soft cloth. No brushes. Brown and white or black and white shoes present a problem. It is probably best to clean the white part first and, when that has dried, to tackle the rest, using a neutral cream.

For stains caused by shoe polish see "Stains," p. 236.

Shower Curtains Always spread a wet shower curtain out as smoothly as possible to dry. Watch for mildew or a musty odor. Special types of shower curtains are cleaned as follows:

Duck (light canvas) shower curtains are washed with hot soapy water like any other heavy cotton material. Dry them in the sun, if possible, and iron them, dampened, with a hot iron. If mildewed, use a chlorine bleach, rinse thoroughly and proceed as directed above. The newest duck curtains are water-resistant and mildewproof so look for the labels if you are buying new ones. To mildewproof cottons at home see directions given under "Mildew."

Waterproof silk curtains are placed on a smooth flat surface and sponged with lukewarm suds, made with a mild detergent or soap. Rinse with clear lukewarm water and hang on the shower bar to dry.

Rubber curtains are washed in thick suds made of mild soap or detergent and lukewarm water. Be careful not to rub or squeeze the material together, but, rather, work it about gently in the water until clean. Rinse in cold water and hang on curtain hooks to dry.

Rubberized fabric curtains are washed like rubber ones. They may be pressed while damp with a warm (not hot) iron.

Plastic and plastic-coated curtains should be spread flat on a smooth surface and sponged with a damp cloth or mild suds. Rinse with clear, warm water and rehang to dry. Do not press. Some are machine washable. See "Plastic Sheeting."

Water-resistant cotton, rayon and silk shower curtains can be washed in mild lukewarm suds. Rinse in water of the same temperature and press, while damp, with a warm iron.

(Since it is difficult to distinguish between the many fabrics used for shower curtains, you should always look for the label giving instructions and file it for reference.)

Silicones Silicones have been described as "liquid glass" and as "chemical cousins of glass." Both are derived from the mineral element silica.

Silicones have countless industrial uses. They resist water, electricity, oxidation, weathering, chemicals, undesirable contacts, and are indifferent to high heat and bitter cold.

As invisible domestic helpers they now appear in furniture and floor waxes which are easier to apply and more durable; in metal polishes; on frypans and baking tins that do not require greasing; in hand creams, baby lotions, hair dressings, lipsticks, suntan oils, hand creams, and increasingly on textiles. Silicone creams and cosmetics stay on when you go swimming and the lotions protect working hands. Silicone textile finishes give resistance to wear, water, weathering, and stains.

There are no special instructions for silicone-treated cloth. It is unharmed by ordinary solvents. Pans with silicone linings should not be scrubbed with steel wool or abrasive powders. When the coating wears off, it can be replaced at the factory, or you can then use the pan like any other. Silicone dusters and polishing cloths lose some of the fluid with which they have been treated when washed, so deal with them gently. They are inexpensively replaced.

Silicone sprays are sold under various trade names for coating oven walls, lids of electric frypans, etc.

Silk The manufacture of silk, queen of all fabrics, was once a secret of the imperial house of ancient China. Legend says that in 2640 B.C., the Empress Si-Ling-Chi accidentally dropped a cocoon into boiling water and discovered how to unreel silk. As time passed, silken fabrics became available to the humble and even the coolie had his pongee.

Today silk again is in the luxury class. Handle the silks that you have with care and they will be beautiful for a long time. Silk, reeled from the cocoons of delicate worms and adapted to a bewildering variety of exquisite and colorful weaves, is a strong and durable material.

Silks not known to be washable should be handled by a reliable dry cleaner. Hand-launder washable silks with lukewarm to cool water and an unbuilt synthetic detergent made for wool. Synthetic detergents are much better for silk than soap because silks are damaged by alkalies and even the purest soap is alkaline in reaction.

In washing silks do not rub the fabric but squeeze and work it about in the suds. Rubbing is likely to break the fibers and dull the finish. Rinse carefully in water of the same temperature, then remove excess moisture by squeezing and patting it between dry towels. To stiffen silks use gum arabic or gelatin. See "Starch and Special Finishes."

Do not wrinkle silks more than necessary. They may be difficult to press. Do not hang silks in the sun or place them near any source of artificial heat. But do dry them as quickly as possible. Rapid drying in front of an electric fan prevents the formation of water marks and aids in retaining the glossy finish. Exquisite bits of sheer silk, especially those whose colors are inclined to run, are sometimes dried by shaking them gently until of the proper dampness for ironing.

Silks should be uniformly damp when they are pressed. Iron them before they are dried completely for best results. (If allowed to dry, dampening may cause water spots.) If they are too wet when ironed, the material will be stiff and papery. Use a warm (never hot) iron and press on the wrong side, preferably

169

with a piece of clean cheesecloth protecting the fabric. Silk scorches easily and too hot an iron will turn white silk yellow.

Pongee is a soft silk made from cocoons of wild silkworms. In Chinese the word means "own loom." Pongee has a rough, rather pleasing appearance in spite of its classification as a cheap silk. This fabric water-marks easily so be sure that the dampness is evenly distributed when you iron it and iron it on the wrong side. Or you can iron it dry. If ironed too wet, pongee becomes stiff.

Silver Silver is ranked commonly next to gold among the precious metals, though other metals are rarer and more expensive than either. It is soft, white, lustrous and easily worked. For centuries silver has been cherished by women for tableware and enduring ornaments. Softly shining silver, good china and immaculate linen can make a feast of the simplest meal.

Sterling silver is a term used to specify that the metal contains at least 925 parts of silver to 75 parts of copper. The term is derived from an English penny, coined in the Middle Ages. "Sterling" became the standard for lawful British coins. Pure silver is rarely used, as it is too soft.

There is no magic formula for keeping silver bright. Metallurgists have worked for years to produce a stainless silver, but without luck so far. So if you want your silver

to look its best you will have to give it a reasonable amount of care.

Sterling silver should be used daily. Constant use gives it the deep mellow tone of fine antiques . . . the "patina" that is really a meshwork of very fine scratches. Wash your silver promptly after each use, using hot suds and a soft cloth. Rinse it in hot water and dry it immediately. If you follow this procedure, you will not have to polish it often. Flat silver should be rotated in daily use so that the finish will mellow uniformly. Keep it, preferably in a lined rack, in a special silver drawer. Dust ornamental pieces regularly and wash them once a week to keep them bright.

There are several methods of cleaning tarnished silver but hand rubbing with a prepared polish (liquid, powder or paste) is best. "Dip shines" are tricky to use. They ruin some finishes and damage stainless steel knife blades as well as other materials if allowed to contact them. This is because they contain a very strong, corrosive acid. "Dip shines" are heartily condemned by manufacturers of fine silver services.

The electrolytic method is quick and easy but jewelers do not approve of it either because it kills the finish of silver. Every trace of oxidation is removed, leaving the pattern dead and the silver dull, white and lusterless. Hand rubbing, on the other hand, gives silver a depth of luster that is beautiful and desirable and leaves enough oxidation to bring out the beauty of its decoration.

When you polish your silver, take time to do it carefully. To protect your hands wear gloves if you like. Wash the silver first in hot soapsuds, then apply a reliable polish with a soft cloth, sponge, or chamois. Rub each piece briskly, but not hard, using even, straight strokes. Do not rub silver crosswise or with a rotary motion. A silver brush (made especially for this purpose) is useful for cleaning hard-to-reach crevices, chased surfaces and beaded edgings. After applying the polish, rub the silver with a clean soft flannel cloth or piece of chamois until it is clean and bright. Last of all wash each piece again carefully in hot suds to remove every trace of polish. Your brush will come in handy here, too, to insure that no powder is left clinging to raised patterns. Polish left on silver causes it to tarnish again quickly.

Silver does not need to be polished each time it is cleaned. Often it is only necessary to wipe off the tarnish with your silver preparation.

Dull, or satin, finish silver becomes bright after many polishings. Reliable dealers are agreed that there is no satisfactory method of restoring satin finish at home, so it's back to the jeweler's with it if you want it dull again.

Gold linings, more often than not, are quickly rubbed out of pitchers, bowls and salt dishes by energetic sisters who can't resist giving the inside a swipe. Keep your polish away from these delicate washes for the gold is soft, the lining thin, and it will vanish even with constant rubbing, polish or no. Gold linings can be restored by your jeweler.

Lacquered silver will not tarnish and, of course, requires no polishing. When you wash it use lukewarm (never hot) suds made with a mild soap or detergent. Your jeweler can apply the lacquer, which is mainly suitable for large, ornamental pieces.

A finish which makes silver tarnishproof and resistant to damage from acids, salts, and other substances has been developed by Tiffany's, New York. This finish is applied at the factory and lasts several years. It is recommended for bowls, ash trays, candelabra, vases, trophies, and similar articles not subjected to abrasive treatment. It is not suitable for flatware or trays. Silver with this finish can be wiped clean with a damp cloth or washed like china. It will stand very hot water.

Electrolytic cleaning This method is presented with some misgivings because jewelers disapprove of it for the reasons already given and because I am in agreement with them. However, it is a time-saver and *is* completely harmless. Some may want to use it in spite of its shortcomings. The finish can be improved somewhat by polishing the silver a little after cleaning it. The electrolytic method calls for a porcelain pan in which a piece of aluminum foil has been placed, salt, and baking soda.

Put into the pan one teaspoon of salt and one teaspoon of baking soda for each quart of water required. Bring the water to a boil, then put in the silver, making sure that it is covered completely. Boil two or three minutes, or until the tarnish has disappeared. Remove the silver, wash it in hot suds, rinse carefully and dry with a soft cloth. Two teaspoons of washing soda or one teaspoon of trisodium phosphate per gallon of water can be substituted for the salt and baking soda combination. In this case boiling may not be necessary.

This method of silver cleaning involves an electrochemical reaction by which the tarnish (silver sulfide) is removed from the silver and deposited on the aluminum foil.

Caution: The electrolytic method should not be used on flat silver with hollow handles that may be fastened with cement. It should not be used on antiqued silver and is not desirable for hollowware.

Storing silver Tarnish is caused by the action of certain gases in the air on the surface of silver. Therefore, if air is kept away, tarnish is diminished. Cloth and paper tissues, treated with silver nitrate, deter tarnish and are useful if silver is to be stored. Both may be purchased from your jeweler or at any department store. The cloth may be had in rolls or made up into bags and cases. Wrapping each piece of clean, bright silver in saran plastic film is almost as effective. It is self-sealing and you can easily identify the silver you want to bring out and use. Press out the air as you wrap. Never secure any wrapping with rubber bands. Rubber, a deadly enemy of silver, can corrode it in a few weeks through several layers of paper or cloth. When the corrosion lines cross etched patterns, the damage is permanent.

Other enemies of silver are table salt, eggs, olives, salad dressings, gas, sulfur, vinegar, fruit juices, perfumes and toilet water. Don't let any of these contact silver long. Sea air and leaking gas tarnish silver rapidly. Watch your fruit and flower bowls. Acids generated by decaying flowers, leaves, and fruits will etch into your silver, causing ugly little pit marks. So use an inner container, or change the water frequently on flowers in silver bowls and vases and do not keep them an instant after they begin to wilt. Watch your fruit bowl for decayed grapes and seeping juices that might cause damage if left in it too long.

Pearl, ivory and horn handles on silver knives or forks should not be allowed to soak in water. They usually are fastened with cement which might be loosened. No other care than ordinary washing is required of such handles, but do not put them in your dishwasher.

Silver plate Silver-plated articles should not be confused with solid silver, or sterling silver. In silver plate a coating of silver has been applied to another metal. The process used today is called "electroplating." The article to be plated is placed in a solution containing silver and, through an electrolytic process, part of the silver is made to adhere to the surface. Sheffield plate, prior to about 1850, involved an altogether different method. A sheet of silver was fused to a copper ingot and the ingot was then rolled thin. Sometimes the silver was fused to both sides of the copper. This method was superseded by electroplating and Sheffield plate is no longer made.

The care of silver plate is the same as for solid silver, except that it should be polished, perhaps, with less energy. The plating is solid silver, softer than sterling.

Silver polish A fine grade of whiting on a damp cloth plus a little household ammonia or alcohol makes an excellent silver polisher. It keeps England's famous silver bright and shining.

Commercial polishes vary in composition but practically all contain fine abrasives like whiting, rouge or diatomaceous earth. Treated polishing cloths are handy for a quick job on lightly tarnished silver and to give added luster to polished silver.

Avoid polishes that contain harsh abrasives, such as silica.

Silverfish and Firebrats Silverfish are wingless, scaly insects, silvery gray in color, with two long antennae in front and three long hairlike appendages behind. When fully grown they are from ⅓ to ½ an inch in length. They like damp cool places and flourish in basements. Firebrats are a mottled gray, very similar in appearance to silverfish. They like warm areas, the attic in summer and the area of the furnace in winter. Both insects are nocturnal and the damage they do is similar. The same insecticides will control them.

They attack foods and other materials that are high in protein, sugar, and starch: flour, cereals, paper that is coated with glue or paste such as wallpaper and bookbindings, starched cotton and other fabrics, especially rayon.

Silverfish and firebrats can be controlled with household sprays or dusts. The results may not be immediate but, properly applied, the insecticide will leave a killing residue that should achieve control within 2 or 3 weeks. If not, repeat the treatment.

Select a household surface spray containing lindane, diazinon, ronnel, malathion, or propoxur. Spray door and window casings, baseboards, closets, and openings around pipes. Oil-based sprays should not be used near an open fire, electric motor, gas pilot flame, or other areas where they might ignite. In such places use a dust containing not more than 6 percent of chlordane, 1 percent of lindane, or 5 percent of malathion. Blow it into cracks and onto the surfaces of areas suggested for spraying. See "Insecticides" for precautions.

Silver Nitrate See "Stains," p. 237.

Sink Clean the kitchen sink with soap and hot water after each use. If stained, use a mild scouring powder. Coarse abrasives damage the finish, making the sink more and more difficult to clean. Rinse with plenty of water, preferably hot. Wipe dry.

To whiten a sink, fill it with lukewarm water, add a little chlorine bleach and let it stand for a while. (Some cleaning powders contain chlorine.) Iron rust stains, if light, often can be removed by rubbing them with a cut lemon. If more stubborn, apply a 5 percent solution of oxalic acid (poison) on a bit of cloth or paper. Rinse thoroughly after a few seconds as acids will eat into the porcelain finish.

For a sink so hopelessly stained that a new one seems the only solution try this formula. Mix cream of tartar and hydrogen peroxide (available at the drugstore) to a paste and scrub the sink with it, using a hand brush and plenty of elbow grease. The result will surprise you.

Stainless steel sinks seldom require more than washing with hot suds, rinsing, and drying.

Sink faucets usually are chromium- or nickel-plated. Clean them with soap and water, rinse and wipe dry. Scouring powders should never be used as they quickly wear off the plating.

See also "Drains," "Steel—Stainless," "Monel Metal."

Slate Slate is sometimes used for the hearth and facing of fireplaces. A little lemon oil, applied carefully after the slate has been washed and dried, makes it dark and lustrous. Be sure to wipe the slate with a clean cloth after applying the oil to remove every trace of excess polish. Do not use wax, because heat affects it.

For the care of slate tiles see "Stone Floors."

Sleeping Bags Garments and sleeping bags insulated with Dacron polyester II fiberfill should be washed with mild soap or detergent and water. They should never be dry cleaned.

To wash them by hand, press them gently into lukewarm (100° F.) suds made with mild soap or detergent. Continue to press the article through the water until it is clean. A second washing may be required if the article is extremely soiled. Rinse thoroughly in warm water, pressing the water out by hand. Do not wring or twist the article. Hang it on a line to air dry. Dacron absorbs little water and dries quickly. Press the water gently from the bottom by hand.

Machine-wash Dacron polyester stuffed articles only in tumble-washers of the heavy-duty, front-loading type normally found in laundromats. Home washing machines and agitator types should not be used, to avoid possible damage to the bag or garment, or to the machine. Use a mild soap or detergent and a warm gentle cycle. After rinsing, they can be dried outdoors on a line, or tumble-dried in a machine. The dryer should be the heavy-duty type found in laundromats. Set for low heat.

When washing and drying by machine, damage will be minimized if the machine is fully loaded because there is less tumbling. Be sure zippers are closed when washing or drying and that the filling and outer fabric are safety-pinned together if the outer fabric is not sewn to the lining.

While Dacron polyester has excellent recovery after depression, storage can ultimately reduce it. Air-dry the bag, fold it, and store it for best results. Roll it or stuff it in a sack only to transport it.

Slip Cover Have your slip covers dry-cleaned if you are not sure that they are washable. If both fabric and bindings are colorfast and shrinkproof, or allowance has been made for shrinkage, they can be safely washed.

It is not difficult to wash slip covers by machine. The first step is to vacuum them or brush them thoroughly, paying particular attention to seams and bindings. Step two is to remove conspicuous spots and stains by wetting them and brushing them with soap or detergent. Ripped seams should be mended, zippers or other fasteners closed.

For washing, use soap or a synthetic detergent, and warm water if the color is delicate. Wash the covers and rinse them twice. If very soiled, you may want to give them a second brief washing, followed by rinses. Do not spin them too long to avoid setting wrinkles.

Slip covers dried on a line should be turned wrong side out and placed in the shade. Pin the front of a chair seat straight to one line and the top of the back to a parallel line. This encourages quick drying and an even distribution of moisture.

Chintz and linen fabrics may require all-over ironing. Iron glazed chintz on the right side to bring up the sheen. If it does not have a permanent finish use a light starch containing wax. (See "Chintz.") For slip covers of other materials that do not need all-over ironing, iron the ruffles or pleats while the material is still damp, then place the slip covers on the chairs to finish drying. This saves work, and the slip covers fit better.

Smocking In ironing, set the iron on the smocking gently, then fluff it up with your finger tips.

Soap Soap is usually made by heating, or emulsifying, fats or oils with lye. The quality of the soap depends upon the kind of fat that is used in making it, the manner in which it is prepared, and the amount and character of foreign materials that are added to it to improve its cleansing action or give it special qualities. A soap is said to be "neutral" when there is a correct balance between the fat and lye.

Soaps for general cleaning and laundry purposes are classified as "built" and "unbuilt." Unbuilt soaps contain from 93 to 97 percent pure soap, a little moisture and salt. The built soaps contain alkaline water softeners . . . phosphates, borax, washing soda, etc., which aid in removing soil, especially in hard-water areas.

Use the more expensive unbuilt soaps for laundering fine fabrics. They are safer for colors and kinder to the hands. Use built soaps for washing heavily soiled clothes.

Too much soap is as bad as too little in laundering clothes. Use just enough to maintain good suds.

See also "Water and Water Softeners."

Soap Jelly Soap jelly, which has a number of uses in the home, can be made easily by dissolving about three tablespoons of white soap flakes in one cup of boiling water. This basic formula can be varied as desired. To increase its cleaning ability add a teaspoon of ammonia or two teaspoons of borax. To give it mild scouring properties add one quarter of a cup of whiting. This variation is good for flat paints.

Soap Stains See "Stains," p. 237.

Soda and Soda Compounds Let's take a peek at the important chemical family of soda, or sodium, compounds that are often presented by manufacturers under various trade names as super-do cleansers. Behind the trade names there is less magic and less mystery than the "ad" writers would have us believe. A few are very old household friends.

First and foremost, what is sodium? Actually, it is a silver-white metal, extremely unstable. It is the base of alkali soda and is an important agent in the production of such metals as aluminum and magnesium. It has a strong affinity for chlorine, in combination with which it is *sodium chloride*, and that, my friends, is common salt, abundantly available. All soda compounds are derived from *sodium chloride*.

The four best known members of the sodium family are *sodium chloride*, or salt, *sodium bicarbonate*, *sodium carbonate* and *sodium hydrate*.

Sodium bicarbonate is baking soda, or bicarbonate of soda. It will remove stains from china, clean your teeth, deodorize drains, clean your refrigerator, eliminate tummy aches due to gas, help make biscuits and cakes, and create bubbly drinks. It will also make jewelry sparkle; relieve the pain of bee stings, light burns, and scalds; extinguish flash fires; clean glass, tile and porcelain, and kill odors.

Sodium carbonate is washing soda, an effective cleaner. It also is referred to as sal soda and as washing crystals. Washing soda has many uses, enumerated in this book, among them the routine cleaning of drains and traps, washing certain types of floors, cleaning gas burners and greasy pots and pans. Probably its most notable use is as a water softener, for it is completely soluble. In hard-water areas it is invaluable in the laundry. Soda ash is partially purified sodium carbonate.

Sodium hydrate is caustic soda, sold as lye. Sodium hydrate can give you a nasty burn and is not to be confused with its milder sisters. It is used to open sluggish drains.

176

Follow the directions on the container exactly to avoid trouble.

While these are the four main sodas in household use, there are many others with which we should have, at least, a bowing acquaintance. This, as we have said, is a very important family.

Sodium hydrosulfite, for instance, is a dye-stripping agent, or color remover, useful as a bleaching agent and for the removal of stains. It can be bought at drugstores under trade names such as "Rit" and "Tintex." See "Color Removers."

Sodium hypochlorite is the chemist's Javelle water or Labarraque solution. It is our old friend, "household bleach," or chlorine bleach, which is sold as Clorox, Purex, Fyne-Tex, etc. Washing soda and chloride of lime, with water, compose it. See "Chlorine Bleach."

Sodium perborate is a safe bleach for all types of fabrics. See "Sodium Perborate Bleach."

Trisodium phosphate, an effective water softener and cleaner, is sold at paint stores as TSP, or as a "paint cleaner" under trade names. At grocery stores its equivalent is Oakite. One tablespoon dissolved in a gallon of water makes an excellent cleaner for flat paint, but removes the gloss from enamel paint. TSP is an excellent cleaner for glazed and unglazed tile, porcelain bathroom fixtures, etc. It has many other uses similar to those outlined for washing soda.

Sodium thiosulfate is the "hypo" solution used by photographers. It is purchasable, in crystal form, at drugstores and photo supply shops. Hypo crystals are useful in removing chlorine and iodine stains. They are safe for all fibers and harmless to colors. Directions for using these crystals are given in Section II, on "Stains," under "Iodine."

Sodium pyrophosphate and *sodium metaphosphate* are desirable as water softeners because they combine with the minerals that make water hard, forming soluble compounds which are washed away. Some softeners, in combining with such minerals, form little gray lumps or flecks which adhere to the clothes and are difficult to remove. See "Water and Water Softeners."

Sodium Perborate Bleach Sodium perborate bleaches are safe for all fabrics but hot solutions should not be used on heat-sensitive fabrics such as those containing wool, silk, or Dynel. In using laundry preparations sold at groceries for ordinary bleaching, follow the directions on the package. For stain removal use pure sodium perborate crystals bought at a drugstore. Do not use metal containers. Always test colors first.

For *stain removal* on *washable* materials dissolve one to two tablespoons of sodium perborate in a pint of hot water. (For silk, wool, and Dynel use lukewarm water.) Saturate the stain with this solution, or soak the stained article in it until the stain is removed. Since this bleach works slowly this may mean several hours or overnight. If silk or wool is yellowed by the solution, sponge it with 10

percent acetic acid or white vinegar. Rinse. For a *strong* treatment on washable materials that will stand very hot water, sprinkle sodium perborate directly on the stain, then dip it into hot-to-boiling water. This should remove the stain in a few minutes. Rinse thoroughly and repeat if necessary.

On nonwashable materials, for a mild treatment, sprinkle the stain with sodium perborate and cover it with a cotton pad dampened with water. Use lukewarm water on heat-sensitive materials, hot on others. Keep the pad damp until the stain is gone (several hours or more), then rinse. Or apply the solution described for washables with a medicine dropper and keep the stain damp until it disappears, then rinse. Sponge silk or wool with acetic acid or white vinegar if it has yellowed, then rinse with water. For a *strong* treatment place the stained material on an absorbent pad, dampen the stain with cool water, sprinkle it with sodium perborate, and saturate it with boiling water, using a medicine dropper or spoon. Rinse and repeat if necessary.

Section II on "Stains" will tell you when to use this bleach.

Soft Drinks See "Stains," p. 237.

Softeners See "Fabric Softeners" and "Water and Water Softeners."

Solvent A solvent is a substance, usually a liquid, which is used to dissolve another substance. First and foremost of the entire category is water, the safest and best. Try it first on all washable materials. Spot removers and cleaning fluids also are solvents; so are many of the chemicals recommended for various stains.

See also "Cleaning Fluids."

Soot See "Fireplace" and "Chimney." Also see "Smoke and Soot" in "Stains," p. 237.

Spandex Spandex is a generic term for synthetic elastic fibers used in girdles and as a core for some stretch yarns. Some of the trade names are Glospan, Lycra, Numa, and Vyrene. Chlorine bleach yellows it. See "Girdles."

Spectran See "Polyester."

Spiders Spiders destroy injurious household insects and most of those found in the United States are harmless. An exception is the black widow spider, whose bite is extremely painful, and sometimes fatal. The female, which has the poisonous bite, is shiny black, about ½ inch long, with a globular body and long slender legs. Usually, but not always, its underside has a red, orangish, or brownish-yellow mark shaped like an hourglass. Call a doctor immediately if anyone is bitten by one.

Black widow spiders seldom enter the living quarters of homes, but sometimes are found in basements, window wells, beneath porches and lawn benches, in old lumber, trash piles, sand piles, and outdoor toilets. Clean up all such places.

The brown recluse is another spider to avoid, if possible. Its bite may be intensely painful from the start, or several hours may pass before the pain is noticed. This spider and several close relatives are found in an area of the United States bounded on the east by western Georgia, northward into Kentucky and westward to Kansas and Texas. If severe pain continues after a bite from a small (⅜ inch) brown spider, call the doctor immediately.

All spiders can be controlled by spraying infested areas with a household surface spray containing lindane. Do not spray spiders above your head on ceilings. A sprayed spider can drop down and still be capable of biting. See "Insecticides" for precautions.

Sponge (v.) When instructions say to sponge a stain with water or other solvent, your success in removing a stain will depend greatly upon your technique. This is how it should be done.

Place the stained material on a clean folded cloth so that the solvent can be applied, if possible, to the reverse side and the stain can be dissolved without having to go through the cloth. With a pad of cloth or cotton moistened with solvent, gently wipe the solvent into the stain, working from the center toward the outer edge. Use the solvent sparingly and work it irregularly into the edge of the stain to avoid forming rings. Repeated applications of small amounts of solvent give the best results. Do not rub so hard that the fabric will be roughened, and move or change the pad underneath as the stain is absorbed. Dry the area quickly.

If a stain such as paint or tar has hardened, cover it with a pad moistened with solvent and let it remain until the stain has been softened. Apply fresh pads as they are needed. Then sponge the stain with solvent. On very delicate materials, dampen a pad or white blotter with solvent and place it on the stain. Do not rub. Replace the pad or blotter as required.

178

On materials that tend to form rings use solvents sparingly. The sponging pad should be scarcely damp. And take special care to sponge the edge of the stain irregularly so that no clear line will form as the material dries. Always dry the treated area as quickly as possible. Ring formation on some materials can be prevented by placing a fresh absorbent pad under the area treated and rubbing it gently with the palm of your hand. (Be sure the material is perfectly flat and unwrinkled.) Or place it on the palm of one hand and rub it gently with the other, following the threads of the material. Sometimes an absorbent powder is mixed with the solvent to make a crumbly paste which is applied to the stain and worked gently into it with the finger tips. Such a mixture should be sufficiently dry that the solvent does not seep out. Let this mixture dry on the stain, then shake or brush it off. Repeat if necessary. This method is not recommended for dark nonwashable materials because final traces of powder are difficult to remove.

If rings have already formed you may have trouble eliminating them. On washable materials try dampening them with water and then working in a liquid detergent. On other materials try rubbing the cloth between your hands or scratching it

lightly with your fingernail. Sometimes the application of the absorbent-solvent mixture already described will work.

Sponge (n.)—**Natural sponges** are the skeletons of odd little sea animals found adhering to rocks and shells under water, and to rocks about the shore when the tide is low. These are dried and bleached for commercial use.

Wash sponges in clean, soapy water. If very dirty, let them soak in soapy water to which ammonia has been added (one tablespoon per quart). Rinse thoroughly in clear water, squeeze out as much of the water as possible and dry in the shade. If used surgically, your sponge should be disinfected by boiling it five or ten minutes. Sponges, when not in use, should be hung by a string run through them.

Cellulose sponges and sponge mops should be soaked carefully before using because they are brittle when dry. They are not harmed by ordinary cleaning soaps and powders but strong solutions and strong bleaches damage them.

Rinse cellulose sponges after each use, and to freshen them and prolong their life, put them in the washer with your clothes. Hang up your cellulose mop after you have washed it. Do not let it dry hard in the sun or near a radiator. Keep it moist between jobs for maximum service. Do not use it on rough surfaces.

Cellulose sponges can be bleached in a mild solution of household bleach, if necessary, but don't soak them too long. Rinse carefully afterward. They can be sterilized by boiling.

Sponge and foam rubber mops and sponges should be washed in warm, mild suds and rinsed carefully. Store them in a cool, dry place. Strong chemicals are likely to damage them. Grease, oils, acids and gasoline are all damaging to rubber.

Sponge Rubber Sponge rubber is made from crude rubber by a milling operation. Chemicals are added to the rubber to soften it and to permit the "blowing of holes" in the rubber.

Spoon (v.) In removing spots and stains, the word spoon means using the bowl of a stainless steel spoon to loosen stains. Place the stain, with nothing beneath it, on a working surface such as a glass pie pan. Hold the bowl of the spoon in your hand and rub it quickly back and forth over the stain, about ½ inch in each direction. Do not press down with the spoon; this might damage the fabric.

Stainless Steel See "Steel."

Stains Stains on fabrics are covered in Section II, where they are listed alphabetically. General instructions are given in the opening pages of that section. Chemicals and absorbents used for stain removal are discussed under individual headings in the main section of this book.

For stains on materials other than cloth, look up the material to be treated, such as "Marble," "Tile," "Furniture," "Wallpaper," etc.

Stairs If the stairway is covered, follow the directions given for the particular type of covering, such as "Linoleum," "Rubber," etc.

Stair carpets and pads should be taken up once a year for a good cleaning. Send them to a dry cleaner, or, if you want to do the job at home, follow these directions: Clean both sides of carpet and padding with the vacuum cleaner or a good stiff brush. Wash, if necessary, following the directions given under "Carpets and Rugs." Hang outdoors to dry or air thoroughly. Replace the padding and then the carpet, turning it around so that wear will be distributed evenly.

The balustrade and rail of the stairway should be dusted like furniture. About once a month it should be cleaned and polished.

Starch and Special Finishes Manufacturers of laundry starch supply excellent directions for the use of their products and, since starches differ, these directions should be followed for best results.

Starch for finishing cloth can be obtained from many sources, but cornstarch is usually used. Substances such as beeswax and paraffin are added to it to increase the gloss and make starched textiles soft and pliable. Other treatments make possible starches that do not require boiling. Finishes other than starch include gelatin, gum arabic, and gum tragacanth.

Laundry starches come in various forms. There are dry starches which require cooking, starches that can be dissolved in hot water, and starches that are added to cold water. Also available are liquid starches in bottles and spray-on starches in pressurized containers. Study the labels, select the kind that best suits your need, and follow the directions on the container.

If a number of articles are to be starched, use your washing machine. It saves time and insures even distribution of the starch if the fabrics are similar. Partially fill the washer with water, then add the starch solution required for the load. Agitate the washer for a few seconds to mix the starch and water. Add the clothes, damp from the previous final rinse and extraction, and agitate for about 2 minutes.

If you are using an automatic washer which provides a spray rinse during extraction, first turn the water off. Remove by spinning or wringing out enough of the starch solution to prevent dripping.

Starched articles can be put into a tumbler dryer, but do not include with them clothes that have not been starched. Remove starched articles from the dryer while they are still damp enough to be ironed, unless the directions for the starch you are using say they should be completely dry.

Instructions for removing traces of starch from the washer and dryer are given under "Washing Machine" and "Automatic Dryer."

Special finishes such as gelatin, gum arabic, and gum tragacanth (bought at drugstores) are sometimes used to restore a crisp appearance to voile, organdy, batiste, silk, and rayon. These finishes are transparent and thus especially fine for colored fabrics. Follow the directions exactly; if too much is used, the material will be sticky.

Gelatin Add 1 pint of cold water to 1 ounce of gelatin and heat until the gelatin has dissolved. To 1 part of this mixture add from 8 to 15 parts of hot water, depending upon the material and the amount of stiffness desired. Add a little borax if the mixture is to be saved. This is especially good for sheer cottons.

Gum arabic Add 1 pint of cold water to 1 ounce of powdered gum arabic and heat until the gum has dissolved. To 1 part of this solution add from 5 to 10 parts of hot water, depending upon the material and the stiffness desired. Use it when cooled. Add a little borax if the mixture is to be stored. This is especially good for silks and rayons.

Gum tragacanth Add 1 pint of cold water to one sixth of an ounce of powdered gum tragacanth and heat until dissolved. To 1 quart of this solution add from 8 to 12 parts of hot water, according to the finish desired. Cool before using. Add a little borax if the mixture is to be saved.

Statuary Dust plaster of Paris and ceramic pieces, using a clean dry cloth or a soft brush. *No water.* Wash china ornaments with unbuilt synthetic detergent or mild soap and warm water, using a cloth or soft brush. Rinse with warm water and dry. Do not use ammonia on china ornaments that are decorated with silver or gilt. Lacquered bronze needs only dusting. See "Bronze," "Marble."

Steam Iron A steam iron eliminates the need to sprinkle clothes, since the steam supplies the necessary moisture. It is ideal for pressing woolens, and for ironing other heat-sensitive fabrics such as silk and the synthetics. The moisture produced by the iron helps safeguard these materials against "invisible scorch" which so often shortens their life. Press all of these materials on the wrong side, unless you use a press cloth, to prevent shine. Exceptions to this rule are light-colored wool crepes, tweeds and flannels. In

pressing woolens use a light stamping motion. Do not glide the iron over the material. And leave it slightly damp. Use an untreated press cloth for silks and synthetics. A chemically treated press cloth is excellent for woolens.

A steam iron gives good results on light cottons and linens, but dry ironing does a better job on the heavier cottons and on linen damask. However, these, too, can be steam ironed if time-saving is important. Dampen them a little first.

Velvet and felt hats, suede shoes and handbags may be given the steam beauty treatment with a steam iron. Set the dial for rayon and, with the iron placed on the board so that the tip overhangs, hold the hat in the steam and turn it around slowly. Steam the crown first, then brush it with a soft brush or rubber sponge to raise the nap. Next do the brim. Suede and doeskin gloves and suede pocketbooks can be steamed the same way. Use a stretcher for the gloves and hold the leather about a half inch from the iron. When thoroughly steamed, brush up the nap. For care see "Electric Iron."

Steel—Tempered The enemies of tempered steel (knives, spatulas, egg beaters, etc.) are acids, which corrode the metal, and moisture, which causes rust. Keep steel spot-

less with scouring powder. Wash tempered steel immediately after use to prevent stains and dry meticulously to prevent rust.

Stainless Stainless steel is an iron alloy containing chromium. It seldom requires more attention than washing in hot suds, rinsing and drying. Stainless steel is rust-proof, but salt and acids in foods can cause pit marks if left in contact too long. If spots do appear, clean the utensil with fine steel wool or steel wool and a fine scouring powder. Polish with a soft cloth. Special cleaners are made for stainless steel cooking utensils.

In using stainless steel pans, do not let gas flames lick up the sides and cause heat stains. These cannot be removed.

Stainless steel tableware, increasingly popular, should be washed promptly to avoid pitting from salts and acids in foods. It never tarnishes, but too much detergent in electric dishwashers sometimes films it, giving it a dull appearance. To remove this film use a good silver polish. Do not use steel wool on stainless steel tableware.

Vanadium Vanadium steel is a stainless steel containing up to 4 percent of vanadium, a light gray metal that increases the toughness and tensile strength of the steel. Spatulas, pancake turners, knives and ladles are often made of vanadium steel.

Steel Wool Steel wool consists of fine filaments of steel, often packed into pads and sold with or without an impregnation of soap. It is the best cleaner and polisher for aluminum and is good for removing stuck food from other metals. At hardware stores it is available in different degrees of fineness for abrasive purposes.

Rust retardants are often added to pads treated with soap to prolong their safe use—or you can put the pad in a cup of soda water. Use about three tablespoons of baking soda in a cup of water. The steel wool will then not rust.

Stone Floors Stones used for flooring—quarry tile, bluestone, slate, flagstone, magnesite—are porous and so is the concrete in which they are usually set. When washed with soap-type cleaners, a scum forms on the concrete which cannot be completely rinsed away. Washing soda can be used to clean them, or a synthetic detergent. Such floors are usually protected with a cement sealer such as Tri-Seal and waxed to provide gloss. Self-polishing wax is recommended, but polishing waxes can be used. See also "Marble."

Stove See "Gas Range," "Electric Range," etc.

Stove Polish Graphite is the basic ingredient of most stove polishes. If finely powdered, it can be used without other substances. Just mix it with a little water. Other carbons such as bone black and lamp black are sometimes added to deepen the color, but are of doubtful benefit since they are burned off much more easily than graphite. Stove

polishes can be bought in powder, liquid, paste, cake or stick form. Avoid those containing flammable liquids, such as turpentine.

For the removal of stains caused by stove polish see "Stains," p. 237.

Strawberry See "Fruit and Berry" in "Stains," p. 228.

Straw Hats Keep them well brushed and they will be damaged less if caught in the rain. To clean them, wipe with a cloth dipped in warm suds, made with a synthetic detergent or soap. Rinse with a cloth wrung out of plain water. Do not get a straw hat too wet or it may shrink.

Limp straws can be stiffened by brushing them over with a light coat of clear shellac, diluted with an equal amount of alcohol. To brighten the color and renew the gloss of dark straws, rub them with a dark cloth dampened with alcohol, diluted with one quarter the amount of water, then polish them lightly with a piece of dark-colored velvet.

Stretch Clothing Most of the stretch clothing now on the market is made with stretch-textured nylon or polyester fibers. Stretch-textured means that the fibers are heat set in corkscrew coils that resemble miniature steel springs. When extended and released, they return to their original form. Prior to weaving, these heat-set yarns are untwisted. When a fabric made with them is stretched, it too returns to its original dimensions. Sometimes the elastomeric fiber spandex is used.

By combining these fibers with others—cotton, wool, silk, synthetics—almost any fabric or weave can be made stretchable. The

183

stretch can be longitudinal, horizontal, or both.

Stretch clothing is washed or dry cleaned according to the material of which it is made. Washable stretch clothing requires no special techniques. It can be pressed with either a dry or steam iron at the rayon or synthetic setting (275° to 300° F.). Some stretch clothing, such as baby wear, never needs ironing.

Suede An undressed leather, with a nappy, velvet surface. Large suede garments such as coats should be sent to a dry cleaner. For cleaning accessories such as shoes and handbags, see "Shoes." See also "Leather."

Sun Lamp The manufacturer's directions for your particular lamp should be followed carefully, but here are some basic instructions. Dust the reflector frequently to keep it clean and polish it occasionally with a suitable metal polish. Clean the bulb in mercury arc lamps about once a month (when the bulb is cold and the lamp disconnected), using a clean cloth moistened with denatured alcohol. Do not use soap and water and do not handle it or oil will be left on the glass.

Sweaters *Synthetic* Sweaters made of the various synthetic fibers differ in what they will stand, and instructions on the inner tags should always be followed. All can, of course, be dry-cleaned or washed, according to preference. Handwashing is nearly always recommended as best, but most of them can also be machine-laundered. (Do *not* machine-wash sweaters

with delicate trimmings such as beads and sequins.)

Safe for all synthetics is lukewarm water with soap and a softener, or detergent. Squeeze the sweater gently through the suds; never rub or twist it. Rinse it thoroughly in lukewarm water, and for a soft, fluffy texture, add a fabric conditioner, following the directions on the box. Squeeze out excess water and, preferably, lay the sweater flat to dry.

Orlon acrylic and nylon sweaters are preferably washed by hand in lukewarm water with a synthetic detergent. Squeeze the suds gently through them. Rinse *thoroughly* in lukewarm water and use a fabric conditioner in the last rinse for best results. Roll in a towel to remove excess moisture. Dry flat. If you wash the sweaters by machine, omit the final spin-dry cycle, remove them dripping wet and dry as for hand washing. No blocking is necessary. If you are going to use a dryer, let the sweaters go through the spin-dry cycle. Dry at a low temperature setting for about 20 minutes and remove immediately.

Orlon sweaters containing special acrylic fibers (labeled Sayelle, Civona, or Wintuk) can be machine washed in warm water with a detergent. (If washed by machine, they must be dried by machine. Use the regular setting.) If the sweaters are washed by hand, rinse them thoroughly in cold water. Squeeze out excess water gently. Roll in a towel and squeeze again. Spread flat, bunch into shape, and allow to dry. Avoid stretching. Do not place on hangers. Such knitwear must be dried thoroughly to insure automatic blocking. If stretched during washing or wearing, wet thoroughly, squeeze, and tumble dry to reshape.

Dacron knits are usually washable. (Check the label.) In a machine, use warm water and standard detergents. Do not spin or wring. Gently squeeze out excess water and tumble dry at a medium temperature setting. Or hand wash the knits in warm water and let them drip dry on rustproof hangers.

Sweaters Wool Unless you are very expert, measure your sweater before washing it the first time. The best way to do this is to lay it flat on a large piece of plain wrapping paper and draw a line around it. Later you will pin your sweater to this pattern.

Preferably, hand-wash all sweaters made of untreated wool. Use plenty of lukewarm water (95° to 105° F.) and an unbuilt synthetic detergent, or a detergent made especially for woolens such as Woolite, Woolfoam and Wool-n-Wash. Synthetic detergents are better than soap for woolens because they are free of alkalies, which damage wool, and do not require water softeners, which also are alkaline.

The soak-wash method recommended for blankets is very effective and safe for woolen sweaters. First moisten with lukewarm water and detergent any especially soiled spots. A soft little brush comes in handy here. Then lay the sweater in your detergent solution and let it soak for 10 or 15 minutes, turning it once or twice. (Do not rub, scrub, or twist it. The less handling wool receives, the better.) Rinse twice by the same soak method, then gently squeeze out excess water and roll the sweater in a

turkish towel and knead it gently. For heavy sports sweaters use two towels, one folded and placed inside, to help absorb the moisture.

If you are using a pattern, place this on a turkish towel or cotton pad and pin the sweater down, patting and easing it into its original shape. Dry in a warm, airy place, away from heat and sunlight. When the sweater is almost dry, turn it occasionally to speed the process. Woolens are best dried quickly.

If untreated wool sweaters are to be machine washed, follow this procedure after pretreating spots. Soak for 5 minutes in a cool detergent solution, then extract the water. Soak-rinse twice for 5 minutes, extracting the water after each rinse. Do not agitate the washer during washing and rinsing. Remove and dry flat as described for hand washing.

Instructions for sweaters made of the new machine washable wool yarns vary according to the treatment given them by the manufacturer. Some treated woolens can stand hot water. Your guide is the label.

Woolen sweaters may be pressed lightly with a warm iron, if desired. Use a dampened press cloth and take care not to press them absolutely dry or they will lose their fluffy, nubby look. After pressing,

185

allow them to air, then fold them neatly and place them in a drawer. Do not use hangers, especially for hand-knits, if you want them to keep their shape. See also "Pilling."

Sweet Oil A mild edible oil such as olive oil.

Synthetic When this term is used it means that the product is not a natural one, but one that has been built up of various chemical elements in imitation of the genuine product. Synthesis, in chemistry, is the exact opposite of analysis. In analysis, the chemist takes a compound to pieces to determine the elements that compose it. In synthesis, he builds it back again.

We hear a great deal of synthetic products today: flavorings used in cooking, plastics, cloth, and even synthetic jewels.

Synthetic Detergents Synthetic detergents are made from petroleum and natural fats and oils by chemical processes more complicated than those involved in making soap. Because of the broader range of materials and methods used in producing them, they can be varied to suit many household tasks. They dissolve easily in either hot or cold water, are effective in hard water without the addition of softeners, do not create scum if enough is used, and do not leave a film on washed surfaces.

Their ingredients are varied to cope with specific problems and they are available in liquid, powder, and tablet form—to wash clothes, shampoo hair, rugs, and upholstery, and clean dishes, pans, floors, walls, and woodwork.

Laundry detergents are of two types—light duty (unbuilt) and heavy duty (built). Use light-duty, alkali-free detergents for laundering lightly soiled delicate fabrics, fabrics of doubtful colorfastness, silks, and wools. Those made for dishes are mildest.

Heavy-duty detergents contain alkaline salts and other substances that increase their cleaning power. They are for clothing that is moderately or heavily soiled, and are safe for many fine fabrics. Some produce rich suds, others almost none. There is no real difference in the cleaning ability of the two types, but use a low-sudsing brand if the manufacturer of your washer suggests it. High suds interfere with the mechanical action of some washers, particularly front-loading (tumbler) models.

For lightly soiled synthetics and for clothes with durable-press finishes, which are best laundered in cold water, use a cold-water detergent.

For a partial list of detergents made especially for wool, see "Woolens (*Untreated*)."

For *stain removal* liquid detergents are best. On *washable* materials, first dampen the stain, then rub in the detergent. Rinse the area thoroughly, or put the article in the wash. If the stain is embedded, rub the fabric between your hands, bending it so that all the fibers in the yarn are reached. Rinse thoroughly. On very heavy fabrics and rugs, work the detergent into the stain with the edge of a spoon.

For stains on nonwashable materials, dilute the detergent with an equal amount of water and work it in, but use as little as possible. It is hard to rinse out the detergent without wetting a large part of the fabric, if too much is used. Rinse by sponging the spot with cool water or by forcing cool water through it with a medicine dropper or syringe. Alcohol is the best rinse for materials not damaged by it, and they dry more quickly.

Synthetic Textiles—What They Are Synthetic textiles are textiles woven from man-made fibers in contrast to those woven from natural fibers such as cotton, linen, wool and silk. The synthetic fabrics on the market today were developed in chemical laboratories from raw materials such as wood, cotton linters, coal, glass, limestone and various plastics. Years of painstaking research lie behind each one.

By a special technique, which the chemist calls "polymerization," the molecules of the compound are bunted around until thousands are linked end to end in giant molecules known as polymers. The resulting compound is then "extruded," which means that it is directed, or forced, through tiny holes, or spinnerets, to form almost invisible filament. The filament is stretched, twisted and plied into thread for weaving.

Rayon was the first synthetic textile. It is derived from cotton linters and wood pulp. Nylon, Orlon, and Dynel are others. In making today's fabrics, synthetics are combined with synthetics, as well as with natural fibers, to give them various desired qualities, such as wrinkle resistance, increased strength, softness, body or drape.

Each synthetic has its individual characteristics, which qualify it for specific jobs, and each differs from the others in the treatment it will stand. In many instances, the synthetics are better than natural fibers. Often they are cheaper to produce. But to get your money's worth from them in pleasure and service, you will have to know how to care for them.

Always look for the identifying label when you buy synthetic materials and follow the manufacturer's instructions for laundering or dry cleaning.

Synthetic textiles produced in the United States for home use fall into these classifications: glass, rayon, acetate, nylon, acrylic, modacrylic, polyester, spandex, olefin, saran, etc. Each class is listed in this book as well as the more important trade names such as Orlon, Dacron, Acrilan, and Kodel. Under law the exact fiber content of clothing and yard goods must be stated, and instruction given for cleaning it.

Talc A soft mineral, consisting of hydrous silicate of magnesium. Talc is used for soothing skin powders and also as an absorbent for removing certain stains. See "Absorbent."

Tapestry A fabric, often handloomed, in which the woof of colored threads is added to the warp in such a way as to produce a

187

pattern. Have tapestries dry-cleaned.

Tar See "Stains," p. 237.

Tatting Tatting is a type of knotted lace, hand made with a shuttle. Press it into shape with your fingers and set the iron down on it gently to dry it out.

Tea See "Coffee, Tea" in "Stains," p. 227.

Tea Towel See "Dish Towels."

Teflon Teflon is the du Pont trade name for an unusual plastic which was discovered accidentally in 1938. Scientists working with refrigeration gases found a white waxy solid in a supposedly empty cylinder. Tested, the material would not yield to conventional solvents and was unaffected by extremes of temperature. Further tests revealed other outstanding qualities and indentified the mysterious substance as a fluorocarbon resin.

The key unit is a minute particle containing myriads of carbon and fluorine atoms tightly bonded together. This togetherness tames the fluorine, an element so active that, alone, it will burn water and concrete. United with carbon it produces an organic material which is singularly inert. Fluorocarbon polymers resist attack by corrosive chemicals, retain their strength in extremes of heat and cold, provide superior electrical insulation, and are so slippery that practically nothing adheres to them.

Teflon played a vital role during World War II, then entered peacetime industries and the space program. Bakers and candy makers

began to utilize its nonstick qualities in the 1950s, and the Teflon-coated frying pan appeared in 1961.

Much of today's cookware—glass, porcelain, and metal—is made slick and pretty with Teflon-enamel finishes.

For cleaning and care see "Pots and Pans." See also "Fluorocarbon."

Teflon Fiber Teflon and Gore-Tex are fluorocarbons, man-made fibers whose use is mainly scientific.

Telephone Don't forget to dust the telephone when you are doing the other furniture. If gummy, clean it with a damp cloth and soap. After use, replace the receiver carefully or your friends will get a busy signal and party liners will suspect you of listening in.

Television Set Clean the face "glass" with a clean soft cloth wrung out of mild soapsuds. Rinse it with a cloth wrung out of clear water, and wipe it dry with another cloth. Never use cleaning fluids or chemical cleaners: these can severely damage the glass. Do not use furniture polish on the face glass or spatter such polishes on it. They often contain solvents that are damaging. Gritty or harsh dust-cloths alone can cause scratches.

To maintain the finish of the cabinet use a fine furniture polish. Do not place rubber articles or articles likely to contain harmful chemicals on top of your television cabinet and do not drape it with a cover. Cloths or scarves that hang down behind obstruct the holes designed to ventilate the tubes and keep them from overheating. In placing your set, for this same reason, make sure that air can circulate freely between it and the wall. Do not place your set near any device that might overheat the chassis or damage the cabinet.

Termite If you have reason to suspect that your house or garage is infested with termites, call a reliable exterminator without delay. This is a job you cannot handle yourself. Termites, also called white ants, operate like an army, with battalions of soldiers and workers. The workers and the soldiers are wingless. Sexual adults have two pairs of gauzy wings, equal in size. (Ants have wings of unequal size.) Their bodies are thick rather than small waisted. Termites feed on wood and completely destroy it.

The presence of a termite colony may be indicated first by large numbers of reproductive (winged) termites, emerging or swarming from the soil or wood. Discarded wings on the floor beneath doors and windows, even when the insects themselves are not seen, is another indication that a colony is nearby. While some termites leave small piles of wood dust, the subterranean termite leaves little or no indication of its presence. A telltale sign, however, is the shelter tube, an earthlike construction one-quarter to one-half inch or more in width, which these termites build from the soil to the wood where they are working.

Terra Cotta Terra cotta floors are composed of glazed clay tiles of a red or red-yellow color. They are non-porous but, because they are set in concrete, such floors are often sealed. They can be waxed, if desired. Self-polishing wax is recommended because it is less slippery than polishing waxes. See also "Sealers."

Terrazzo Terrazzo flooring is made by mixing marble chips with cement. When hard, the mixture is ground down smooth and polished. Terrazzo often is made in blocks, separated by metal strips. This allows for contraction and expansion of the blocks under temperature changes. Allow a newly laid terrazzo floor to set for one week before washing it. At this time a marble sealer, such as Tri-Seal, can be applied, if desired. (See "Marble.")

Sweep terrazzo with a soft broom or clean it with the floor brush of your vacuum cleaner. Mop it occasionally with clear water or light suds made with a mild synthetic detergent. (Soap leaves a scum on marble, acids dissolve it.) Self-polishing wax is generally recommended for terrazzo floors because it is less slippery than polishing wax. If you prefer another type of wax, check the instructions on the container to see if it is suitable for terrazzo.

Varnish and lacquer should never be used to seal terrazzo because they discolor it.

Terry Cloth Wash bath and beach robes made of terry cloth like any other cotton material. Shake them out lightly and hang them to dry on rustproof hangers or tumble dry. When dry, fluff them out again and fold carefully. No starch. No ironing. Fabric softener, if desired.

Terylene See "Polyester."

Textura See "Polyester."

Thermos Bottle See "Bottle–Vacuum."

Ticks Only brown dog ticks ever become a household pest in the United States. After feeding on a dog, such ticks drop off and hide in cracks and crevices, behind baseboards, and under carpets, rugs, and furniture. They breed in these places and each succeeding generation finds the dog and repeats the cycle.

Brown ticks seldom bite people and they do not carry human diseases. Their presence in the house, however, is annoying and they can make your dog's life miserable.

Control begins with the dog. Have your veterinarian treat him in a bath containing a suitable insecticide, or bathe him yourself. Buy an emulsifiable concentrate containing 50 percent of malathion. Mix 1 tablespoon of the concentrate in each gallon of water. Dip the dog into the mixture, being careful not to immerse its head. Sponge its ears. If the dog is too large to dip, prepare the mixture in a bucket and pour it slowly over its back so that it will soak through to the skin.

Next spray the areas in the house where ticks may be breeding, using a household surface spray containing malathion, lindane, or diazinon. Pay particular attention to cracks in the floor, baseboards, window casings, and places where the dog likes to sleep. A malathion spray can be applied to rugs, carpets, and upholstered furniture— but be sure the label says that it

190

will not stain. Repeat in 2 or 3 months. See "Insecticides" for precautions.

Ties See "Neckties."

Tile Glazed ceramic tiles usually need only to be wiped with a clean, damp cloth or sponge. However, if soap, grease or dirt has caused a cloudy film or slight discoloration of the surface, use trisodium phosphate or a packaged water softener such as washing soda or Oakite. One teaspoon in a pail of water should turn the trick. If heavily soiled sprinkle a little softener on a moist cloth and wipe the tiles clean. Rinse and wipe dry with a clean soft cloth.

Cleansing powders also can be used, but must be carefully rinsed away. Do not use acid solutions on tile; they damage it.

Unglazed ceramic tiles, used for floors, can be scrubbed, mopped, or wiped clean easily with water containing trisodium phosphate, washing soda or other softener. Often a moist cloth or sponge is sufficient. If very soiled, scouring powders may be used. Afterward, of course, you will have to rinse carefully to remove traces of the powder. Wipe dry.

Cellulose sponges and mops are ideal for tile because they never leave ravelings on the cement in which the tiles are set.

Tile installations which are adjacent to oiled or waxed floors often acquire a scummy appearance, owing to wax being tracked into them. This dirt or scum can be removed and the tiles restored to their original freshness by the generous use of scouring powder applied with a wet cloth or steel wool.

If *stains* on your tile floor do not yield to trisodium phosphate or to scouring powders, try these remedies.

Paint spattered on tile should be wiped up immediately and the spot scoured. For old or stubborn paint stains several methods are suggested by tile experts and it will be a tossup as to which works best for the stain on your tile. All chemicals suggested can be bought in small quantities at drugstores or, in larger amounts, from chemical supply houses. The cheapest grade, known as the commercial grade, will do.

Buy at your hardware or paint store a commercial bleaching compound called "Tile Bleach." Following directions on the container, attempt to remove the stains from a small area, experimentally. A good paint remover will sometimes work. Again test it on a small inconspicuous area.

A third suggestion for removing a paint stain is to saturate a thick, white cloth, or layer of cotton batting, with hydrogen peroxide and place it over the stain. Place a second cloth, moistened with ammonia water, over the first to hasten the bleaching action. Repeat the operation if required.

Method four is somewhat involved. Cut a piece of white cotton flannel, larger than the stain, and saturate it with one part acetone and one part amyl acetate (highly flammable). Place this over the stain and cover with a piece of glass, marble, or dry porous tile. If the cloth becomes dry, saturate it again and re-cover as before. The solvent may spread the stain, in which case the second cloth should be larger.

A fifth suggestion for paint stains is to obtain and mix the following chemicals: trisodium phosphate (one part), sodium perborate (one part), and powdered talc (three parts). Prepare a strong soap solution with hot water and add to the dry ingredients to form a thick paste. Cover the stain with this paste and let it stand until dry. Repeat if required, remoistening the same powder with soap solution. Alternating this treatment with the hydrogen peroxide treatment sometimes hurries the job along.

(And the moral of that is: Don't spill paint on tile.)

Iron stains, the characteristic color of iron rust, often yields to scouring powder. So try that first. If it doesn't work try sodium citrate and glycerin. You dissolve one part of sodium citrate crystals in six parts of water and add to this solution an equal part of glycerin. Mix it thoroughly. Take part of this solution and mix it with whiting (using a putty knife) until you have a thick paste. Spread a layer, about one eighth of an inch thick, over the stain and let it dry. If necessary, repeat.

For *inkstains* try method five, described for paint stains.

Grouting (mortar or cement) that has become stained or discolored is practically impossible to restore. You can try scouring powders or rubbing the joint lightly with folded sandpaper, or swabbing with a weak acid solution. Tile Bleach, paint remover, and hydrogen peroxide might also be helpful. Wax is not recommended as a finish for ceramic tiles.

Tin Tin is a metal which approaches silver in whiteness and luster. It is easily worked and can take a high polish. Tin resists oxidation but is corroded by acids. It is used in many alloys and as a coating on iron.

Tin pie pans, tart molds, bread pans and other kitchen accessories should be washed in soap and water, rinsed and dried thoroughly to avoid rust. You aren't supposed to keep tin utensils bright and shining. They heat better when they have become darkened. Besides, if you scrub tinware with scouring powders you will remove the tin. It's just a plating. Remove burned foods from tin vessels by boiling them up for three to five minutes (no more!) in water to which a little baking soda has been added.

To remove rust from tinware rub it with a piece of cut raw potato that has been dipped in a mild abrasive. To remove accumulations of grease wash the utensil in a solution of hot water and washing soda. Use one fourth of a cup of soda to one quart of water.

Decorative tinware of the type being imported from Mexico can be coated with clear lacquer or with hard wax to protect the finish. Lacquer is best if the tinware is to be used outdoors.

Tin Foil See "Metallic" in "Stains," p. 233.

Toaster See "Electric Toaster."

Tobacco See "Grass, Flowers, Foliage," in "Stains," p. 229.

Toilet Before adding a cleaner or disinfectant, flush the toilet to wet the sides of the bowl. Sprinkle the cleaner on the wet surfaces and in the water. Let it stand for a few minutes, then clean the bowl with a toilet brush or swab. If stains remain, sprinkle on more cleaner and let it stand for at least an hour, preferably overnight, and again brush or swab. Repeat if necessary. Such stains are usually caused by hard water and do not appear if the toilet is cleaned regularly.

For cleaning, preferably use a standard commercial preparation (Vanish, Saniflush) and follow the directions on the label exactly. Do not ever try to improve their action by adding any other cleaning or bleaching agents. Toxic gases could be released. Store bowl cleaners carefully; many are poisonous. Do not use them for stains in sinks or bathtubs; they damage the finish. Clean the outside of the bowl, the rim and the seat with hot soapsuds or a mild scouring powder. Rinse and wipe dry to avoid streaks.

Toilet bowl brushes should be washed promptly after use in hot soapsuds, rinsed thoroughly, and hung to dry. Use paper toweling for the rim and outside of the toilet and discard them.

Tôle Tôle is painted metal, used most often for lamp bases and trays. See "Lamp—Electric."

Tools If you like to putter about with tools, perhaps you ought to know the fundamentals for their care. Rust, next to the borrower, is their worst enemy. If a spot appears, remove it promptly with fine emery cloth. To prevent rust wipe tools now and then with a cloth

moistened with any good oil. Olive oil is perfect; vaseline is all right. Linseed oil is worse than none for metal, but it is good for wooden handles.

Store sharp tools so that the cutting edges won't be damaged . . . planes on their sides, chisels in racks, etc.

Trash Compactor The exterior and interior walls of the General Electric trash compactor are finished with baked-on synthetic enamel. They should be cleaned with a high-grade wax cleaner. (Do not use harsh or gritty abrasive cleaners or scouring pads.)

To clean the top front of the ram disc, first remove the bucket from the door. Take off the top ring and handle from the bucket and set them aside. Put the bucket back inside the cabinet and shut the door. Push the starter button and let the machine run for about four seconds. Turn the key to "off" and open the door. This should allow clear access to the top of the disc for cleaning. (*Warning:* Look out for glass fragments which may be on top of the ram disc.)

Close the door, turn the key to the on position, and press the starter button. The ram should return to its upward position. Open the door and replace the top ring and handle on the bucket. Replace the bucket on the door.

To clean the cabinet interior, first lift out the trash bucket. Wash the ram and the interior with soap or detergent, and dry. (Look out for glass particles in the ram or lying in the bottom of the cabinet.)

The trash bucket can be cleaned as follows: Remove the top rim and handle and wash the bucket with hot soapsuds. Dry thoroughly. Insert new bag. (Particles of glass may be embedded in the surface of the bucket; use care when cleaning.)

Compactors not of General Electric origin may vary slightly in materials and arrangement, but they are essentially similar in function.

Trevira See "Polyester."

Triacetate A man-made textile fiber. See "Arnel."

Trichloroethane Do not use on Arnel and Kodel. See "Chlorothene" and "Cleaning Fluids."

Trichloroethylene See "Cleaning Fluids."

Tripoli Tripoli is another name for rottenstone. See "Rottenstone."

Trisodium Phosphate See "Soda and Soda Compounds."

Tucks Iron vertical tucks lengthwise. Iron rows of tucks from the top down, in sections.

Turkish Towels Wash turkish towels like any other cotton material. Fluff them with a vigorous shake and hang them straight on the line (or tumble dry). Stretch woven borders gently. When dry, give them another good shake and fold them neatly. No starch. No ironing.

193

Turmeric See "Stains," p. 238.

Turpentine Turpentine is a resinous juice obtained from pine and fir trees. It is used as a solvent in certain paints, varnishes and waxes and as an ingredient of furniture polishes and washes. Turpentine will remove wax from floors that need a complete rewaxing job. It will remove paint stains and grease. In treating furniture, turpentine is valuable because it has the ability to penetrate the finish and restore the original color of the stain.

Caution: Turpentine is flammable and poisonous.

Typewriter Clean the platen (large rubber roller) and the little rubber rollers that feed in the paper by wiping them periodically with a clean cloth, moistened with alcohol. This will keep them free of ink, and resilient. Some platens are removable. This makes it possible to brush out easily the inevitable accumulation of dust and erasings.

Type can be cleaned with alcohol or cleaning fluid. Slip a blotter or folded paper under the type bars and scrub the type with a stiff-bristled typewriter brush. The paper will absorb any excess fluid. A doughy compound also is available at typewriter stores for this purpose and (very easy to use) a cleaner that is sprayed on.

Once a month oil the carriage rails. To do this move the carriage over to the extreme left and place *one* drop of typewriter oil on the rails. Do *not* oil the type bars.

Precaution: When making erasures move the carriage over so that erasings will drop out of the ma-

194

chine. If using a portable, replace the lid after use to safeguard it against dust. Cover larger models with a dust jacket. When your typewriter is not in use the paper release lever should be down, or in the released position. Constant pressure on the paper feed rolls tends to flatten them and make them less efficient. Brush out dust and erasings regularly.

Umbrella The heck with old wives' tales. Open up your wet umbrella when you come in out of the rain and give it a chance to dry decently to avoid streaks. If a rib slips out of place you can cement it in easily, using one of those handy tubes of quick-drying household cement that you can buy in any hardware store or drugstore.

There are umbrella specialists in every city who will supply new handles, new covers and make any sort of repair, so don't run to buy a new parasol at the first sign of trouble.

Upholstery See "Furniture—Upholstered" and "Vinyl."

Urea See "Melamine and Urea."

Urethane Urethane foam, polyfoam, or "plastic" foam is used for package cushioning, rug underlays, sometimes for furniture cushioning and mattresses. It is a plastic material. Small items are washable.

Urine Stains See "Stains," p. 238.

Vacuum Bottle See "Bottle—Vacuum."

Vacuum Cleaner Pamper your vacuum cleaner. Think how much it does for you! If you don't keep it clean and in good working order it will get even with you by making a joke of your house-cleaning efforts. Just dumping the bag, or container, regularly is not enough.

Before you start on a floor pick up pins, buttons and other objects that might make it choke. Move it slowly in straight, even strokes, lengthwise of the rug, and go over each section at least seven times. Avoid swishing the wand like a broom if your machine is of that type.

Disposable paper bags have largely eliminated the need to empty dust bags. If you still use a cloth bag, turn it upside down on a newspaper, hold the mouth firmly in place (use your feet) and gently shake out the dirt. This is Rule One. But remember that the air you use in the suction process may be filtered through the bag and that, if the pores of the fabric are clogged with dust, your machine will operate less efficiently. Rub the sides of the bag together gently to loosen embedded dirt. Now and then turn it inside out and give it a good brushing with a stiff whisk broom. (Outdoors, of course.) This will be a good time to check on its condition. Hold it to the light and inspect it for rips and tears. If you find any, it's time to invest in a new bag. Never wash a dust bag.

If your vacuum cleaner has a water container for dust, empty it after using, wash the container with soap and water, rinse and dry it, then return it to the cleaner.

Vacuum off all hair and lint from the brushes. If the brushes become worn get new ones or treat them to new bristles. Wipe off other attachments before storing them.

Filters used on some types of vacuum cleaners need replacing every six months. In between they should be removed now and then and vacuumed.

Upright vacuum cleaners should be inverted for cleaning. Remove hair and threads that get wound around the brush and rotating cylinder. Once a week the roll should be removed from the nozzle and the bearing at the end should be examined for hairs or threads. A little rubber belt usually is used to secure this roll and care must be taken that it is replaced correctly when the roll is put back into place. And be sure the belt itself is in good condition. It is a good idea to keep a few on hand so that you can replace a belt that is cracked or loose. Buy the kind that is made for your particular machine.

Many women put the various attachments of their vacuum cleaners on a shelf or in a drawer and forget all about them. This is partly because it is a bother to tote them from room to room. Some of the newer models have solved this problem by devising ways for them to ride pickaback.

The attachments are great labor-savers and enable you to do a really thorough job. The little duster will

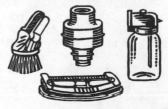

whisk dirt and dust from lamp shades, the insides of drawers, from moldings, the crevices of brick fireplaces, from hard-to-reach corners and carved surfaces. The floor brush will also dust the walls, gobbling webs, spiders, and even hornets.

Not only stuffed furniture but draperies, curtains, mattresses, blankets, coats and hats can be cleaned with the upholstery attachment. An enterprising salesman once told me that this part would even remove fleas from a dog, but, since none was available, we were unable to test the theory and the possible canine reaction. The spray attachment can be used for spraying rug shampoos, liquid wax, insecticides and mothproofing compounds.

Vanadium A metal added to steel to make it more flexible and tougher. See "Steel–Vanadium."

Varnish See "Paint, Varnish" in "Stains," p. 234.

Vase Look up the material of which the vase is made.

Vaseline See "Petroleum Jelly."

Velcro Cockleburs gave Swiss inventor George de Mestral his inspiration for the Velcro fastener. It consists of two woven nylon tapes—one covered with hundreds of tiny loops and the other with hooks—that lock securely when pressed together and are peeled open lengthwise. The tape can be cut to size in patches and lengths, and can be stitched, glued, or stapled to cloth, metal, wood, or plastics, to form closures.

Velcro can be substituted for zippers, buttons, snaps, toggles, and hooks and eyes on clothing. It can do things that zippers can't do—fasten down a square, for instance, and provide adjustable fasteners by varying the amount of overlap. This is a boon for such items as brassières, wrap-around dresses and housecoats, skirts and petticoats, diapers, and reversible belts.

Experiments have determined that only half a pound of pressure is needed to peel the tapes apart, while a 16-pound yank is required to open them sideways. This means they won't pop open under stress.

Velcro is washable and dry cleanable. Bleaches do not hurt it and it does not melt or fuse under normal pressing temperatures. But close the fastener before washing to avoid pickup of lint, fuzz, and threads, and during pressing to minimize the danger of breaking the little hooks.

Vellum Vellum is a fine grade of parchment made from the skins of lambs, kids, or very young goats. See "Parchment."

Velon Velon is a saran vinylidene chloride monofilament used mainly in webbing for outdoor furniture, automobile seat covers, insect screens, and venetian blind tape. It is cleaned by wiping with soapy water; the furniture can be hosed down. The monofilament is nonabsorbent with excellent chemical, weather, and mildew resistance. Its colors tend to darken a little with prolonged exposure to the sun.

Velvet Washable velvets and velveteens are handled like corduroy. The label on the garment should be your guide in determining whether the material will stand water. Those that are nonwashable should be sent to a dry cleaner. If the nap is merely crushed, you can fluff it by steaming it over the spout of a teakettle.

To steam velvet follow these directions. Tie a piece of muslin or several layers of cheesecloth over the spout of the kettle. When the water is boiling rapidly pass the crushed velvet back and forth through the steam, making certain that the steam goes from the wrong to the right side. Velvet is never pressed. Let the material dry thoroughly before wearing it.

For laundering washable velvets see "Corduroy."

Venetian Blinds To dust, drop the blind to its full length, tilt to full-light position and dust with a divided venetian blind brush which does several blades at a time. Or turn the blades flat and dust them with the round dusting brush of your vacuum cleaner. Turn the other way and dust the reverse side.

To wash painted or plastic blinds use a sponge or soft cloth, wrung out in suds made of a mild detergent or a good paint-cleaning solution (Oakite, washing soda), washing one slat at a time . . . both sides. Rinse and dry carefully. Some venetian blind cleaners wax as they clean.

If the blinds are of natural wood

finish, clean them with liquid wax, one slat at a time, changing the cloth as it becomes soiled. Rub up with a soft cloth.

Tapes can be scrubbed with a brush made of plastic. Use soap or detergent.

Venetian blind tape and cord can be bought by the yard, if you wish to renew them. Be sure to measure carefully the distance between the cross-tapes if you want the blinds to be the same length. Better yet, take a sample with you. Replacing tapes is a tedious job and is to be recommended only if you are handy at such operations and anxious to save money. Otherwise you can have them redone professionally.

Verel Verel is the trade name for a modacrylic fiber spun from an acetone preparation. It is a soft, resilient, low temperature fiber, highly resistant to acids, alkalies, and other chemicals. It will not support flames and is resistant to damage from sunlight, age, mildew, moths and other insects, and rot. These qualities suggested carpeting as a prime role for the fiber.

According to its producers, tests have disclosed that Verel carpeting is equal to wool for wear (second only to nylon), with higher strength and stretch and better elastic recovery. In addition it is readily dyeable in both dull and light lusters in a range of bright and pastel colors.

Verel fibers are smooth, and shed dust and dirt easily. They are easily shampooed, and most ordinary stains can be removed with a soft cloth or sponge and a detergent solution or cleaning fluid. Do not use acetone for spot removal.

197

Vinegar Vinegar is often useful in cleaning because it cuts soap film. A little in a bowl of water will help remove cloudiness from furniture. It also is useful in stain removal to counteract alkalies and restore altered colors. Vinegar is about 5 percent acetic acid. For stain removal select white vinegar. For vinegar stains see "Acid" in "Stains," p. 224.

Vinyl Vinyl plastics are made from such raw materials as coal, limestone, natural gas, petroleum, and brine. The first vinyl plastic was made by the French scientist Regnault more than one hundred years ago.

Vinyls may be rigid, semirigid, film, sheeting, or a coating. They may be of any color or colorless—transparent, translucent, or opaque. Sturdy, long wearing, and resistant to abrasion, they are hard to break if rigid, and hard to tear if flexible. They resist the penetration of water, but must be guarded against high heat from oven or flame. Special types are made for outdoor use.

Flexible vinyls appear in the home as upholstery, raincoats, curtains, garment bags, packaging material, inflated toys, jackets, boots, pants for babies, dresses, sun hats, bikinis, skirts, men's vests, walking shorts, and trousers. Rigid vinyls are used for phonograph records, roll flooring, and floor tiles.

Vinyl film can be bent back and forth many times without sustaining breaks or tears, and rigid vinyls will return to their original shape after a blow, but sharp knocks should be avoided.

Such plastics are not harmed by common chemicals, resist acids, alcohol and stains from food, ink, and dirt. They have a low absorp-

tion rate. They are fire-resistant—some types stop burning as soon as the flame is removed, while others actually snuff out fire. Vinyls are light in weight and their colors will withstand long exposure to the sun without fading. All of these qualities recommend them for upholstery.

Vinyl film can be stamped in dainty patterns, and the material can be hemmed, tucked, pleated, and seamed by heat. When closely boxed, vinyls may develop a slight (not unpleasant) odor but this disappears with airing.

Hand-wash vinyl plastics with warm water and soap or synthetic detergent. Keep hot dishes and burning cigarettes away and, in cleaning, do not use ammonia, nail polish remover, acetone, or abrasives. Some vinyl products have a tendency to stick to, mar, or discolor lacquered surfaces when in close contact under certain conditions. If you are using moth or insect sprays, be careful not to spatter vinyl surfaces.

Vinyl upholstery needs only wiping with a damp cloth, but it can be washed when necessary with warm water and mild soap. Sponge a good-sized area and let the soapy solution remain for a minute or two, then rinse with a damp sponge. If the soil is not removed, rub it again or scrub it lightly with a soft-bristled brush.

Common stains can be removed as follows: chewing gum—scrape off as much as possible and remove the residue with naphtha, kerosene, or lighter fluid; paint and shoe polish—wipe up immediately and remove the rest with turpentine (do *not* use brush cleaner or paint remover); tar, asphalt, road oil— remove immediately with turpentine or lighter fluid to avoid a permanent stain; ink—wipe away immediately with water or alcohol; nail polish and remover—to minimize the damage, blot carefully or daub up instantly (wiping spreads the damage).

Vinyl plastic floors are nonskid and easy on the feet. They resist abrasion, acid, grease, and alkalies. They are washed with warm water and either a soap or detergent. Waxing is optional. Either self-polishing or polishing waxes can be used, but self-polishing waxes are preferred.

Viscose Rayon See "Rayon."

Viyella Trade name for a wool and cotton fabric made in England. Viyella is 55 percent wool and 45 percent cotton. It washes almost like cotton and doesn't shrink. Wash with warm suds made with soap or a synthetic detergent. Iron on either the right or wrong side with the temperature setting on "wool."

Vycron This is the trade name for a polyester fiber made from a polymerized resin. Vycron is used for suitings, dress fabrics and raincoats of the wash-and-wear type, and for upholstery. It dyes well and the fabrics have excellent colorfastness. They are wrinkle-resistant, pill-re-

sistant, and very strong. Consult the label as to whether to wash or dry-clean. Washable Vycron should be ironed at a temperature of 300° F. (lower than silk). See "Synthetic Textiles."

Waffle Iron See "Electric Waffle Iron."

Walks Sweep walks with a heavy broom and wash them down occasionally with spray from the garden hose.

Wallpaper See "Walls and Ceilings."

Walls and Ceilings Some bright day, when your energy is high, it may strike you suddenly that your walls need cleaning. Assemble your ammunition, clear the decks, and go into action while the mood is upon you. Whatever the wall, your first step is to turn back the rugs (or take them out), shove the furniture to the middle of the floor and cover it and take down the pictures.

For *painted walls* you will need: a wall brush, either hand or vacuum, or cloth-covered broom; two sponges; two pails, one for your washing mixture and one for rinsing; a good mild soap or a chemical cleaner. (See "Paint Cleaners" for information about preparations suitable for flat and enameled paint.)

Your first step is to dust the walls. Cobwebs and dust threads are attached by one end and hang down. They will be removed most readily if you dust from the bottom of the wall up. After dusting carefully begin washing, again from the bottom up. The reason for this is

199

that if dirty water runs down over the soiled part it leaves streaks that are hard to remove. Squeeze your sponge or cloth as dry as possible and clean a small area (not more than three square feet) at a time, using a circular motion. Rinse with a sponge squeezed out of clear water and wipe the area dry. Proceed to the space adjoining this and repeat, taking care to overlap the edges of the area just cleaned. Continue until the wall has been finished.

Note: If you are using soap and water, you might add borax to the suds to soften it and make the job easier. Use one tablespoon of borax per quart of water and add it to the rinse water too. Scouring powders damage paint so do not use them unless the walls are extremely dirty and a new paint job is indicated. A little whiting, or a mild scouring powder, usually will remove scuff marks. And, of course, remember to change the water in your pails as soon as it gets dirty or you will frustrate your efforts. If you are using a commercial paint cleaner, follow the directions exactly. Too much will damage, or even remove, the paint.

If you are cleaning a painted wall with the idea of repainting it, give it a final wash with turpentine. This will remove any greasy film and help bind the paint to the wall.

Walls finished with *calcimine* and similar washes cannot be Paints of the Kem-tone type, which

cleaned. They must be redone. have an oil base, though they are mixed with water, can be cleaned but are difficult. See "Calcimine," "Whitewash."

Papered walls You may not know whether the paper on your walls is washable, but even if it is so labeled it is a good idea to test it in an inconspicuous place before proceeding with an all-over job. Squeeze a sponge out of clear, lukewarm water and rub very lightly. Use as little water as possible to avoid soaking the paper off the wall. If the pattern doesn't blur and the test is otherwise successful, go ahead with the washing, working from the bottom of the wall up. At least one grade-A decorator concurs with me in my belief that no papers are really washable.

For thin papers clear warm water with no soap is recommended. Strokes should be overlapped and gently patted dry. Do not rub. For the heavier washable papers use a suds made of mild white soap. Apply with a soft sponge, squeezed out of the suds, and wash a small area at a time, proceeding with a very light touch. Rinse with a sponge squeezed out of clear water. Pat dry with a clean soft cloth.

Nonwashable papers can be cleaned with a commercial cleaner that looks like a lump of dough and can be bought in paint and hardware stores. Follow the directions on the container. Or you can use any of the following: art gum; the inside of a loaf of stale bread, preferably rye; wheat bran sewed in a bag; or pipe clay. Overlap your strokes and proceed with great care or the wall will look streaky.

Stains on wallpaper Grease spots

should be removed from wallpaper promptly. Make a paste by mixing fuller's earth, french chalk or other absorbent powder with cleaning fluid. Test an inconspicuous place to make sure the colors won't bleed, then smooth the mixture on the spot. Allow it to dry thoroughly, then brush it off. For a bad spot two or three applications may be necessary. To remove crayon marks, try sponging them lightly with a soft cloth moistened with cleaning fluid. (Test first.) It may be necessary to repeat the sponging a number of times. Washable papers may be given a final soap and water treatment. If the cleaning fluid leaves a ring on nonwashable wallpaper, try the fuller's earth poultice described for grease stains. Ink spilled on wallpaper should be blotted up promptly. Be careful not to smear it. Apply fuller's earth or French chalk. Brush off the absorbent as quickly as it takes up the ink. This may not remove the stain completely. Try ink eradicator (obtainable at a drugstore) to finish the job, but remember that it is likely to remove the color, too.

Clean light smudges and pencil marks with art gum. Brush off food stains as well as possible and sponge any greasy marks that remain with cleaning fluid, or apply a poultice made with it, as described for grease stains.

Wallpapers that have been lacquered can be washed safely with warm suds. Rinse and wipe dry. Wall waxes, available at paint and wallpaper stores, also make cleaning easier. Spots on these can be wiped off with a damp cloth.

Wood-paneled walls, if waxed, require little attention other than dusting. If they become soiled, or

begin to look dry, clean them with liquid wax, and rub to a soft polish. Varnished or shellacked wood paneling that is not waxed can be cleaned with a polish made by mixing half a cup of turpentine with a cup of boiled linseed oil (see "Linseed Oil") and about a tablespoon of vinegar. Apply sparingly. Let it stand for fifteen minutes, then rub until no smudge is left by a clean, dry finger.

Fabric-coated walls should be cleaned according to the directions provided by the manufacturer for the covering. If you do not know who manufactured the covering, ask for a cleaner made especially for this type of wall.

Walnut Stains See "Stains," p. 238.

Wash and Wear The term wash and wear is applied to garments made of synthetic textiles with a "memory" which enables them to return to their original wrinkle-proof state when properly washed and drip dried. Such textiles include nylon, polyesters, acrylics, and their blends.

When instructions have been provided by the manufacturer, follow them. Otherwise, use these directions, based mainly on material provided by the du Pont company for Dacron, Orlon, nylon, and high-percentage blends of these fibers:

Before washing, to insure best results, pretreat badly soiled areas by rubbing in heavy-duty liquid detergent or a paste made with a detergent powder. Cleaning fluids can be used on oily stains. Remove any trim, such as ribbon bows, which may not be washable.

Hand wash articles of delicate

201

trim or construction. Always wash white and colored clothing separately. If touch-up ironing is needed, use either a steam or dry iron at a rayon or synthetic setting.

Hand washing Use plenty of lukewarm water (100° F.) and a heavy-duty synthetic detergent, or soap with a softener such as Calgon. Do not wring or twist the garment. Rinse thoroughly in lukewarm water. Place the garment, dripping wet, on a nonstaining hanger. Shape the collar and cuffs. Gently adjust seams.

Machine washing If your washer has a special synthetic setting, use it. Otherwise use warm water and a heavy-duty detergent or soap with a softener such as Calgon. Do not crowd the clothes. At the end of the rinsing cycle, and before beginning the final spin, stop the machine and remove the garments dripping wet and place them on hangers. Adjust collars, cuffs, seams.

Drip-drying gives the best results, but a tumbler dryer can be used. If clothing is to be tumble dried, use the complete washing and spin-dry cycles. Set the dryer for low or medium heat and add the clothes. When they are dry, let them tumble without heat for 10 minutes. Remove them from the dryer immediately and place them on hangers.

Bluing and optical whiteners can be used on white synthetics and any bleach is safe provided the garments have not been given a durable-press finish and do not contain spandex fibers. If in doubt, use a peroxy bleach.

Severe discoloration of white

synthetics (due to improper washing or inadequate rinsing) can often be corrected by an alkali soak. (Do not use this method if the fabric contains rayon.)

Dissolve 1 cup of Calgonite or Electra-sol (compounds made for electric dishwasher) in 1 gallon of warm water (130° to 140° F.), using a plastic or enameled container. Completely submerge the discolored articles in this solution and let them soak for 30 to 45 minutes, or overnight at room temperature. Without drying, wash by machine. *Caution:* Do not let this alkali solution remain in contact with your skin for long and avoid getting it into your eyes.

See "Nylon," "Dacron," etc. See also, for special pointers, "Sweaters *Synthetic*," "Pillows," "Blanket (Synthetic)," "Nylon Coat," "Comforter," etc.

Wash Basin See "Bathtub."

Washing Machine Whatever its make, the consideration you give your washing machine will help determine its length of life and the job it does on your clothes. Overloading strains the motor, and the clothes are not properly washed. Too much soap or detergent spreads a blanket of suds and makes soil removal difficult. If your machine has a lint trap, clean it often. These are primary rules.

In using your particular machine you should follow the manufacturer's directions for best results. If yours have been lost, write to the manufacturer, giving the model number which is stamped somewhere on the washer. The directions which follow are for general care.

Automatic Washers When washing is completed, turn off both faucets to eliminate pressure on the hoses. Occasionally wipe the exterior with a clean damp sponge or cloth. Use of an appliance wax is optional. If you use it, do not apply it to plastic parts.

During normal use, the inside of a front-loading (tumbler) washer is self-cleaning. Occasionally remove the agitator from top-loading washers and clean the washer basket underneath. Wipe out the inside of the agitator.

General Electric says that about every 4 to 6 months the agitator should be removed and inspected for lint which may have accumulated on the underside. The slotted section at the top of the metal shaft has been given a slight coating of lubricant to prevent the parts from sticking together. If this looks dry, apply a very light coating of grease or petroleum jelly around the slotted portion of the shaft before replacing the agitator.

Replace the agitator carefully by lowering it straight down on the shaft so that it fits into the slots. Then push down until the agitator snaps into its normal position.

If the machine has been used for starching or tinting, it will need special attention. Washing a load of clothes after starching will re-move any excess starch from the basket. Or start the washer at the final rinse and let it complete the cycle. To remove traces of tint, use detergent and chlorine bleach. For top-loading washers use 1 cup of detergent and 1 cup of bleach; for front-loading washers use ½ cup of detergent and ½ cup of bleach. Start at wash and complete the cycle. Wipe off any tint that may have spilled on the exterior with a diluted bleach solution and rinse well with a clean damp sponge. If the rubber around the door remains discolored, wipe it with a diluted bleach solution and rinse thoroughly. The clothes guard of top-loading washers may be permanently tinted.

Nonautomatic washers should be cleaned when the last load has been removed. Lift out the washing mechanism (unless directions say not to), wash and dry it. Remove any hard-water deposit from the tub, using soapsuds on a cloth dipped in a strong solution of water softener. Rinse the tub and wipe it dry. (Never use an abrasive.) Clean lint and ravelings from the drain screen or trap. Drain off any remaining water by lowering the hose. Replace the washing mechanism in the tub, preferably leaving it off the shaft. Disconnect the electric cord. Release pressure on the wringer rolls because if left compressed they are likely to become flattened, and the rubber may stick and tear. Always leave the rollers clean and dry.

Washing Soda See "Soda and Soda Compounds."

Wasps and Hornets Wasps and hornets are beneficial insects that destroy many garden pests. Only a few of the many varieties sting. However, they should be destroyed if they build their nests in the attic rafters, porch corners, and near locations where children play. The nests may be circular combs of cells, large globular paper-like constructions, or little joined cells of mud. Some species nest in the ground.

Uncle Sam suggests cloak-and-dagger tactics for the job of destroying a hornets' nest. Wear dark clothes, carry a flashlight, and wait for your zero hour, one hour after dark when the insects are asleep. Your lethal weapon will be a surface spray or dust containing chlordane. Use your flashlight cautiously as you reconnoiter your enemy. Work fast, then beat a hasty but orderly retreat.

For a nest on a porch, under the eaves, or in the attic, where the insecticide will not come into contact with plants, use either an oil- or water-based surface spray. If the nest is in a tree or shrubbery use a water-based spray to avoid damage to foliage. Spray the nest thoroughly, as close to the opening as possible.

For a nest in the ground (yellow jackets, cicada killers) use an insecticide dust containing chlordane. The entrance to such a nest is a hole up to the size of a quarter. A few puffs of dust should do the trick. Cover the hole with a shovelful of moist earth afterward to keep the wasps from escaping. The colony should be killed within 24 hours.

The night treatment minimizes the danger of your being stung by escapees. If anyone with asthma, hay fever, or other allergies should be stung, his physician should be promptly notified. See "Insecticides" for precautions.

Watch A watch should be cleaned and oiled regularly . . . men's watches every twelve or eighteen months, small wrist watches every eight months. The tiny watch on your wrist needs more frequent attention because it works harder (31,000,000 ticks a year) and is constructed more delicately. It will warn you when the time for overhauling is overdue by refusing to run. Even the best oil thickens with time and the delicate mainspring of a small watch cannot overcome the resistance of congealed oil. A large watch, on the other hand, because of its more powerful mainspring, will keep on running for a while after almost all of the lubrication has disappeared, just as an automobile will, and with equally disastrous results.

Men's pocket watches should be wound once a day, preferably in the morning and at the same hour. Small wrist watches will give their best service if they are wound both at night and in the morning. This practice keeps the mainspring taut and helps overcome damage from the many shifts of position a wrist watch experiences.

Many persons injure their watches, especially small wrist watches, in setting them. The winder should never be pulled out, because there is always the danger that it will break off or come out

Wasp   Hornet

erals and form an insoluble compound (precipitate), and those that do not form a precipitate but keep the minerals in solution.

Precipitating softeners, such as washing soda, borax, and Raindrops, should always be dissolved in the wash water before soap is added because once soap scum is formed they cannot dissolve it. Nonprecipitating softeners, among them Tex and White King, prevent scum from forming and dissolve scum left on clothes by previous washing. (Add softener to the first rinse too.)

Water hardness varies and it is important to use the right amount of softener. Too little will not correct the trouble and too much may make the water alkaline. A simple test, suggested by the Department of Agriculture, will determine the proper amount of softener to use.

To 1 gallon of hot water (140° F.) add ½ teaspoon of the softener you intend to use; stir to dissolve. Put 2 cups of this solution in a quart jar and add ½ teaspoon of the soap you have selected. Shake the jar vigorously for 10 seconds. If good suds result and they hold for 5 minutes, the water has been softened. Repeat the experiment, using less softener, to see if a smaller amount will do the job.

If ½ teaspoon of softener fails to produce good suds, repeat the experiment with fresh hot water, using 1 teaspoon of softener in 1 gallon of water. Continue experimenting until you have determined the proper amount of softener. You save on soap (and detergent) if the water you use is soft.

Home owners in hard-water areas can solve the problem once and for all by installing a water-softening system. Such systems are available

altogether. The proper way to set any watch is to place the thumb nail and middle finger nail just below the winder and press them together. This forces the winder out slightly to permit the setting of the hands, after which it should be snapped back into position.

A few "don'ts." Don't open the back of your watch; moisture and dust are harmful. Don't fail to remove your wrist watch before washing your hands. Should your watch become accidentally wet, send it to your jeweler promptly to prevent rust and a large repair bill. Don't wind your watch too tight; you may break the mainspring. A loose hold on the stem acts as a safety valve.

Water and Water Softeners Water is said to be "hard" when it contains an excessive mineral content (usually calcium, magnesium or iron), which counteracts the action of soap and makes successful laundering difficult. More soap is needed in hard water, and a scum is deposited on the clothes.

The problem can be solved by using synthetic detergents instead of soap or by adding a softener to the water. Water softeners are of two types: precipitating—those that combine with the hard-water min-

205

from manufacturers specializing in this field. They make use of complex soda compounds in a form that resembles clay. These compounds are called zeolites.

For the care of water-softening systems see "Zeolites."

Water Color Paintings One of the things that makes an art museum curator practically wild is the perennial query about cleaning water colors, or what can be done to restore them after they have been washed with soap and water. You *cannot* clean them. Leave them alone.

Water Heater Have your hot-water heater cleaned and serviced once a year by your fuel company when the heating system is checked and cleaned. The burner, flue and chimney should receive attention and the water should be drained to remove any sediment.

Automatic gas and electric heaters require little or no attention, once they are correctly installed. If the water is hard, it may be necessary to have the heating element checked occasionally and the lime deposit removed.

Water heaters are of many types . . . oil, coal, wood, etc. Cleaning and caring for them properly is a job for a capable serviceman, not for the homemaker or inexperienced household mechanic.

For average use the setting on the thermostat control should be about 140° F. Higher temperatures put extra wear and tear on the tank and plumbing lines and are a hazard to small children. If, however, your water heater is linked with a hot water heating system, the thermostat control may have to be set much higher in the winter to

secure adequate heat. Ask your fuel serviceman about this matter.

Water-Repellent Finish Follow the washing, or dry-cleaning, instructions on the label of garments with water-repellent finishes. Some stand up under repeated washing and dry cleaning. Others are removed, but can be restored by your dry cleaner. If the garment is washable, follow instructions for the fabric of which the garment is made. See also "Raincoats," "Zelan," "Silicones."

Water Softeners See "Water and Water Softeners.

Water Spots See "Furniture." Also see "Stains," p. 239.

Wax Two basic types of wax are made for floors: *polishing waxes,* which require buffing, and *self-polishing waxes,* which dry to a glossy finish without buffing.

Polishing waxes may be either liquid or paste. The ingredients of these are the same, but the liquid wax contains more solvent. Polishing waxes provide a beautiful and lasting finish and, if properly applied and maintained, do not ever need to be removed. Paste wax is highly concentrated, very durable, and economical to use. Liquid polishing waxes are excellent for cleaning floors. The naphtha in them dissolves surface grime so that it can be wiped away, while the wax in the mixture remains on the floor to be buffed. Polishing waxes can be used on many types of floor and are the best kind for wood. They can be identified by their pungent odor.

Self-polishing waxes use water as a carrier for microscopically small particles of solid wax. The water keeps the particles separated, and when it evaporates, a shiny film of wax remains on the floor. These waxes have practically no odor and do not require buffing. Such waxes are most often used on types of flooring not harmed by water, which require frequent cleaning.

Water-based self-polishing waxes must be periodically removed because each application builds up on the previous one. Unlike the solvent-based waxes, a new coating does not remove the old. When a floor begins to look shabby—usually after 6 to 8 coats, or once a year—remove the old wax completely. To do this, use the following mixture: 1 cup of ammonia and ¼ cup of powdered floor cleaner (Spic 'n Span, Soilax) added to each half gallon of cool or cold water. Apply the cleaner generously with a cloth or sponge over a 3 foot by 3 foot area of floor space. Let it soak for 3 to 5 minutes. Immediately after soaking, loosen the softened wax by scrubbing it briskly with steel wool (grade 0, 1, or 2) or with plastic or nylon scouring pads. (Scrubbing with a sponge mop or brushes will not provide enough abrasion to lift the softened wax.) Wipe up the solution and dissolved wax promptly with a cloth or sponge. Rinse the floor with clear water until no residue remains. It may be necessary to go over the floor again if it is not completely clean. To test, scrape a coin across the floor. If there is a residue, the wax has not been fully removed. Try again.

Similar in use are polyethylene emulsions which provide a tough spot-resistant finish that will last through numerous damp moppings. Such finishes may be applied, when the floor is clean and thoroughly dry, to linoleum, asphalt, rubber, vinyl and cork tiles, plastic sheet flooring and terrazzo.

In buying paste wax for floors or furniture, remember that you can get light and dark shades. Use light shades for blond woods, dark for mahogany, walnut, etc.

Many different kinds of wax are used in making the prepared waxes we know, and the hardest of these is carnauba, obtained from the Brazilian wax palm tree known botanically as *Copernicia cerifera*. Carnauba is valuable because it makes possible self-polishing and high-gloss wax polishes.

Wax Applicator Long-handled applicators eliminate knee action in waxing floors. Some have hollow handles so that liquid or self-polishing waxes can be poured in and dispensed evenly by pressing a lever. For cleaning operations with liquid wax there are steel wool pads that slip over the base to scrub the floor gently as the wax goes on. Push a cloth across the floor and the grime is taken up. Nylon and chenille pads, washable and replaceable, make light work of the chore of applying self-polishing waxes. Always wash applicators promptly before the wax hardens.

Waxer Weighted buffers are to be had for polishing wax floors but an electric model makes things easier. These can be rented. See "Electric Waxer."

Wax Stains See "Greasy Stains," p. 222.

Weevils See "Pantry Pests."

Wet Spotter Wet spotter is prepared by mixing 1 part of glycerin, 1 part of liquid hand dishwashing detergent, and 8 parts of water. Shake well before each use. This mixture will remove many types of stain. It can be stored conveniently in a plastic squeeze bottle with a small cap.

White Sauce See "Combination Stains," p. 223.

Whitewash Whitewashed surfaces cannot be cleaned; they must be given a fresh coating. Whitewash formulas vary. For instance, you would use different mixtures for inside and outside jobs and a special blend for walls that are inclined to be damp. The following recipe is for average inside use.

Mix thoroughly one pound of powdered glue and one gallon of water. In another container mix twenty pounds of hydrated lime with two gallons of water, stirring carefully until all lumps have been eliminated. Combine the two mixtures and mix until very smooth. Thin with water to a suitable consistency and apply with a whitewash brush.

Whiting Whiting is a very fine preparation of chalk. It is used in cleaning powders, polishes, in making putty and oilcloth. It can be bought by the pound at paint stores.

In preparing whiting the chalk,

from the chalk cliffs of Dover, is dried in the air or in a kiln and then ground. After that it is levigated (floated off on the surface of water) and again ground. Fine whiting, moistened with ammonia, is all our English cousins ever use to polish their famous silver. For this purpose it is sold in England in little blocks and tuppence buys a block large enough to keep the silver gleaming for months. There are many other household uses for whiting, noted in this book.

Whiting is known, in trade, by different names, depending on the amount of labor that has been expended to make it fine and free from grit. The grades are: ordinary, or commercial whiting, Spanish white, gilders' whiting and Paris white, the best grade. Gilders' whiting is suitable for polishing silver.

If you have trouble finding whiting in ordinary hardware stores, go to a paint store of the type patronized by professional painters.

Wicker Wicker furniture and wicker baskets are made of osiers, rattan twigs, or thin, flexible strips of wood. Unless finished with a paint or varnish damaged by water, they should get an occasional wetting to keep them from becoming dry or brittle. See "Furniture— Wicker."

Windows Aerosol sprays take the muss and fuss out of window washing and reduce the amount of equipment that must be carried about. You spray the cleaner on, then wipe the glass clean with soft paper towels or with window wipes. Because they are so convenient to use and because they keep the hands out of water, many women consider them well worth the extra cost.

Otherwise, many simple home mixtures will clean windows. Professionals, who polish off a hundred a day, are adamant in their view that clear, cool water is best. And the heartiness of their conviction was demonstrated some years ago in Westchester County, New York, when a window washer actually murdered a woman who kept telling him to put in a little alcohol. This would seem to indicate a hands-off policy, if you have located a professional to do your windows for you.

If you are doing the job yourself, use plain water or water containing vinegar, washing soda, borax, kerosene, alcohol, ammonia, or trisodium phosphate. Use about a tablespoon of ammonia or vinegar for each quart of water, about two teaspoons of borax or kerosene, one to two teaspoons of washing soda or trisodium phosphate, and about a quarter of a cup of alcohol per quart of water. The alcohol mixture is recommended if windows are to be washed during freezing weather. Alkaline solutions (soda, ammonia) and solutions containing alcohol should be handled carefully because they damage painted, lacquered and varnished surfaces.

Follow this procedure if you are using a liquid mixture of the home-made variety. Dip your chamois, sponge or soft lintless cloth into the water and squeeze it as dry as possible. Wash the top, the bottom, then the middle, of the pane. If the window is very dirty, rinse and repeat. Polish immediately with a clean, damp chamois or paper towels. Change the washing water as soon as it becomes dirty.

Rubber squeegees are useful for large windows. Hold the squeegee firmly, stroke downward, and wipe the edge after each stroke. Some squeegees have long, hollow handles into which the cleaning solution can be poured, an additional boon to the hasty or bored as it eliminates dunking and splashing about with a brush on large expanses like sun porches.

Paint and putty stains Remove fresh paint stains with turpentine or cleaning fluid. Soften old stains with turpentine and scrape them off with a razor blade. (You can buy a holder at the five-and-ten to eliminate hazards.) Putty smears will yield to ammonia.

A few "don'ts" Don't scrub dirty glass with a dry cloth; you will scratch the panes. Don't work on windows when the sun is shining on them; they dry too fast and show streaks. *Don't* use soap, *ever*; the panes will be smeared and the smears are hard to remove. Don't "sit out" a window to clean it; you might lose your balance, and truck drivers will wave to you. Clean the outside by raising and lowering the sashes.

Window Screens Dirty screens shut out sunlight and soil window-panes when it rains. Brush them now and then with a hand brush, or with the dusting brush of your vacuum cleaner. For a thorough job (as before putting them up) brush them on both sides with kerosene,

after dusting, using a small paintbrush. Wipe carefully with a clean, soft cloth to remove any surplus. This treatment also helps prevent the formation of rust on iron screens.

Spar varnish applied to copper screens will prevent the unsightly greenish-gray stains caused by water trickling down from the mesh onto painted frames.

Window Shades Some window shades are washable, while others are not. If yours are the washable variety, clean them this way: Take them down, lifting the slotted end of the roller first, then pulling the other end out of the socket. Spread the shade on a flat surface and scrub it with a stiff lather, using a cloth or brush. Wash a small section at a time and overlap the strokes. Care must be taken not to get the fabric too wet. Rinse with a clean damp cloth. Hang and allow to dry thoroughly before rerolling.

If your shade is stubborn about rerolling, or refuses point-blank to do so, the spring in the slot end of the roller probably needs rewinding. Use a pair of pliers, or your fingers, but don't wind it too tightly or your shade will become vicious. An easier way is to remove the shade (or just lift the slotted end of it) while partly unrolled, roll it up and replace it. This amounts to rewinding.

Nonwashable shades can be cleaned with corn meal, with a commercial cleaner or with art gum. If the shade is beyond satisfactory cleaning, take the roller to a window-shade man and have it redone. No need to toss away a good roller. Shades that are worn or stained at the bottom can be removed from the rollers and

turned. Hem the "top" and tack the "bottom" to the roller.

Window Sills Clean your window sills according to the finish (paint, varnish, lacquer), then wax them to prevent damage from moisture. Hard wax, well rubbed in and carefully polished, is best. (This wax coating must be removed when woodwork is to be repainted. Just wipe it off with turpentine.)

Wine Stains See "Stains," p. 239.

Wintuk Wintuk is the trade name for an Orlon acrylic fiber by du Pont, engineered for knitwear. It looks and feels like fine Shetland, merino, or lamb's wool; it dyes well, is light in weight and absorptive. Wintuk sweaters can be washed by hand or machine and do not need to be blocked. For instructions see "Sweaters Synthetic."

Wood and Coal Range Maybe you have been stuck with an old-fashioned wood or coal stove during a vacation in the mountains and allowed it to wreck your good time completely. If not, you may be called upon to use one someday, for, believe it or not, plenty of them are in use today in rural America.

The first thing to remember is to keep the water reservoir filled with clean water at all times. If you don't, it will rumble and growl its displeasure, scaring you almost out of your wits.

The iron top of a wood stove is cleaned, when cool, with a damp cloth. Rubbing it over with waxed paper (a bread wrapper will do nicely) restores its gloss. Occasionally you can wipe the outside with a cloth wrung out of soapy water, using a fine steel wool where necessary to remove spots. Some wood stoves have enameled tops. Go easy with steel wool on these.

If your fire does not burn well, or smokes, investigate the dampers. Or maybe you forgot to take out the ashes. They're behind that little door under the firebox, and if you forget them too long, you'll have trouble. The grate might burn out and then where would you be?

This is probably all you will need to know about wood and coal stoves, if yours is to be merely a nodding, or vacation, acquaintance. But suppose you get stuck with one for a substantial length of time; you'll have to know more about its "innards."

Polish the chromium or nickel trim, according to directions given for these metals, and keep the iron top neat and shining. Stove polish is for that. Its chief ingredient is graphite, or black lead, which never burns. It is sold in cake form or as a liquid (diluted in benzine, which is highly flammable). Follow the directions given on the package in applying it. Or, if you don't want to fool with the stuff, a slightly oiled paper or cloth will do nicely.

The oven is cleaned in the same way as a gas or electric oven is cleaned. (See "Electric Range.") So far, so good. But here goes for a really thorough cleaning. Don't think of home and Mother!

First, the reservoir. The fire, of course, must be out. Remove all water from the tank and all settlings from the bottom of it. Rinse with clear water, and refill with fresh water. Now for the stove, saints preserve us, but this is what Great-Grandmother had to do.

You will need a brush with a long flexible handle, a metal rod with a smooth crossbar at the end,

a small coal shovel, a metal pail, a round scraper (an old saucer will do) and plenty of paper. Better put something over your head.

Shut the kitchen doors and windows and close all drafts on the stove. Shake down the ashes and cinders and empty the ash pan, pushing the debris into the metal bucket with your little shovel and metal scraper.

Remove the lids and lid frames from the top of the stove and scrape each one individually free of accumulated soot. Just let the soot go down into the top opening, left by the lids, for attention later. Now scrape the soot from the top and sides of the oven with your scraper, brushing it to the floor of the compartment under the oven. Replace lid frames and lids.

Now for the stovepipe. Loosen it from the chimney end, after removing the braces, and ease it gently first from the range and then from the chimney opening. Take it outdoors and separate it into sections. Gently scrape out the soot from each section, being careful not to dent the metal. Resist any impulse to bang it about. Wipe the outside with a clean cloth and apply stove polish, or stove enamel if desired. Put the pieces back together.

Back to the kitchen now. Clean the soot from the chimney opening with your old saucer and attack the chimney similarly as far as you can reach. Replace the pipe, first at the stove end, then at the chimney end, and anchor her down. Now spread your papers on the floor under the front of the range, remove the door to the flue opening under the oven and scrape out the soot with your long-handled scraper. Replace the door and go empty your soot far off, where the wind won't return it to you. Relight the stove. Assemble soap and towels. Wait for hot water.

Note: If there is any sort of man at all about the place, this is an occasion when a woman would be justified in going very, very feminine and helpless. The cleaning directions, by the way, are based on material prepared by Uncle Sam.

Wooden Floors, Woodwork For the proper care of a wooden floor it is helpful to know whether the finish is lacquer, shellac, varnish or sealer. However, if wax has been applied to any of these finishes, the routine cleaning and polishing procedure is the same for all.

Waxed floors should be dusted with the brush attachment of the vacuum cleaner, a soft brush, or an untreated mop. An oiled mop damages the finish. They should be polished monthly with a weighted buffer or electric polisher, which can be rented in most towns if you do not own one. At this time worn spots can be rewaxed. Rewax the entire floor twice a year. Use solvent-based liquid or paste wax, according to your personal preference. These two polishing waxes are identical in composition, except that liquid wax contains more solvent. (Do not use a water-base polish.)

If a waxed floor has been well cared for it is not necessary to remove the old coat before applying more. A good method is to go over the floor first with liquid wax (sometimes called "cleaning wax"). Apply the wax to a small area at a time and wipe it carefully with a clean dry cloth. Change cloths as they become soiled. The solvent in the wax removes the soil and a fine film of wax remains on the floor. Let it dry the length of time stipulated on the container, then buff. If desired, paste wax can now be applied. This will give a beautiful and lasting finish. Fine floors are often given a second and even a third coating of hard wax.

Interim care of a waxed floor includes prompt removal of spills with a damp cloth. If the spill contained milk, dip a cloth in a mild detergent solution, wring it out, and wipe the spill. Rinse the cloth in clear water, wring it out, and wipe again to remove detergent film.

White spots sometimes appear on wooden floors after they have been waxed. These are mostly due to unnoticed food spills, especially those containing milk or sugar. To remove them, pour a little liquid wax on them and rub them gently with very fine steel wool, following the grain of the wood. Polish by rubbing with a clean cloth. Scratches are treated like stains.

Word of warning: In waxing a floor it is better to use too little than too much wax. Apply it with a slightly dampened pad of cheesecloth (wax inside) in a very thin layer. Too much wax will make the floor sticky and difficult to polish to a hard finish.

Oiled floors and woodwork are dusted with an oiled cloth or mop and washed, when required, with a suds made of mild soap. Rinse thoroughly with a cloth or mop wrung out of clear water, wetting the surface as little as possible. Dry thoroughly with a clean soft cloth. Cover a small portion of the floor at a time and proceed in this way until the task has been finished.

When completely dry, apply a fresh coating of warm oil. (Those with a paraffin or linseed oil base are best.) The oil may be applied with a cloth or a mop and should be rubbed in thoroughly. Any excess oil should be wiped up carefully to avoid a dust-catching, slippery surface.

If a wax finish is to be substituted for an oil finish, clean the floor carefully with liquid wax, then apply paste wax and buff.

Gloss lacquers give floors a durable finish and are resistant to heat and water. They can be washed with a mop wrung out of mild lukewarm suds and rinsed with clear water. They do not have to be waxed, but may be, if desired. If unwaxed, dust with a treated mop. Lacquered floors can be patched. They can be recoated, after cleaning, without removing the old lacquer. Lacquer can be applied to a shellacked floor, but not to a painted or varnished surface.

Varnished floors can be waxed, if desired. If not waxed, they can be dusted with a treated mop. Unless the varnish is waterproof, these floors should not be washed unless it is absolutely necessary. Wash waterproof varnish like lacquer. Wash other kinds, a very small area at a time, using the greatest care not to let the water stand. Use mild suds, a cloth well wrung out. Rinse and dry each small segment quickly. Varnished floors can be patched but it is very difficult to make a good job of it.

Shellacked floors are ruined by water and should never be washed. Unless kept protected constantly with wax they spot, crack, and wear away easily. They cannot be patched satisfactorily and water whitens them.

Sealed floors are usually waxed. These finishes penetrate the wood, do not scratch easily and can be patched. Properly applied, they give a beautiful and lasting finish which can be washed as described for lacquered surfaces.

Painted floors can be washed with soapsuds made from a mild soap, or oil soap, or with one of the materials discussed under "Paint Cleaners." Use a cloth or sponge and as little water as possible, clean a small area at a time, rinse and wipe dry. Painted floors are often waxed to make cleaning easier. For glossy enamel paint use plain hot water or hot water containing one teaspoon of washing soda per gallon of water. Rub gently. Stubborn spots on the painted surface may be rubbed lightly with whiting or a very mild scouring powder.

Unfinished wood floors are difficult to keep clean and are not often found in homes. They can be swept with a corn broom or vacuum cleaner brush, and can be washed. For such floors detergents are better than soap. Use as little water as possible so as not to raise the grain, and scour bad spots with a brush and scouring powder. Rinse carefully. A little chlorine bleach added to the rinse water will whiten the wood.

Woodenware. Wood absorbs water and is cracked or warped easily if it remains long in contact with it. Woodenware such as pastry boards, rolling pins, salad bowls and salad sets should be cleaned promptly after use. Wipe them with cold wa-

213

ter, wash quickly in lukewarm suds, rinse with cold water and dry immediately.

Do not soak woodenware in water or put it in an electric washer. Do not stand it on edge to dry. Do not stack or store individual salad bowls until they are thoroughly dry. Do not heat or chill wooden bowls. This care applies to finished as well as to unfinished woodenware.

Salad bowls are often finished with waterproof varnish, but many gourmets prefer them to be unfinished on the inside so that seasonings will be absorbed. Or they season the interior by rubbing it with olive oil.

Wooden Work Surface A wooden work surface that is extremely durable can be had by treating the wood with boiled linseed oil. First remove any existing finish down to the clean, bare wood. Heat the boiled linseed oil (you buy it as *boiled* linseed) in a double boiler or by putting it in a cup and placing the cup in boiling water. Linseed oil, raw or boiled, is highly flammable and should never be placed over an open flame.

Apply the hot oil to the surface, then rub it down with steel wool. Repeat this treatment twice (three coatings), allowing a full day each time between applications.

Such a surface can be cleaned by wiping it quickly with lukewarm

water or mild suds. Reoil occasionally.

Woodwork See "Wooden Floors, Woodwork."

Woolens (*Treated*) Machine washable woolens—available as clothing and yard goods—are produced by grafting a very thin chemical coating onto the fibers of wool yarn or fabrics. The Department of Agriculture, which originated the treatment, calls this the Wurlan process, but Wurlanized woolens also appear under trade names.

Wurlanized woolen dresses, sweaters, shirts and socks look like other woolens but do not shrink, mat, or pill when they are machine washed. In an advanced test stage are blends of Wurlanized wool with cotton and rayon that have been treated for durable press. The best qualities of each fiber seem to be combined. This will mean durable-press, part-wool garments and permanently pleated skirts.

Instructions for machine washable woolens vary because of differences in techniques used by the manufacturer. Look for tags inside clothing giving washing and drying instructions when you buy them. Directions for yard goods are usually given on the end of the bolt. The manufacturer is the best authority for his particular fabric. If the article is marked Wurlanized, it can be machine washed like cotton. If the process has been modified, the instructions usually say to use warm water and a mild soap or detergent in a short-cycle wash. Some of these woolens can be put into an automatic dryer; others cannot. Here too, follow the manufacturer's instructions. If directions are missing, ask the buyer of the department of the store where you bought the garment for washing and drying instructions.

Woolens (*Untreated*) Washable woolens and wool blends can be handled successfully at home if a few simple rules are followed. Careless treatment will cause them to shrink, mat, pill, and roughen, and they can never be restored.

Wool fibers are damaged by alkalies in soaps and water softeners, by water that is too hot, by sudden changes in the temperature of the water, by chlorine (household) bleaches, by rubbing, twisting, or just too much handling when they are wet. (A peroxy bleach can be used on white woolens.)

For washing woolens use a mild synthetic detergent. By mild we mean "unbuilt," containing no alkaline softeners. (See "Synthetic Detergents.") Some of these are made especially for wool (Woolite, Woolfoam, Wool Wash). If you use them, read and follow the directions given. The water used should be cool or lukewarm. Hot water shrinks wool and makes white wool yellow. If you are not sure just how warm "lukewarm" is, test it with a thermometer: the reading should be about 95° F. Wool absorbs a great deal of water, so be sure to prepare an abundance of suds. Be certain too that the detergent is dissolved completely.

Before placing the garment in the water, pretreat spots, because they might not show when wet. Moisten them with lukewarm water, apply a little detergent, and brush them lightly with a soft brush. Sometimes a brief soak in the detergent solution (5 to 10 minutes), during which the garment is turned once or twice, will

clean it. At any rate, handle it as little as possible. Drain off the wash water and soak-rinse it twice. Squeeze it very gently, roll it in a turkish towel to absorb excess water, and hang it to dry in a warm airy place—away from sunlight or any source of artificial heat. Or lay it flat on a towel or pad.

Woolens should be steam pressed, never actually ironed. Use a steam iron if you have one, following the instructions given for wool. Or use an ordinary iron (not too hot) and a press cloth. A chemically treated press cloth will give practically professional results; heavy muslin will do, if you haven't a treated one.

Some experts advocate using two muslin press cloths. If you are pressing the right side of the material, the first cloth goes over the material dry and the second, moistened uniformly, is placed on top of the first. Press by setting the iron down carefully on the press cloth, lifting it and setting it down again, until the entire surface has been pressed. Do not lean heavily on the iron; it is not necessary and it marks the cloth. Now lift the press cloths and gently shake or beat out the steam from the wool, using the palm of the hand. Some moisture should always be contained in wool after pressing if it is to have a fresh look. Hang the garment carefully on a hanger with the fastenings closed, to finish drying.

Fabrics of unusual weave should be pressed on the reverse side. In this case the first press cloth is placed under the material and the second, dampened, on top of it.

Chemically treated press cloths are available at any good store dealing in housewares. Such cloths should never be washed or dry-cleaned. Brush them off well, wipe them with a wet sponge and then iron them dry on a clean paper or piece of cloth. Follow the simple directions supplied with these timesavers in using them.

See also "Blanket," and "Sweaters Wool."

Zefran See "Polyester."

Zelan Zelan is the trade name for a coating applied to fabrics to make them water-repellent. It also makes them resistant to perspiration and nonoily spots. Such fabrics are used notably for raincoats, snowsuits, and ski jackets.

Nonoily spots can be removed from Zelan-coated fabrics by sponging them with a damp cloth. Grease and oil spots can be removed safely with cleaning fluid. Zelan-coated fabrics are dry-cleaned in pure fluid, without soap.

Zeolites Zeolites are complex soda compounds in a form resembling clay. They are used extensively in commercial laundries and in private homes in connection with water-softening systems. Hard water is filtered through a thick layer of zeolites and, by chemical action, the calcium and magnesium which make water hard are absorbed by the material, while soda compounds pass from the zeolites into the water. These soda compounds soften the water before it reaches the taps.

Zeolites lose their strength as they work and when this happens a strong solution of salt is passed through them and the chemical action is reversed. The calcium and magnesium compounds which have collected in the zeolites are thrown into the water. This water is discarded and the system is again ready to do its water-softening job.

In the older zeolite systems solutions of salt are added to the tank manually every week or two. In the newer models the flushing is done automatically from a brine tank, to which salt is occasionally added. If you buy or rent a house that has a water-softening system, make a point of finding out what care it requires.

The installation of zeolite tanks involves considerable expense, but in areas where the water is extremely hard, such a system is worth considering. Zeolites usually can be purchased only in connection with commercial installations.

See also "Water and Water Softeners."

Zinc Zinc is a hard, brittle, bluish-white metal, sometimes seen as a covering for work surfaces. Regular washing with hot soapsuds will keep a zinc surface clean. If required, a mild scouring powder can be used. Tarnished zinc can be brightened by rubbing with vinegar or lemon juice, diluted with a little water. Let the acid remain on the surface for several minutes, then rinse with clear water and polish.

Zipper It took fifty years to perfect this gadget, which is based on the principle of the hook and eye. Remember this steadfastly if you get into trouble with one.

Close zippers before washing or pressing a garment, and when it is going to a dry cleaner, and they will be less likely to get out of commission. The trouble spot is usually at the bottom of the zipper. During rough treatment the ends of the "track" (or whatever) are loosened and the thing goes haywire.

A zipper made of two metals can be a hazard to clothing, warns the Department of Agriculture. Aluminum in the track and copper or nickel-plated copper in the slide can act as electrodes. Salt in liquid starch (or minerals in water used for dampening) serves as the carrier of a tiny electric current in the cloth. A small amount of acid is formed, and brown spots or holes appear when a hot iron is used. Zippers of one metal and nylon zippers pose no such problem. No-iron materials sidestep it. But too hot an iron may melt a nylon zipper.

If a zipper has run off the track and the usual jiggering fails to restore it, better spare your nerves and take it to an expert. Good dry cleaners understand these gadgets and can make repairs. Or you can get a new zipper if the situation is hopeless.

Should a zipper jam with you inside the garment, don't panic. Call for help, if necessary, but remember that there is usually a way out without shears.

STAINS:
HOW TO
REMOVE THEM
FROM TEXTILES

Materials for Stain Removal

Absorbents
Corn meal
Cornstarch
Powdered chalk
Talcum powder
Fuller's earth
French chalk

Bleaches
Chlorine bleach
Hydrogen peroxide
Sodium perborate
Color remover

Other Chemicals
Acetic acid (10 percent) or white vinegar (5 percent acetic acid)
Ammonia *
Iodine *
Oxalic acid *
Sodium thiosulfate ("Hypo")

Solvents for Nongreasy Stains
Acetone *
Alcohol (rubbing) *
Amyl acetate (chemically pure) *
Turpentine (flammable) *

Cleaning Fluids for Grease, etc.
Nonflammable
Perchloroethylene *
Trichloroethane *
Trichloroethylene *
Flammable
Usually trade-marked petroleum naphtha mixtures

Washing Agents and Accessories
Absorbent cotton or cloth, paper towels and tissues
Glass rod
Liquid synthetic detergent
Medicine dropper or small syringe
Soaps
Sponge

Chemicals on the above list can be bought at the drugstore. Other materials are available at the grocery or hardware store. Keep them together on a handy shelf, out of reach of children. Chemicals marked with asterisks are poisonous. Keep flammable solvents tightly stoppered and away from sources of heat.

For additional information about these and other materials, and directions for their use, see the main section of this book. The directions which follow for the removal of stains from fabrics are based on a bulletin published by The United States Department of Agriculture.

Three Main Types
of Stain
and How to Treat Them

Greasy Stains On *washable* materials such stains may, or may not, be removed by hand or machine laundering. You will save yourself trouble if you pretreat them first by rubbing in a detergent. Or rub liquid detergent into stains that appear after washing and then rinse them with hot water. Often, however, a grease solvent (cleaning fluid) will be needed. This will remove the spot equally well after the article has been laundered. Let the material dry and sponge it repeatedly if necessary. Fabrics with special finishes often tend to hold greasy stains and persistent effort is required to remove them.

If a yellow stain remains after the solvent has been used on old or heat-set stains, use a sodium perborate or chlorine bleach, or hydrogen peroxide. On materials for which it is safe, the strong sodium perborate bleach is usually the most effective.

Sponge *nonwashable* materials repeatedly with cleaning fluid, allowing them to dry between applications, or use an absorbent. (See p. 16.) If a yellow stain remains, use one of the bleaches described for washable materials.

Nongreasy Stains On *washable* materials, some of these stains are removed by laundering while others are set. Play safe. Always sponge such stains promptly with cool water. This simple treatment will remove many of them. Or soak them in cool water for 30 minutes or more. Some may need to be soaked overnight. After sponging or soaking, work undiluted liquid detergent into the stain and rinse. If the stain remains, you will have to use a bleach. Old stains and stains that have been ironed are in the difficult-to-impossible category.

On *nonwashable* materials, sponge the stain with cool water or put a sponge under it and squirt cool water through the cloth with a small syringe or medicine dropper. If this does not remove the stain, work liquid detergent into it and rinse. A final sponging with alcohol helps to remove the detergent, and the fabric dries faster. Dilute the alcohol with two parts of water for acetate; test colors to see if it is safe for dyes. If the detergent treatment does not remove the stain, you will have to try a bleach.

Combination Stains (Greasy and nongreasy mixtures) On washable fabrics, treat the stain first for the nongreasy portion, using cool water and detergent as described in the two preceding paragraphs. Rinse the spot thoroughly and let the material dry. Then sponge the remaining greasy part of the stain with cleaning fluid. Let the cloth dry and repeat if necessary. A bleach is sometimes needed to remove all traces.

On nonwashable fabrics, sponge the stain with cool water, or put a sponge under the stain and force water through it with a small syringe. If a greasy stain remains, sponge it with a grease solvent. Let it dry. Repeat if necessary. For final traces use a chlorine or peroxy bleach.

Acid Acids do not usually stain white fabrics, but if very strong they may weaken or destroy textile fibers, especially cotton and linen. On colored materials they are apt to change the color of the dye. Spilled acids, therefore, should be removed at once.

Rinse the material thoroughly with cold water to remove as much of the acid as possible. Next sponge it with ammonia or baking soda solution (1 tablespoon of soda to 1 cup of water) to neutralize the remaining acid. Again rinse with water.

Strong acids (sulphuric, hydrochloric) may damage or destroy some fibers before being rinsed out. The amount of damage will depend on the type of fiber and acid and the concentration and temperature of the acid solution. Often, however, thorough rinsing before the acid dries prevents serious damage. Solutions of weak acids (vinegar, acetic acid) will not damage fibers.

Both weak and strong acids can change the appearance of dyes. The use of ammonia after rinsing with water neutralizes any acid left in the fabric and sometimes restores lost color. If the acid spot is light, or the material waterspots easily, dampen the stain and hold it over an open bottle of ammonia. The fumes should neutralize the acid and restore the color. Should

the color be affected by the ammonia, sponge the stain quickly with white vinegar or acetic acid diluted with one part of water. Rinse with water.

Adhesive Tape Sponge with cleaning fluid.

Airplane Cement See "Glue, Mucilage, Adhesives."

Alcoholic Beverages Always wipe up spilled drinks promptly and sponge fabrics with cool water to avoid a serious stain. In treating such spills and splashes follow the directions given at the beginning of this section for nongreasy stains. Another method is to sponge the stain with rubbing alcohol if the color is not affected. For acetates dilute the alcohol with two parts of water. If a trace remains, use a sodium perborate or chlorine bleach, or hydrogen peroxide. Alcohol in these beverages sometimes makes dyes run and fade; there is no remedy for this damage.

See also "Wine."

Alkalies Alkalies can damage fabrics and alter colors. Silk and wool are especially sensitive to them. Damage will vary with the strength of the alkali.

Rinse or sponge the spot promptly with cold water. This is usually sufficient for mild alkalies such as ammonia or washing soda. However, if the color has been altered, or to be absolutely safe, neutralize the spot by applying white vinegar or lemon juice to it.

Strong alkalies like lye may damage or destroy fibers before they can be rinsed out. The amount of damage depends on the kind of fiber and alkali and on the concentration and temperature of the alkali solution. Often, however, prompt rinsing will prevent serious damage. Both strong and weak alkalies may change the color of some dyes. The use of white vinegar, after rinsing with water, neutralizes any alkali left in the fabric and sometimes restores changed colors. Fabrics most affected by alkalies are silk and wool.

Antiperspirants and deodorants Wash or sponge stains caused by antiperspirants (or deodorants) with warm water and liquid detergent. Rinse carefully. If the stain is not completely removed, use a chlorine or sodium perborate bleach, or hydrogen peroxide. Rinse. Some antiperspirants contain aluminum salts which are acidic in nature and may damage the fabric or color. It is sometimes possible to restore colors by sponging them with ammonia. (Dilute the ammonia with an equal amount of water for use on silk or wool.) Sponge or rinse thoroughly with plain water.

Argyrol A fresh stain can usually be washed out with water and detergent. If not removed, dampen the stain with water, and apply a few drops of iodine with a glass rod. Let it stand for a few minutes, then apply sodium thiosulfate (a few crystals dissolved in half a cup of water). Rinse or sponge with water. This method is good for all

fabrics. If stains on silk and wool are not treated promptly, a yellow or brown discoloration will remain.

Asphalt Paint See "Tar."

Ballpoint Ink See "Ink, *Ballpoint.*"

Beauty Clay Usually washes out. Sponge nonwashables with plain water.

Beer See "Alcoholic Beverages."

Beet Follow the directions for nongreasy stains, p. 222.

Berry See "Fruit and Berry."

Black Walnut See "Walnut (Black)."

Blood Soak or rub *washable* materials in cold water until the stain is almost gone, then wash with warm water and a detergent. To old or stubborn stains apply a few drops of ammonia and wash again with detergent. Use a bleach if necessary.

On *nonwashable* materials sponge the stain with cold or lukewarm water. Sponging with a little hydrogen peroxide usually will remove any final traces of stain. If not, use a sodium perborate or chlorine bleach, depending on the material. Blood stains that have been set by heat are very difficult to remove, but on cottons and linens a warm solution of trisodium phosphate, or Oakite, usually will remove such stains.

For blood stains on thick materials such as carpets and rugs, use an absorbent mixed to a paste with cold water. (See "Absorbent" p. 16.) Spread the paste thickly on

225

the stain, let it dry, then brush it off. Repeat until the stain is gone.

Bluing Follow directions for nongreasy stains, p. 222.

Butter Follow directions for greasy stains, p. 222.

Candle Wax With a dull knife scrape away as much of the wax as possible. Place the stain between two pieces of white blotting paper (paper towels, facial tissues) and press with a warm iron. Use fresh paper as the wax is absorbed. Sponge final traces of the stain with cleaning fluid. A quick method on fabrics that will stand it is to pour boiling water through the stain. Dry, and remove final traces with cleaning fluid.

If a dye stain remains from colored wax, sponge it with alcohol diluted with two parts of water. Then rinse or sponge with water.

Candy Follow directions for combination stains (p. 223) for chocolate and syrup. For other candy and syrup stains follow directions for nongreasy stains (p. 222).

Carbon Paper Regular Work undiluted liquid detergent into the stain and then rinse. If the stain is stubborn put a few drops of ammonia on it and retreat with detergent. Rinse and repeat if necessary.

Duplicating Sponge the stain with alcohol, diluted with 2 parts of water for use on acetates. If a stain remains, rub it with soap or detergent and rinse. Repeat if necessary.

If a bleach is needed, follow the above treatment with a chlorine or peroxy bleach, depending on the material.

Carrot Follow directions for nongreasy stains, p. 222.

Catsup, Chili Sauce Follow the directions for nongreasy stains, p. 222.

Cellulose Tape Sponge with alcohol. Test colors first. Dilute with two parts of water for use on acetates.

Cherry See "Fruit and Berry."

Chewing Gum Choose one of the following methods:

If water does not spot the material, rub the gummy portion with a piece of ice and scrape, or rub, the gum out of the fabric. This method is very good for carpets and other heavy materials.

Saturate the stain with cleaning fluid, repeating applications as necessary. If a sugar stain remains, sponge it off with water. This method is good for all fabrics and can be used when the material will not wash.

Chlorine Resin finishes are often applied to cottons, linens, and rayons to convert them to wash and wear, or to give them wrinkle resistance, sheen, crispness, and durable embossed or sculptured designs. If chlorine bleaches are used on such treated materials they are likely to be weakened and yellowed. This is because the resins in some finishes absorb and retain the chlorine in the bleach.

If you have inadvertently used a chlorine bleach on an article with such a finish, rinse it immediately and thoroughly with water. After rinsing, soak it for half an hour or longer in warm water containing sodium thiosulfate. (Use 1 teaspoon for each quart of water.) For fabrics that will stand it, make the water hot. Rinse thoroughly.

An even more effective treatment for white or completely colorfast fabrics is to use a color remover, following the directions on the package.

On some materials the yellow chlorine stains do not appear until the material is ironed. Ironing before the chlorine is removed weakens the fibers.

Chocolate Follow the directions for combination stains, p. 223.

Cocktail See "Alcoholic Beverages."

Cocoa Follow the directions for nongreasy stains, p. 222.

Cod-Liver Oil Fresh cod-liver oil stains can be removed easily from any fabric by sponging the material with cleaning fluid. Washables can be laundered in the usual way afterward. Or put liquid detergent on the stain while it is still fresh. Rub lightly between the hands, rinse carefully in water, then wash.

Cod-liver oil stains are almost colorless when they are fresh.

When they are old they are light brown in color and almost impossible to remove even with bleaches, especially if the material has been washed and ironed, or pressed.

If bleaching is desirable see "Sodium Perborate Bleach," "Chlorine Bleach," "Hydrogen Peroxide," all in Section I, for instructions.

Ounce of prevention: Administer cod-liver oil to your cherub at bathtime.

Coffee, Tea To remove fresh tea and coffee stains containing cream from washable materials, follow the directions given for combination stains, p. 223. If cream is not involved, follow the directions for nongreasy stains, p. 222.

Another method, if safe for the fabric, is to stretch the stain over a bowl, fasten it with a rubber band, and pour boiling water on the stain from a height of 1 to 3 feet. (Careful of your tootsies!)

Correction Fluid, Mimeograph Sponge the stain with acetone or amyl acetate. Use amyl acetate on acetate, Arnel, and Verel. Use acetone for other fabrics.

Cosmetics (*All types*) Apply a liquid detergent directly to the stain if the material is *washable*, or dampen the stain and rub synthetic detergent or soap into it until thick suds are formed. When the outline of the stain is gone, rinse thoroughly. Repeat as many times as necessary. Sometimes it helps to let the fabric dry between treatments.

Sponge *nonwashable* materials with cleaning fluid repeatedly until no more color can be removed. If a trace remains, work synthetic detergent into it and rinse.

227

Crayon Follow the directions for cosmetics.

Cream Sponge nonwashables with cleaning fluid. When the solvent has evaporated, sponge carefully with cool water. Rinse washable materials with cool or lukewarm water, then launder.

Cream Sauce Launder washables with warm water and soap or detergent. Sponge nonwashables with warm water. Allow to dry, then sponge with cleaning fluid.

Cream Soup See "Cream Sauce."

Curry See "Turmeric."

Dandelion See "Grass, Flowers, Foliage."

Deodorant See "Antiperspirant."

Dyes Follow the directions for nongreasy stains, p. 222. For fresh stains, a long soak in detergent suds often does the trick. If a bleach is needed, use a chlorine bleach if the material will stand it, or a color remover.

Egg Scrape off as much as you can with a dull knife, then sponge the spot with cold water, or soak the article in it. If the material is washable, launder in the usual way. If nonwashable, allow it to dry after sponging with water, then sponge with cleaning fluid.
  Caution: Never use hot water on an egg stain; it will set it.

Epoxy Cement This stain cannot be removed.

Eye Shadow See "Cosmetics."

Face Powder See "Cosmetics."

Fingernail Polish See "Lacquer."

Fish Oil Follow the directions for cod-liver oil.

Fish Slime Soak the stain in a solution made by adding half a cup of salt to two quarts of water. Or sponge the stain with this solution. Rinse with plain water and wash with warm water and soap. Or follow the instructions for nongreasy stains on p. 222.

Flypaper Sponge with cleaning fluid. Washable materials may then be laundered.

Food Coloring Follow the directions for nongreasy stains, p. 222.

Fruit and Berry Follow the directions given on p. 222 for nongreasy stains. Or, if the material will stand it, stretch the stained part over a bowl, secure it, and pour boiling water on it from a height of 1 to 3 feet.
  Always sponge fresh stains promptly with cool water before they have time to become set. Some, such as citrus, are invisible when dry; aging or heating turns them yellow and then they are hard to remove. Never use soap and water first on fruit stains. It may set them. Ironing makes matters worse.

Furniture Polish Treat it like a grease stain, p. 229. If wood stain is included follow the directions under "Paint."

Glue, Mucilage, Adhesives Stains caused by airplane glue and household cement can be removed with acetone from all fabrics except acetate, Verel, and Dynel. Chemically pure amyl acetate can be used on other fabrics, but if the cement contained acetone, the material may already have been damaged.

For casein glue follow the directions for nongreasy stains, p. 222.

Wash plastic glue with soap or detergent and water before it has hardened. Some types cannot be removed if they have hardened. The following treatment will remove some dried plastic glues. Immerse the stain in a solution of 10 percent acetic acid or vinegar and water. Keep the solution at or near the boiling point until the stain is removed. This may take 15 minutes or more. Rinse with water.

Scrape away the gummy part of rubber cement stain, then sponge with cleaning fluid.

Other types of glue and mucilage may be removed by following the directions for nongreasy stains except that the water should be hot rather than cool.

Grape See "Fruit and Berry."

Graphite See "Pencil."

Grass, Flowers, Foliage Sponging with alcohol will remove most plant stains from washable and nonwashable textiles. Dilute it with two parts of water for acetate, and always test colors first to see if they are affected. Or work liquid detergent into such stains on washable materials and rinse. If a stain remains, use a mild sodium perborate or chlorine bleach, or hydrogen peroxide. Detergents and bleaches also can be used on nonwashable materials, but always try the alco-

hol treatment first if safe for the dye.

Gravy Soak gravy stains on washable materials in cold water to dissolve the starch, then wash. If a stain remains when the fabric is dry, sponge it off with cleaning fluid.

Sponge stains on nonwashable materials with cool water. Then sponge with cleaning fluid or apply an absorbent.

Grease and Oil Treat fresh oil or grease stains promptly according to the material. For stains caused by axle grease, road oil, etc., see "Tar." Otherwise, follow the directions given for greasy stains, p. 222.

For stains on fine materials or those that will not wash use either cleaning fluid or an absorbent. Cover the spot with the absorbent and let it remain until it becomes gummy. Brush it off. Repeat this process several times, if necessary.

For oil and grease stains on carpets use a coarse absorbent such as corn meal.

Spots containing grime or metal filings, such as Pop and Junior acquire in the shop, yield to treatment more readily if they are rubbed first with Vaseline. Sponge afterward with cleaning fluid or work the stain around in a small bowl of it.

Huckleberry See "Fruit and Berry."

Ice Cream Follow the directions given for combination stains, p. 223.

Ink *Ballpoint* Apply lukewarm glycerin. If the fabric is strong enough, tamp or use a spoon. Blot the stain frequently with an absorbent cloth. It is important to remove loosened stain immediately. Keep the stain moist with glycerin and continue as long as stain is being removed.

If the stain is not gone, flush with water and apply wet spotter (p. 208). For fabrics that will not be damaged, tamp lightly with a brush. Use a spoon, very gently, for delicate fabrics.

Add several drops of ammonia and continue to tamp or use a spoon. Flush with water. Repeat from "wet spotter" until no more stain is removed. Flush with water.

Use chlorine bleach on remaining traces.

Drawing (India, black) Go to work at once on these stains because if they dry they are very difficult to remove. If the material is washable, put an absorbent pad or sponge under the stain and force cool water through it with a small syringe or medicine dropper. This will remove loose pigment and prevent the stain from spreading. Wash repeatedly with liquid detergent or soap, then soak the stained article for several hours in warm water containing ammonia (1 to 4 tablespoons for each quart of water). Dried stains may require overnight soaking.

Another method, which works on some stains, is to apply ammonia directly to the stain (after removing loose pigment as described), work in liquid detergent or soap, rinse, and repeat if necessary.

On nonwashable materials, after forcing water through the stain to remove loose pigment, sponge the stain with water and ammonia (1 tablespoon per cup). Rinse with plain water. If this does not remove the stain, moisten it with ammonia, then work in liquid detergent. Rinse and repeat if necessary. If the ammonia affects colors, sponge the material first with water, then with white vinegar. Rinse carefully.

For *colored drawing inks* follow the directions for nongreasy stains on p. 222. If a bleach is needed, color remover will be the best if it does not fade the dyes. If a test shows it is not safe, select another bleach.

Marking ink There are two common types of marking, or indelible, ink: those with an organic dye (usually aniline black) as a base, and those containing silver nitrate.

Directions for aniline black inks usually say not to iron articles marked with it until after they have been washed. If directions for using the ink say that articles marked with it must be placed in the sun, or pressed with a warm iron before being washed, the ink is probably of the silver nitrate type.

To remove the stains of nitrate inks, follow the directions given under "Silver Nitrate." Aniline black inks are impossible to remove after they have dried.

Mimeographing and printing inks, when fresh, can often be removed by the method given for greasy stains, p. 222, or by sponging them with turpentine. Treat stubborn stains like paint stains, p. 234.

To remove the inks from unbleached muslin feed and flour sacks, soak them in kerosene for several hours, then work them in hot soapsuds. Rinse and dry in the sun.

Writing inks vary in chemical composition so no general rule can be laid down for removing them. For materials that will wash, try first the methods outlined for nongreasy stains on p. 222. If a bleach is needed it may be necessary to try more than one kind. Use a chlorine bleach first on materials that are not damaged by it. For others try sodium perborate or hydrogen peroxide. The strong treatment of any of these bleaches may be needed, a process which may leave faded areas on some colored fabrics. Certain inks require color remover; others yield to oxalic acid. If a yellow stain remains after bleaching, treat it as an iron rust stain. (See "Iron Rust.")

For nonwashable materials, first blot up small stains with an absorbent material such as facial tissue, or cover the stain quickly with an absorbent powder to soak up excess ink and keep the stain from spreading. Then follow the directions for washable materials or, especially on rugs, continue the absorbent treatment. Keep removing the stained absorbent powder and ap-

plying more until no more ink is absorbed. Then mix some of the powder with water (or half water and half alcohol) to form a paste and put it on the stain. Allow the paste to dry, then brush it off. Repeat a number of times if necessary.

Iodine Iodine makes a brown or yellow stain on unstarched materials and deep blue or black on those that have been starched. Ironing turns the stain dark brown.

Fresh iodine stains on fabrics can be removed by the following simple method. Moisten the stain with water and place it in the sun, on a warm radiator, or in steam from a boiling teakettle. The stain will be gone in a few minutes.

Sometimes an iodine stain will yield to a detergent after a long soak in cool water.

Materials injured by water may be sponged with alcohol. (Dilute it with two parts of water for acetate.) Or place a pad of cotton soaked with alcohol on the stain, keeping it wet with alcohol for several hours.

Iodine stains, old or new, on any fabric not damaged by water, can be removed easily with a sodium thiosulfate solution. Dissolve a tablespoon of crystals in a pint of water and either sponge the spot with the solution or dip the stained article into it for about 15 minutes. Rinse carefully. This chemical does not usually damage colors, but test first. It is harmless to all fabrics.

Iron Rust Iron rust stains can be removed from washable white fabrics by any of the methods which follow. If the stain is on a colored material, test your bleach first in some inconspicuous place, such as an inside seam, to determine its

231

effect on the dye. Iron rust stains are almost impossible to remove from materials that must be dry-cleaned.

Lemon juice will remove iron rust stains from the most delicate cottons and linens without injuring the cloth. Moisten the stain with water, squeeze lemon juice directly onto it and hold it in the steam from a boiling teakettle for a few minutes. Rinse with water and repeat as many times as necessary. Another method is to sprinkle salt on the stain, add lemon juice and dry in the sun. Repeat if necessary.

Oxalic acid (poison) can be used for iron stains as follows. Spread the stained material over a bowl of boiling water. Apply a few drops of oxalic acid solution (one tablespoon of crystals to one cup of water) to the stain. Rinse quickly by dipping in the hot water. Repeat until the stain disappears. Or sprinkle oxalic acid crystals directly on the stain, then apply very hot water. *Do not use this method on nylon.* It is very important, when oxalic acid is used, that the material be carefully and thoroughly rinsed. If not, the fabric will be destroyed. Ammonium bifluoride (one tablespoon in a cup of hot water) is an excellent rust remover which can be obtained from your druggist. Soak or sponge the material with the solution. (May take up to ten minutes.) Rinse carefully.

Still another method is to boil the stained article in a solution of water and cream of tartar. Use four teaspoons of cream of tartar to each pint of water. Boil until the stain is removed, then rinse in plenty of water.

232

Lacquer Stains caused by lacquer, including fingernail polish, can be removed from all fabrics except acetate, Arnel, Dynel, and Verel, by sponging with acetone. Use chemically pure amyl acetate for fabrics that will not stand acetone. Nail polish remover may also be used but it may contain acetone. Test before using it on materials damaged by acetone.

Lead See "Metallic Stains."

Lead Pencil See "Pencil."

Leather Stains caused by leather rubbing against a textile are difficult to remove, since they probably contain tannin. If the material is washable, try liquid detergent, applying it directly to the stain. Rub and repeat. Final traces can be bleached with sodium perborate or hydrogen peroxide.

Linseed Oil Sponge the stain with cleaning fluid, then use liquid detergent or put the detergent directly on the stain and rub the fabric between the hands to loosen the stain. Wash in warm suds. Rinse thoroughly.

Lipstick See "Cosmetics."

Liquor See "Alcoholic Beverages," "Wine."

Mascara See "Cosmetics."

Mayonnaise and Salad Dressings See combination stains, p. 223.

Meat Juice Follow the directions for combination stains, p. 223.

Medicine Medicines are composed of such a variety of substances that no single method can be given for stains caused by them. Instructions for iodine, argyrol, mercurochrome, and silver nitrate are given under special headings. The instructions which follow are general and should prove helpful for other types.

Gummy medicines often respond to the treatment for tar stains. Rub in vaseline or lard to soften the stain, then sponge with cleaning fluid. Or dip the stain into the solvent and rub the fabric between the hands. Rinse in the solvent, or launder the material if it is washable.

Medicines in a base of sugar syrup, such as cough medicines, usually can be washed out with soap and water, or sponged off nonwashables. Those dissolved in alcohol (tinctures) sometimes can be removed by sponging with alcohol. Dilute the alcohol with two parts of water for use on acetate. Prescriptions for swabbing sore throats often include silver nitrate. See "Silver Nitrate."

For medicines containing iron, follow the directions for "Iron Rust." Treat those containing coloring matter as dyes, p. 228.

Mercurochrome, Merthiolate, Metaphen These stains should be treated as promptly as possible because they are very difficult to remove when old.

Soak washable materials overnight in a warm detergent solution containing ammonia (4 tablespoons per quart of water).

Sponge nonwashable fabrics with alcohol. (Dilute the alcohol with two parts of water for use on acetate. Test colored materials before using.)

If a stain remains, place a pad of cotton saturated with alcohol on the stain and keep the pad wet until the stain is gone. (An hour or more.)

On colored materials that will not stand alcohol, wet the stain with liquid detergent, add a drop of ammonia with a medicine dropper, then rinse with water. Repeat if necessary.

Metallic Stains on fabrics caused by rubbing against tarnished brass, copper, tin, and other metals can be dissolved by applying white vinegar, lemon juice, acetic acid, or oxalic acid. Rinse with water. Acetic and oxalic acids are stronger than lemon juice and vinegar and will remove more difficult stains. Do not use chlorine or peroxy bleaches. The metal in the stain hastens their action and may cause damage.

Metaphen See "Mercurochrome, Merthiolate, Metaphen."

Mildew Light fresh stains on washable fabrics can be removed by washing with soap and water. Rinse thoroughly and dry in the sun. If the stain is not removed, try a chlorine or peroxy bleach. It is often impossible to remove a heavy mildew stain which includes damage to textile fibers.

Send nonwashable articles to your dry cleaner promptly.

See also "Mildew" in Section I.

Milk Follow the directions for nongreasy stains on p. 222.

Mimeograph Correction Fluid
Follow directions given for "Lacquer" and "Correction Fluid, Mimeograph."

Mucilage See "Glue, Mucilage, Adhesives."

Mucus Follow the directions given for fish slime.

Mud When the mud has dried completely, brush it off. Sometimes this is all the treatment needed. If a trace remains, follow the directions for nongreasy stains, p. 222. Treat stains made by iron-rich clays like rust stains; see "Iron Rust."

Mustard Put the stain on a smooth surface and carefully brush or scrape off dried mustard. Flush with dry-cleaning solvent and, if the fabric is strong enough, tamp or use a spoon. Flush again with dry-cleaning solvent and allow to dry.

If not gone, apply wet spotter (p. 208) and ammonia, tamping or using a spoon if the fabric is strong enough. Flush with water. Repeat until no more stain is removed.

Or wet traces of stain with hydrogen peroxide and add a drop of ammonia. Let it remain for not more than 15 minutes. Flush with water.

Nail Polish See "Lacquer."

Oil Follow the directions for greasy stains, p. 222.

Paint, Varnish Remove paint and varnish stains while they are fresh. They are difficult if not impossible to remove when they have hard-

ened. Today's paints contain a variety of materials and no single method will remove all stains. Look at the label on the paint container to see what is recommended as a thinner; it may be the best thing to help you get rid of the stain.

On washable fabrics, sponge fresh stains with soap or detergent and wash. If the stain is only partially removed by washing, or has dried, sponge it with turpentine until as much as possible of the paint or varnish has been removed. For aluminum paint stains, trichloroethylene (cleaning fluid) may be more effective than turpentine. Do not use this solvent on Arnel or Kodel. While the stain is still wet with the solvent, work liquid detergent into it thoroughly, place the article in hot water, and soak overnight. Careful washing after this treatment will remove most paint stains. Repeat this treatment if necessary.

Nonwashable articles should be sponged with turpentine until no more paint can be removed. For aluminum paint stains trichloroethylene is sometimes more effective than turpentine, but do not use this on Arnel or Kodel.

If necessary, a paint stain can be loosened by covering it for 30 minutes or more with a pad of cotton moistened with solvent. Repeat the sponging. If a trace of the stain remains, put a drop of liquid detergent on it and work it in with the edge of a spoon. Alternate the treatment with the solvent and detergent until the stain is gone.

Unless alcohol is damaging to dyes, it can be used to remove the turpentine and detergent from the stain. Dilute with 2 parts of water if used on acetate. If alcohol makes the dyes run, sponge the stain first with a warm soap or detergent solution, then with water.

Water color paints usually wash out. Sponge materials that will not wash with cleaning fluid or turpentine. Or sponge first with glycerin, then with warm water. See also "Lacquer."

Paraffin Follow the directions given for candle wax.

Peach and Pear See "Fruit and Berry."

Pencil Pencil marks, both black and colored, can often be removed from cloth with a soft eraser. If not erasable, flush with dry-cleaning solvent. Apply dry spotter (p. 69) and rub gently with a pad of absorbent material dampened with dry spotter. Cover the stain with a pad of absorbent material moistened with dry spotter and let stand for 20 minutes. Flush with dry-cleaning solvent and allow to dry.

If a spot still shows, sponge with water and apply wet spotter (p. 208) and a few drops of ammonia. Tamp or use a spoon if the fabric is strong enough. Flush with water and allow to dry. If a trace of stain remains, repeat instructions in this final paragraph until it is gone.

Perfume Sponge washables with water and apply wet spotter (p. 208). Spoon or tamp the material

if it is strong enough. Flush with water. Apply alcohol and cover with a pad of absorbent material moistened with alcohol. Let stand as long as any stain is being removed. Change the pad as it becomes soiled. Keep stain and pad moistened with alcohol. Flush with water.

Nonwashable fabrics should be treated exactly the same as washables except that wet spotter is not used.

Perspiration Perspiration tends to weaken textile fibers if allowed to remain on fabrics and to alter or fade the color of dyes. Always wash or sponge off as promptly as possible, using warm water containing a detergent.

If colors have been changed by perspiration it is sometimes possible to restore them. Sponge fresh stains with ammonia or vinegar. Apply ammonia to fresh stains and rinse afterward with water. Apply vinegar to old stains and rinse with water. If an oily stain remains, use cleaning fluid.

Yellow stains that remain can be removed with a chlorine or peroxy bleach. If safe for the fabric, the strong sodium perborate bleach often is the most effective.

Should perspiration odor cling to washable materials after they have been laundered, soak them for an hour or more in warm water containing three or four tablespoons of salt for each quart of water.

Always remove perspiration stains before ironing. Ironing such a stain will weaken the fabric.

Pitch See "Tar."

Plastic Plastic hangers and buttons, softened by heat or moth-

235

proofing agents, sometimes cause stains on cloth with which they are in contact. They can be removed with amyl acetate or trichloroethylene. (Do not use trichloroethylene on Arnel or Kodel.) Test colored fabrics first to be sure the dyes will not bleed. If sponging the stain with solvent does not remove the plastic, cover the stain with a pad wet with solvent and leave the pad on the stain until the plastic has been softened. Then sponge repeatedly with a fresh pad, moistened with solvent, until all traces of the plastic have been removed.

Plum See "Fruit and Berry."

Pokeberry See "Fruit and Berry."

Printer's Ink See "Ink."

Raspberry See "Fruit and Berry."

Resins Resins and resinous substances can be removed from textiles by means of solvents. Sponge with cleaning fluid, turpentine, or alcohol. Dilute the alcohol with two parts of water for use on acetate. (Test colored fabrics first if using alcohol.) Rinse by sponging with plain water, or launder.

Rouge See "Cosmetics."

Rubber Cement See "Glue, Mucilage, Adhesives."

Running Colors See "Dyes."

Rust See "Iron Rust."

Salad Dressings Follow the directions for combination stains on p. 223.

236

Sauces Follow the directions for combination stains on p. 223.

Scorch To remove light scorch stains from washable materials, follow the directions for nongreasy stains on p. 222.

Light scorch stains on nonwashable materials can be removed by sponging the fabric with hydrogen peroxide (p. 105). The strong treatment may be necessary. (Test first for colorfastness.) Rinse afterward with plain water. Repeat if necessary.

Scorch stains are almost impossible to remove from silk or woolen materials. They cannot be removed if the fibers of the cloth have been burned.

Shellac. Sponge the stain with drycleaning solvent. Apply dry spotter (p. 69), tamping or using a spoon if the fabric is strong enough. Flush with dry-cleaning solvent. Apply alcohol. Tamp or use a spoon if the fabric is strong enough. Flush with alcohol.

Shoe Polish Because shoe polishes vary in their ingredients it may be necessary to try more than one method in attempting to remove stains caused by them.

Try first the method described under cosmetics. If the stain is not removed, try next sponging it with alcohol. (Test colored materials first to be sure the dyes will not bleed. Dilute the alcohol with two parts of water for acetate.)

For stains not removed by alcohol, try sponging with cleaning fluid or turpentine. If turpentine is used, sponge afterward with a warm detergent solution or alcohol to remove the turpentine.

For traces of stain that still remain after these treatments, use a sodium perborate or chlorine bleach, or hydrogen peroxide. If safe for the fabric, the strong sodium perborate bleach is probably the most effective.

Silver Nitrate Stains caused by silver nitrate can often be removed by sponging promptly with cool water, and then washing. If a stain remains, put a few drops of iodine on it and let it stand for a few minutes. Then sponge with a solution of sodium thiosulfate. Use one teaspoon of sodium thiosulfate to one cup of water. Rinse, or sponge with plain water. This chemical can be used on any fabric. It is important to treat promptly stains on silk or wool because otherwise a brownish stain will be left on the cloth.

Smoke and Soot Follow the instructions for cosmetics. An absorbent is sometimes effective.

Soap When soap has not been rinsed thoroughly from a laundered article, ironing sometimes causes a stain resembling iron rust or scorch. This discoloration will come out if the garment is rewashed. Rinse thoroughly this time!

Soft Drinks When soft drinks are spilled, always sponge them off immediately with plain cool water. If they are allowed to dry they are sometimes invisible, but turn yellow with age or when ironed, and are difficult to remove.

To remove stains caused by soft drinks, follow the directions for nongreasy stains on p. 222.

Soup Treat it as a combination stain, p. 223.

Stove Polish If the material is washable, apply liquid detergent directly to the stain and rub it in thoroughly. On materials injured by water, first use an absorbent, then cleaning fluid. Sprinkle the absorbent on the stain, work it into the fabric, and brush it off when it becomes soiled. Apply fresh absorbent and repeat until most of the stain is gone. Then sponge with cleaning fluid, or immerse the stain in it and rub it gently or brush it with a small soft brush.

Strawberry See "Fruit and Berry."

Sugar Syrup Stains caused by sugar syrups are no problem on washable materials. Laundering removes them. Sponge nonwashables with warm water.

Syrup See "Medicine" and "Sugar Syrup."

Tar Scrape off as much of the substance as possible, then follow the directions for greasy stains on p. 222. If traces remain, sponge with turpentine. Washables may then be laundered.

For stains on carpets or rugs use this method: scrape off as much as

possible with a dull knife, then sponge with a cloth soaked with cleaning fluid. Use a light, upward, brushing motion so that the stain will be rubbed out of the rug rather than into it. Change your cloth when it becomes soiled and continue until the stain is gone.

Tea See "Coffee and Tea."

Tin Foil See "Metallic."

Tobacco Follow the directions under "Grass, Flowers, Foliage."

Tomato Juice Follow the directions for nongreasy stains, p. 222.

Transfer Patterns Follow instructions for greasy stains, p. 222.

Turmeric Turmeric is a spice used in curry powder, prepared mustard and often in pickles. It produces a bright yellow stain, which is especially difficult to remove from cotton materials.

For fresh stains on white washable materials, try soaking the article in a dilute solution of ammonia water or alcohol. If the material is not washable, sponge the stain with these agents. Test colored materials first to see if alcohol affects the dye and dilute it with two parts of water for acetate. Rinse with water.

If the stain still shows after this treatment, and for old stains, use a bleach.

Note: Colored materials should be tested in an inconspicuous place, such as an inside seam, before being subjected to bleaches.

Typewriter Ribbon Use method described for carbon paper (regular).

238

Unknown If greasy, treat as a grease stain, p. 229. Otherwise, follow the directions for nongreasy stains on p. 222. See also "Yellowing."

Urine Follow the directions for nongreasy stains on p. 222.

If colors have been changed, sponge the stain with ammonia. See "Ammonia," p. 22.

If ammonia does not help, sponge with acetic acid (p. 17) or white vinegar.

If a bleach is required, follow the directions for "Medicine" and "Yellowing."

Varnish See "Paint."

Vaseline Use the method given for greasy stains, p. 222.

Vegetable Follow the directions for nongreasy stains, p. 222.

Vinegar If vinegar has changed the color of a fabric, use the treatment for acid stains, p. 224.

Vomit Follow the directions for fish slime.

Walnut (Black) Sponge the stain with water.

For delicate fabrics, apply wet spotter (p. 208) and a few drops of white vinegar. Cover with a pad of absorbent material dampened with wet spotter and vinegar.

Let it stand for five minutes, then flush with water. Repeat soaking and flushing until no more stain is removed.

For stronger fabrics, apply wet spotter and a few drops of white vinegar, then tamp or use a spoon. The stain should be kept moist with wet spotter and vinegar. Blot occasionally with clean absorbent material. Continue until no stain is being removed.

Fresh stains on nonwashable materials sometimes can be removed with an absorbent, or sponge them with alcohol. (Dilute with two parts of water for acetate.)

If traces of stain remain, use a chlorine or sodium perborate bleach.

Water Spots Materials that water-spot usually contain sizing or other finishing agents. The water dislodges part of these substances and causes them to be rearranged and deposited in a ring. Fabrics most likely to water-spot are taffeta, moire and other crisp silk and rayon materials.

To remove such spots dampen the entire garment by sponging it with water or by shaking it in steam from a boiling teakettle (not too close to the spout). Press the garment while it is damp.

Sometimes water spots can be eliminated by scratching the fabric lightly with the fingernail, or by rubbing it with a clean, stiff brush. Or try rubbing the material gently between the hands.

Wax (*Floor, furniture*) Follow the directions for greasy stains, p. 222.

White Sauce Treat as a combination stain, p. 223.

Wine A quick method, for materials that will stand it, is to stretch the stained portion over a bowl and secure it with a rubber band or string. Sprinkle salt on the stain, then pour boiling water on it from a height of one to three feet. Use care to avoid being splashed.

Yellowing Yellow or brown stains sometimes appear on clothing and household linens that are stored. For these, and for all yellow and brown stains of unknown origin, try the following treatments in the order given until the stain has disappeared.

1. Wash the article.

2. Use a mild treatment of a chlorine or peroxy bleach, p. 145.

3. Use the oxalic acid treatment described for iron rust stains, p. 232.

4. Use a strong treatment of a chlorine or peroxy bleach, p. 51.

For yellow stains caused by chlorine bleach on resin-treated fabrics, see "Chlorine," p. 226.

Note: Little brown dots that sometimes appear on stored linens are caused by particles of iron in hard water, which eventually rust. Always use soft or softened wash and rinse water for linens that are to be stored.